SUNDAYS AT 2:00 WITH THE BALTIMORE COLTS

THE BALTIMORE COLTS

Official Theme Song

Words and music
By
Jo Lombardi
and
Benjamin Klasmer

Courtesy of John Ziemann

SUNDAYS AT 2:00 WITH THE BALTIMORE COLTS

by Vince Bagli and Norman L. Macht

TIDEWATER PUBLISHERS
CENTREVILLE, MARYLAND

Library of Congress Cataloging-in-Publication Data

Bagli, Vince
Sundays at 2:00 with the Baltimore Colts / by Vince Bagli and Norman L. Macht. — 1st ed.
p. cm.
Includes index.
ISBN 0-87033-476-X (pbk.)
1. Baltimore Colts (Football team)—History. 2. Baltimore Colts (Football team)—Anecdotes. 3. Football players—United States. I. Macht, Norman L. (Norman Lee). II. Title.
GV956.B3B34 1995
796.357′64′097526—dc20 95-359805
CIP

Manufactured in the United States of America
First edition

Hurst C. Loudenslager.
Photograph by Norman and Ruth Anderson

To "Loudy" and Flo, the best friends a team ever had.

—Vince Bagli

To my Aunt Margie: her bones are in old Har Sinai cemetery, but her heart is in Memorial Stadium.

—Norman L. Macht

This sounds corny, and maybe it happens in other places, but these guys played for the town.

—Ernie Accorsi

Photographs by Bob Miller

Contents

1958 BALTIMORE COLTS

TOP ROW: Marchetti, Lipscomb, Parker, Moore, DeCarlo, Brown, Hall, Lyles, Nicely, Spinney, Jordan, Coach J. Bridgers.

SECOND ROW: Coach H. Ball, Coach C. Winner, Nutter, Yelvington, Pellington, Nelson, Braase, Ameche, Szymanski, Unitas, Joyce, Krouse, Donovan, Equipment Manager Schubach, Jr., Head Coach Ewbank.

THIRD ROW: Ass't Trainer Spassoff, Shaw, Sandusky, Sanford, Patera, Eggers, Jackson, Preas, Myhra, Davis, Shinnick, Plunkett, Trainer Block.

BOTTOM ROW: Horn, Sample, Call, Pricer, Taseff, Dupre, Berry, Mutscheller, Walters.

Courtesy of John Ziemann

PREFACE

The Baltimore Colts came into existence on December 28, 1946, when a group of investors led by Bob Rodenberg purchased the bankrupt Miami Seahawks franchise of the All America Conference and moved it to Baltimore. The nickname "Colts" was chosen after a contest, with Charles Evans of Middle River declared the winner.

My association with the Colts began as a fan watching them practice in the wide open expanses of Herring Run Park when the team wore green and silver jerseys in 1947.

A lot of us college boys served as ushers in old Baltimore Stadium during that inaugural season. They paid us $3.00 a game to show people to their seats. The ushers' uniform consisted of a green chauffeur's cap, and when a late summer shower drenched the scene during the second half on opening day, September 7, we realized that the green was not colorfast. It poured down our necks and onto our clothing. On Monday, a lot of us spent the $3.00 we had earned for a new shirt at Brandau's in Waverly.

The Colts won that franchise opener, 16–7, over the Brooklyn Dodgers of the All America Conference. We kicked off to start and, after a Dodger fumble and a mad scramble, recovered the ball in their end zone for a touchdown. The Colts led, 7–0, in the first ten seconds of their history.

The kids in our neighborhood were especially proud when Hamilton's own Bud Grain (Poly and Penn) played guard on that first team. Then Elmer Wingate (Poly and Maryland), who lived two blocks from Grain, made the '53 team. When he was twelve, Elmer was the biggest kid in our neighborhood. He played with us, but we never let him run the ball.

Opening day program, September 7, 1947.
Photograph by Bob Miller

Broadcasting the Colts games on radio from 1959 through 1961, then from 1975 until the team's departure for Indianapolis in 1984, exceeded my fondest dreams as a native Baltimorean. Working with Chuck Thompson was a special bonus. Despite his long experience and Hall-of-Fame future, Chuck prepared for each game with the dedication of a novice. He was truly an inspiration.

The team's first general manager of the modern era, Don Kellett, was the trendsetter in public relations for all subsequent Baltimore sports teams. Never before had any sports organization introduced its players to the public in such a sincerely personal way. Kellett never missed an opportunity to accompany his players—two or three or four at a time—to civic clubs, churches, alumni gatherings—wherever fans or potential fans got together. The season ticket base grew, the team got better, and Kellett had the whole town believing in the Colts' civic contribution.

To me, the Colts' Band and the intensely loyal Colts Corrals were vital in sustaining interest. Remember, in 1951, after four years of play, the owner withdrew the franchise, and Baltimore was without a team for two years. But the Band played on—marched in parades, gave concerts, even went to games in several Eastern cities and performed at half-time, representing the "city without a team."

Meanwhile, the Corrals gathered momentum, opening new chapters in neighborhoods all over the area. They were among the 15,000 season ticket holders who assured the NFL that Baltimore was ready to resume play in 1953.

The Band and the Corrals were always there!

The players have always been there, too. They contributed with unusual civic pride and interest. Of the first twenty-five people I interviewed for this book, sixteen have stayed to make their homes and raise their families in the Baltimore area. None of these men (or their wives) had been native Marylanders, but they chose to stay here after their football careers ended.

Compiling the material for this book has proven again to me how genuinely grateful most of these players are for the opportunity to have played in Baltimore. Every player was easily approached and eager to talk about his experiences as a Colt and a Maryland resident. Collectively, it was like interviewing a huge class—almost a reunion—though I never talked to more than one player at a time.

As I met with each of them, a feeling I've always had was vividly reinforced. The most consistently striking quality about the Colts is the camaraderie among them. The older vets and the more recent performers all share a bond of unity. That bonding manifested itself as they talked about the support of others through their careers, and the successes and problems of many after football. Many have remained close friends, and almost all have kept in touch through their own personal alumni network.

I hope that I have asked the kinds of questions the rest of you fans would ask of the people who occupied so much of our attention on Sundays at 2:00 (the Colts were the only team that started its games at that hour).

During the nearly half-century of Colts football, I talked to all these players and coaches many times. But to have spoken to all of them again, within a five-month span as we worked on this book, made me realize anew how close the bond is among them, and between them and us.

See if you don't get the same impression.

Vince Bagli
Baltimore, Maryland
June 1995

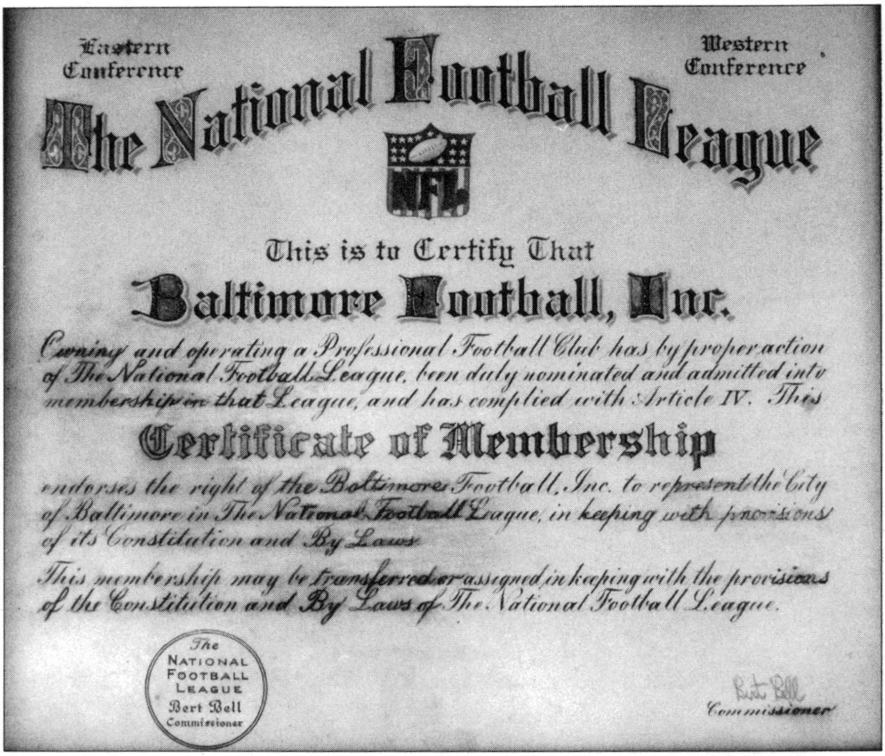
Eastern Conference

Western Conference

The National Football League

NFL

This is to Certify That

Baltimore Football, Inc.

Owning and operating a Professional Football Club has by proper action of The National Football League, been duly nominated and admitted into membership in that League, and has complied with Article IV. This

Certificate of Membership

endorses the right of the Baltimore Football, Inc. to represent the City of Baltimore in The National Football League, in keeping with provisions of its Constitution and By Laws.

This membership may be transferred or assigned, in keeping with the provisions of the Constitution and By Laws of The National Football League.

The National Football League Bert Bell Commissioner

Bert Bell

Commissioner

The Colts' NFL charter, which was rescued from the trash bin by John Ziemann. Photograph by Bob Miller

The 1947 Colts pennant. Photograph by Bob Miller

SUNDAYS AT 2:00
WITH THE BALTIMORE COLTS

The Gladiator, Hall of Famer Art Donovan.
Photograph © 1995 TADDER/Baltimore

Arthur Donovan

Born: 6-5-25
New York, New York
Boston College
Defensive Tackle

6′ 3″, 270 lbs.
Drafted: #4, 1950
Colts: 1953–1961
Hall of Fame: 1968

"[In 1953] they introduced us and we ran through the goal posts and I got a few claps, but they were saying, 'Who's that fat guy from New York? He'll never make it.' "

I grew up in the Bronx. My mother raised us, 'cause my father was the talk of the town, refereeing all the big fights in the 1930s. People used to take him out, wanting to know all about Joe Louis and all those big fighters. But we had a great relationship. I always kissed my father and he expected it. If I didn't, he'd say, "What are you, a big shot now?"

Now, when I see my son, I expect him to kiss me. I like it. The year I was elected to the Hall of Fame, my son was only a little kid and he went out there to Canton with me. He had to go to the bathroom, and when he came out his fly was unzipped. I said, "Arthur, your fly is unzipped." Well, he had a tough time zipping it up, so I bent over and I zipped it up for him. Some guy says, "Look, there's a Hall of Famer zipping his son's fly up." I says, "Hey, I'm his father. What do you expect me to do?"

I grew up in the neighborhood; I had fourteen cousins living on two streets. My grandmother was the matriarch of the whole neighborhood. I got one aunt left, lives next to the church, and when she goes, that's it. When I lived there, there were Italians, Irish, Germans, Jews. Most of the Italian guys that I grew up with are still there. They walk around in uniforms like Italian generals; they're inspectors in the department of sanitation. Great guys.

About four years ago I was up there to see my aunt. I'm riding up the street in the neighborhood and I saw this guy sitting outside a house. He looked sort of sick, sitting on a chair shaking a little. So I stopped the car and got out and said to him, "Are you Nicholas Carlini?"

He says, "Yeah. And I know who you are. You're Artie Donovan. Are you still playing?" I said, "No, Nicholas. I retired a few years ago."

I lived a fifteen-minute walk from Fordham University, and that was the only school I ever wanted to go to. I used to go there at six o'clock in the morning to serve Mass for the priests. Then they'd let us come back in the afternoon and watch football practice. My big idol was the center, Alex Wojciechowicz. He and I went into the Pro Hall of Fame together.

I'll never forget when I was in high school going over to Fordham and working out with a lot of other high school guys. It taught me one lesson. I was down in the locker room underneath the gym getting dressed with my friend, John Brady, and I'm listening to all these other guys telling each other how good they are. I said to myself, "I'm over my head here. I'm embarrassed." I said to John, "These guys are big." He said, "You're bigger than most of the varsity here."

So we go up and Ed Franco, one of the Fordham "Blocks of Granite," was the line coach. We all line up and try blocking him, and I'm thinking, "I can block better than these guys." So my turn comes and Franco says, "Okay, block me."

So I hit him pretty good, and I see he's getting a little mad. He says, "Do it again." This time he knocked me flat.

Afterward, we were all over in the dining room and the head coach, Jim Crowley, came over to me and said, "Arthur, would you like to come to Fordham?"

Well, that was like giving me a million dollars. I said, "Yes, sir, coach, but I'm only a junior in high school."

He said, "Well, next year, then."

But by the time I got out of high school, Fordham had disbanded intercollegiate athletics. So I went to Notre Dame, but they didn't like me there. Frank Leahy was the coach and he had his favorites. We were having a scrimmage one day and this guy from New Orleans kept holding me. I couldn't block him. I says, "Hey, don't hold me." He didn't say anything, but about three plays later he holds me again. I says, "I told you not to hold me." So we have a fist fight.

Leahy breaks it up and says, "Shake hands."

I says, "I'm not going to shake hands with him. I don't like him."

Leahy gets on me: "We don't like your type here."

So that was the end of Arthur Donovan at Notre Dame.

I went into the marines and spent about twenty-six months in the Pacific. I was in the third division, on Okinawa and Guam. We were getting ready to invade somewhere when they dropped the atom bomb, and thank God they dropped it.

I was a Pfc. when I left Parris Island and when I got discharged I was still a Pfc. I got out at Bainbridge, out on Route 40, on December 10, 1945. Fifty years ago. If I'm still around on that fiftieth anniversary, I'm going to go out there to get stone drunk.

I had to come to Baltimore to go to New York, and we got all dressed up in our green marine uniforms. The discharge papers showed all the battles you had been in and the ribbons you were entitled to wear. So I stopped on 34th Street in New York and bought all the ones I deserved. The guy wanted to sell me the Medal of Honor ribbon for five bucks, but I said, "I don't want to get shot." So I just bought what I was entitled to wear and pinned them on and went down in the subway to go to the Bronx and I see a guy from my neighborhood, Tommy Lionelli. He used to deliver false teeth.

I say, "Tommy, how are you?"

He looks at me and says, "Artie. Where you been?"

I tried to go back to Notre Dame. There were four of us who went at the same time. One of them was Gus Cifelli, who played for the Detroit Lions. He still keeps in touch. One of the coaches took us to the administration building. They took three guys into one room and me into another. When I saw that, I said, "Oh oh, they don't want me here."

I went back to New York and a man named Biz Arnold, a multimillionaire comic book publisher, asked me to come down to Park Avenue and see him. So I did. He said, "We have an Arnold Foundation at Brown University, and we would like you to come up and see the school and maybe go there." He took six of us up to Providence, Rhode Island, and he not only picked up all the bills, he gave us each $2,000. But I took one look at Brown and said, "This is an Ivy League school. That's not my cup of tea."

So I went home and said to my mother, "Ma, this man Mr. Arnold gave me $2,000 and he picked up all the bills."

She says, "You take it back to him, Arthur."

That was a lot of money in 1946, but I took it back. I said, "Mr. Arnold, I gotta be very truthful with you. I've always been to Catholic schools and I'd like to go to a Catholic college."

He said, "The coach at Boston College is a good friend of mine." And he gives me $1,000 to go to Boston and look it over. So I take two of my friends from the neighborhood, just out of the service, and we go to Boston and live it up for a week on Mr. Arnold's money. I came home with some money left over, and my mother made me go back down to Park Avenue and give Mr. Arnold the rest of the money.

And that's how I ended up going to Boston College. I was twenty-two. My first year there, we had a class of three hundred, most of us just out of the service. And this Father Murphy stands up and says it was immoral to drop that atom bomb on Japan. We had a ringleader, and we all got up and left the room. We had the president make Father Murphy apologize to us for what he said, because if they hadn't dropped the bomb, maybe half of us wouldn't have been there. Who knows?

The best I ever did in college was second team All–New England, and that's not too good.

I was drafted by the Colts in 1950. The coach was Clem Crowe. We had a few good players, but we couldn't compete. We won one game. After the season the owner, Abe Watner, turned the franchise back to the league, and we all got drafted by different teams. Sisto Averno and I got picked by the Cleveland Browns.

We went to training camp, but we knew we weren't going to make it. They had the same team that had beaten the Rams for the championship the year before. They were going to keep six tackles, and I'm the seventh. The handwriting's on the wall. I thought I was as good as most of them, but evidently Paul Brown disagreed.

We played an exhibition game in Akron against the New York Yankees. After the game Brown traded Sisto and me to New York. We played there for one year, 1951; won one game. Then that guy turned the team back to the league.

This time they sold the whole team to a group in Dallas, and we moved again. After four home games they didn't draw any people, so they threw in the towel, and the commissioner's office operated the team the rest of the year. They moved us to Hershey, Pennsylvania, and we played our last five games on the road. There was nothing else to do in Hershey but drink beer all night long.

Jimmy Phelan was our coach. He was a great man, but football had passed him by. He gave us all these Knute Rockne–type fight talks. When we played the Bears in Akron, he told us, "We're going to go out there and meet the fans individually," 'cause there weren't that many. And he was going on: "We gotta beat the Bears. . . . We gotta beat somebody before the season's over. . ." He's getting us all revved up. "We gotta punch 'em, kick 'em, beat 'em. Let's go!" And we all jump up ready to go and he says, "But for God's sake, be careful." He didn't want anybody to get hurt. We went out there and beat them, 27–23. That was the only game we won.

I'd been on three teams in three years and won three games, and all three teams folded.

Cecil Isbell was one of our coaches. He called a friend of his in Baltimore, Nelson Baker, who owned a bar on Maryland Avenue. Baker told him that Bruce Livie had a campaign going, and they sold 15,000 season tickets to bring the Colts back to Baltimore, and that's what happened, and it was the greatest move that ever happened to me.

I still can remember the first night I was introduced at an intrasquad game at Memorial Stadium in 1953. They introduced us and we ran through the goal posts and I got a few claps, but they were saying, "Who's that fat guy from New York? He'll never make it."

We won three games that year. We had a quarterback, Dick Flowers, who never threw a spiral. He threw a better knuckleball than Hoyt Wilhelm. And we had the best-tanned coach in the business—Keith Molesworth. He never wore a shirt when he coached us. Everybody said, "Look, he's got a better suntan than Buddy Young." Moley was a great fellow.

When Weeb Ewbank came in 1954, we had maybe twelve good football players out of thirty-three guys. Then in the '55 draft we got a lot of fine players: Alan Ameche, George Shaw, Dick Szymanski, L.G. Dupre, George Preas. That was the beginning.

Weasel as he was, Weeb was a great coach and a teacher. He taught us how to play the game. He brought the Paul Brown theory of offense and defense and advanced it. If he told you black is white, you better believe it. And I thought Joe Thomas was an excellent defensive coach.

In '55 we started off winning our first three games. We beat Green Bay out there and we got on the bus and Gino Marchetti says to me, "Hey, Fatso, how good do you think we are?"

I says, "Gino, I don't know, but we got the nucleus here of a good football team and I hope the bubble doesn't burst." Well, it bursted, but we were that close.

We had some problems in '56 and they were going to fire Weeb after we lost to the Rams and 49ers out west. Then [Jim] Mutscheller caught that pass that bounced off Norb Hecker to beat the Redskins and saved Weeb's job.

I think 1957 was the best team we ever had, and we should have won it. We lost in Detroit's Tiger Stadium when Lenny Moore fumbled and the ball, instead of going out of bounds, stayed in. Hopalong Cassady caught a pass that was a crusher. It was the only pass he ever caught. I'll never forget standing on the sidelines with Joe Campanella—they had brought Joe back on account of Bill Pellington had broken his arm—and Joe says to me, "Hey, Arthur, I don't know who's going to win this game, but this is the best goddamn game I've ever seen in my life."

I said, "Joe, I hope we win." But we lost, 31–27.

Then in San Francisco Mutscheller drops the ball on what would have been first down, and they scored when Hugh McElhenny pushes off "Pops Willoughby" Milt Davis right near the end of the game and we lose, 17–13. We called Milt "Pops Willoughby" because he had legs like two sticks.

But it was a great season.

I never had any idea that John Unitas was going to be as great as he was. He was the boss on the field. But off the field, this is the kind of guy he was:

In San Francisco we used to hang out in a bar called The Paddock. A guy named Joe Pate owned it, and they used to show old football and boxing movies. I got in there because way back when I started, we were playing in San Francisco and a kid from my neighborhood named Richie Romanoli came to see me and said, "I gotta take you to this bar. They show old fight movies and your father's refereeing the fights."

So I went, and after that we used to hang out there. One night Pate was going to take a bunch of us to dinner—Dr. McDonnell, me, Mutscheller, Szymanski, Alex Sandusky, Art DeCarlo. We're staying at the Jack Tar Hotel, and we're going out, and Unitas is sitting in the lobby. So I said, "John, you want to go to dinner?"

So John says, "All right. I ain't got nothing to do."

So we're going to an Italian place in North Beach called New Joe's. So we get there, we're in the bar having a few beers and playing the Italian game, fingers, having a great time. Now we go in to eat, and New

Joe is in the dining room, and the only guy he recognizes is Unitas. So we're all eating away, and New Joe says, "Hey, John, my friends here all want to know, isn't it great food?"

And John shrugs and says "I've had better."

We jumped all over him: "Come on, John, at least you could have said 'Yeah, it's great.' "

But that's John.

From the time I started playing I would get the dry heaves before a game and I couldn't control myself. I never got over it. Anybody sitting beside me, I'd give him my pregame meal, steak and all, and I would drink consommé. I was nervous. I don't know why.

In 1956 Pellington, Shula, and I lived together. We're playing the Lions at home. Shula and Pell fix themselves steaks before the game. I went down to Harry Little's sub shop and got myself two big liverwurst submarine sandwiches loaded with onions.

I'm playing opposite Dick Stanfel on the line that day, a great player. The first play of the game I've still got the dry heaves, and I'm down there on the line heaving away and Stanfel says, "Jesus Christ, you stink. What the hell did you eat?" He never touched me the whole game.

We had a great team in the 1950s. Lenny Moore ranks up there with the finest football players I've ever seen. Gino, Parker, Berry were great. Bill Pellington never got the publicity he deserved. Andy Nelson—you name them—we had a great team. Our offensive line was a pass protector line. That's the reason John had so much success. If we had had a punter, I don't believe we would have ever lost a game. We had a punter-by-committee.

Gino was the best pass rusher I ever saw. We had guys who were better against the run; I think Ordell Braase was as good. But as a pass rusher, I don't think Gino had an equal. Gino never showed any emotion. The first time I ever saw him show any was when we were down at Ocean City years later for Tom Brown's camp. The other guys were leaving and I was staying to drive back to Baltimore, and Gino grabbed ahold of me and said, "You know, Fatso, I really love ya." That meant a lot to me.

I loved them all. They used to play tricks on me, and I loved it all.

The biggest thrill I ever had in football was not the 1958 championship game in New York, even though I'm from New York. It was playing in the last home game that year, when we won the western division title by beating the 49ers, 35–27. I had 85 cents in quarters, dimes, and nickels in my locker, 'cause after the game was over, if we won, I was going to call my mother to tell her right away. It was a 55-cent phone call to the Bronx; I talked about ten minutes overtime, and she's crying and my sister's crying and I'm crying on the phone, because it was the first game I ever played in, from all the years I started on a cinder field at P.S. 8 in the Bronx, that I was in a championship game. I think it was the greatest feeling I've ever had.

Then going up there and playing the Giants; I was born four miles up the road from Yankee Stadium. I'd been going to baseball games ever since I was a kid, and bringing my father's bag down when he refereed all those Joe Louis fights there. It was a great feeling. My mother wasn't at the game. She had gone to the game on November 9 that year when we lost in New York, 24–21, and she wouldn't go again. She thought she was a jinx. But my father saw almost all my games.

In that Giants game, they had an idea we were going to put a lot of pressure on quarterback Charlie Conerly, so they kept rolling out to the left, then Conerly would come back and catch us all running to the right. Then he had time to throw the ball, which I thought was a great feat of offensive strategy.

The toughest runner I ever had to tackle was Jim Taylor. John Henry Johnson was right behind him. We didn't play the Browns that much, but Jim Brown wouldn't block or fake like those guys. I'll tell you another tough guy was Tank Younger of the Rams. He'd crack you and so would Deacon Dan Towler. He hit me under the eye and gave me twenty stitches, and I chased him all over the stadium. Then, after we won in '59, he came to see me after the game in the Coliseum. I'm in my little cubicle where we dressed and I'm feeling bad because my mother had died just a month or so before that, and I'm thinking about her, and a knock comes on the door.

I said, "Who's there?" and the first guy who comes in was the singer, Billy Eckstine. Then another guy comes in and it's Towler. I said to him, "Get out of here or I'll blow up your church." But I didn't mean it. We laughed about it.

Of all the guys I played against, Red Stephens, the guard for the Redskins, hit me the hardest. He hit me a shot one time in Baltimore—I don't know whether he hit me or clipped me—but I was in the air for 5 yards and when I bounced I hit my hip and thought I'd displaced it. When I went to practice on Tuesday I was black and blue from my navel all the way down to my ankles, and coach John Sandusky got mad at me, made me practice without the pad on my hip.

One guy I had trouble with was Bruno Banducci from the 49ers. I thought he was holding me all the time, but I watched the movies and he was just blocking me. The last time I played against him was in Baltimore, and I finally had a hell of a day against him. We're walking off the field after the game and he says, "Well, you had a good day today."

Instead of keeping my mouth shut, I said, "Yeah, I finally got you, you guinea son of a bitch, after all these years."

And he says, "Yeah, I just got out of the hospital. I was in there for three weeks with mononucleosis."

Me and my big mouth.

One time in '58 we were playing the Giants in an exhibition game in Louisville, Kentucky, and you know how humid it is there. They had a rookie right tackle named Frank Youso, 6-foot-4 and 260 pounds. He's coming down on me shoulder to shoulder and chest to chest. Usually there wasn't anybody I couldn't get rid of if he was blocking me high.

We get in the defensive huddle and I say to Gino, "This son of a bitch is strong. I can't get rid of him."

Gino says, "I can't get around him either."

I said, "After the game let's tell Weeb if we ever get a chance to trade for him, he's a good football player."

So after the game we're waiting to get on the bus and the Giants are standing there and who's the line coach for them but an old Fordham guy, Johnny Dell Isola. He comes over to Gino and me and says, "So what do you think of our big stud?"

I said, "He stinks. He can't block."

And they cut him! Weeb was going to pick him up, but when the Giants saw the movies of the game, they brought him back.

When we were playing, they were all dirty. Jim David—The Hatchet—was always giving you something after the play was over. Jack Christiansen was always doing something. Charlie Ane, a Hawaiian center for the Lions, hit me pretty hard.

Once, years later, I was in Hawaii and I called Ane.

"Charlie, this is a friend of yours from Baltimore."

"Yeah? Who is it?"

"Art Donovan."

"What are you calling me for?"

"I figured we knew each other from the Pro Bowl game, and I'm here in Honolulu, and I thought we'd go out."

He says, "I'm not going out with you. I don't like you. I didn't like you when I played against you, and I still don't like you."

And he hung up.

I said to my wife, "I can't believe it. This guy still holds a grudge."

Half hour later the phone rings. It's his wife. She says, "Don't mind him, he's crazy. Sure we'll go out with you."

He takes us to a restaurant called The Willow, and we were in the men's room and we're talking about how many children we each have and so on, and some guy's in the john and I hear this voice say, "It can only be one guy—Art Donovan from Baltimore."

I says, "Who the hell are you?"

And the voice says, "Bart Mitchell." It was the blacktop guy, out there for an asphalt convention.

In those old days, there were twelve teams in the league, thirty-three guys on a team. We didn't have any special rivalries, and you didn't get to know anybody else except maybe the guys you went to the Pro Bowl with. But now, when we see each other, we kiss and hug each other. I was up in Detroit to speak in 1994, and who was there but that little weasel, Jim David, the Hatchet Man, and Joe Schmidt, an old Detroit linebacker. We're hugging and kissing at the bar and Schmidt, who has a real good

Art Donovan. Photograph by Vince Bagli

voice, is singing and there was a whole bunch of people there and we had a good time.

I had a pretty good year in 1960, but the handwriting was on the wall. They wanted to go with younger guys. I was thirty-five. They said to me, "You're not getting by the second guy like you used to."

Nobody ever retires; they get rid of you. I didn't want to quit. You don't like to leave, but you try to leave gracefully. I wasn't bitter. I loved every minute of it, and wanted to play one more year.

When Don Shula came in 1963, he wanted me to come back just for a year, but I said no; I couldn't do it. I had the liquor store and all. I don't know if it was just a gracious gesture on his part.

Gino made the mistake of coming back. They used him as a tackle, and Gino didn't know how to play tackle. He knew how to play end.

Herman Ball, an old line coach for the Colts, came to see me when they asked me to come back. He said, "Whatever they want you to do, don't do it. The first time is always the best. It'll never be the same."

I'm glad I didn't do it.

Now people say to me, "Aren't you sorry you're not playing today with all the big money?"

And I say, "What the hell's the money? I got enough money. I can only eat so many hot dogs and cheeseburgers and salami sandwiches. I loved it. I wouldn't have missed any of it."

Jim Mutscheller, short yardage possession specialist, great blocker. Courtesy of Jim Mutscheller

Jim Mutscheller

Born: 3-31-30
Beaver Falls, Pennsylvania
Notre Dame
Tight End

6′ 1″, 205 lbs.
Drafted: #12, 1952
Colts: 1954–1961

"The ball hit a defensive back, Norb Hecker, on the shoulder pads and popped up in the air and I caught it and scored. My moment of glory."

After high school I intended to go to Duquesne, but they dropped football that year. I wanted to go to a Catholic school, and went to Notre Dame, where I played for Frank Leahy.

Being at Notre Dame at the age of eighteen is very impressive. I remember being in the navy drill hall that looks out on the football practice field one day. It was about one o'clock, an hour before practice. I looked out and saw a guy in shorts and a T-shirt running laps around the goal posts. It was Bill Fisher, the team captain. He was injured at the time, but he was working out. I looked at the size of his legs and chest and thought, "I'm in the wrong place."

It was like you would think it's supposed to be at Notre Dame. Leahy was the commander in chief. He had his lieutenants, and things were organized and run like a business, almost a military operation. Leahy was a taskmaster, a perfectionist who couldn't stand it if they lost. He didn't have to suffer in my sophomore year—the first year I could play—in 1949; we were undefeated and national champions.

In 1950 we lost the second game of the year, to Purdue, 28–14. It was a tough year because the team was in transition. It was the end of the time when veterans were coming back from the war and playing football, and we were undermanned. Some of us played both ways because we didn't have enough players.

I was the captain in my senior year; we lost two games, to SMU and Michigan State.

After graduation I went to the marines' officer training school in Quantico, Virginia. I'd had enough of football, but after classes all day and maneuvers and everything else we had to do, they would come down in a helicopter and pick up all the football players and take us to the main base for practice. It was worse than anything in high school or college.

So I was not real excited about playing pro football. I couldn't get myself geared into it. I was twenty-four when I joined the Colts in 1954.

I was not aware of pro football and didn't know much of the background of it. It was a unique experience.

Weeb Ewbank was the coach, and he typed people right away. If you were coming out of the service, he decided you had "army legs" and couldn't run. I lucked into making the team that year because Weeb decided that everything was going to be like the Cleveland Browns, who were winning championships with good backup men.

I became the Colts backup man, not only to the two ends, Lloyd Colteryahn and Dan Edwards, but to the two defensive ends, too, Don Joyce and Gino Marchetti. I was the sub if anybody got hurt, but in those days nobody got hurt. The way things were in Baltimore in those days, they were afraid that somebody else might take their place and they'd get cut.

One of my first experiences taught me a lesson. During a preseason game, I went into the defensive huddle, and Pellington's screaming at Shula and Shula's screaming at Marchetti and everybody's cussing at everybody else. I stood there and decided, "I don't think this is for me. My pursuit should be offense." I weighed 220 at the time. So at the end of that first year, I lost 15 pounds and bought low-cut shoes.

I was on the kickoff team in the opening game in 1954 against the Rams at Memorial Stadium. We kicked off, and after the tackle, the Rams were running their offensive team onto the field and the kickoff team off. Their halfback, Skeets Quinlan, stayed on the field over near the east sideline and down by the closed south end near the Rams bench. Nobody noticed him. On the first play they pulled a sleeper and threw the ball to Skeets, and he ran down the sideline untouched. Our defensive halfback, Don Shula, never saw him. I had just come off the field and was standing there watching, and I realized that nobody would get him. We lost that day, 48–0.

Then in 1955 we got Szymanski, Ameche, Preas, Shaw, and Berry in the draft, and you could see the difference. The offense started moving the ball.

In 1956 we were 4 and 7 after losing two in a row on the West Coast. Our last game was December 23 at home against the Redskins. We were losing, 17–12, near the end of the game. In the huddle, Unitas said, "All of you run down as far as you can go and I'll throw it." We all ran down too far and had to come back toward the ball. It was a big mess of people. The ball hit a defensive back, Norb Hecker, on the shoulder pads and popped up in the air and I caught it and scored. My moment of glory. That game was televised, so the whole country saw my "great" last-minute catch. That was my day of honor.

When George Shaw was injured and John Unitas made his first start [October 21, 1956] against the Bears, his first pass was intercepted by J.C. Caroline. I can't say that I was all that excited that Unitas was going to play in place of Shaw. I had not developed any opinion of him. After the game, I happened to be sitting behind him on the bus, and I overheard

Walter Taylor of the *Sun* papers interviewing him. We'd just gotten killed, 58–27, and you had to be demoralized, but John's talking to Taylor like everything's perfect. He's sitting there sounding so confident, I concluded: "Well, maybe there's something here I haven't seen."

Jim Mutscheller.
Photograph by Vince Bagli

I remember the game we won in Cleveland that year. Bob Gain was a defensive tackle from Kentucky. Their regular defensive end got hurt, so they moved Gain to end. I'd been having some success blocking down the defensive ends, but Gain didn't understand the game. Defensive ends were supposed to rush inside. I could time them and was quick enough to get them. But Gain played like a tackle. His first move was right into me, and he weighed maybe 260. I was running into him all day. That was a long day; when I got done with that game I was goofy.

In 1957 I thought we were the most effective offensively. Raymond Berry was modernizing pass receiving in pro football. Bob Shaw had come as the receivers' coach. He knew the position in a different manner from Weeb, who went with Paul Brown's reliance on cut-and-dried plays. Shaw was more into individual patterns, and Raymond developed as a result, and kept improving on it. I don't think I've ever seen a receiver who could catch the ball better than Raymond.

It was Lenny Moore's second year, and we had L.G. Dupre and Alan and John and Raymond. After we won our first three games, we had a 27–3 lead in Detroit and wound up losing that game in the last couple seconds. We still had the lead and were trying to run out the clock near the end of the game, and Weeb said, "Run the Statue of Liberty. Give it to Lenny Moore and let him run around." So they gave it to Lenny and Roger Zatkoff, a linebacker, came up and hit him and the ball flew and started out of bounds, then rolled back and they recovered and that was that. They scored and beat us, 31–27.

The next Sunday, Green Bay beat us 24–21 at the end when Babe Parilli throws the ball to Billy Howton and Henry Moore stood there and watched Howton run right by him. It was amazing.

In the overtime in the 1958 game against the Giants, John called the pass to me in the huddle. It was a diagonal out, not a down and out. We were on about the 8 yard line, and on a diagonal it was difficult to tell if you would get into the end zone before the ball came. It was supposed to be thrown at my outside shoulder, so if the defensive back, Linden Crow, was on my back, John could throw it out of bounds. The field was frozen and I couldn't do anything but slide out of bounds after I caught it. Then Alan Ameche scored. I looked at the game film not too long ago. Alan scored early in the game, too. He played really well all game, with his blocks and runs.

Playing inside, you have a linebacker on your head all the time. You have to block him straight ahead, and try to move him one way or the other. We blocked down a lot on the defensive end. I would block down on an off-tackle play. If the play's going the other way, you're downfield trying to knock somebody down.

In practice every day I had Bill Pellington on my head and Gino inside me. Pellington was our most intimidating player.

The most intimidating team we played was the Chicago Bears. Guys like Ed Sprinkle, Dick Butkus—their mission was to put fear into people. Butkus was devastating in the middle; he played like an animal, but very good. He and Ray Nitschke of the Packers were intimidators. When Bill George was playing, the Bears would run all kinds of screwy defenses, not the same kind of intimidation game. Then you had the coach, George Halas, screaming at everybody from the sidelines: the officials, his own players, us, everybody.

I had a sore forehead my whole career. The suspension tanker type helmets spun around on my head. I was doing a lot of blocking, and the helmet would spin when it hit against the other guy's shoulder or legs and cut my ear. I got a cauliflower ear out of it. So I went to the helmet that was padded inside so it wouldn't spin.

I played through 1961; I had a knee operation the year before, and I could tell I wasn't playing the way I had been. Since then I've sold insurance.

Baltimore was the ideal place to be in pro football. I talk to guys I had gone to college with, who played ten or fifteen years with other teams. They said they were never really happy, never had the enjoyment that we had here. It was a perfect time and a perfect place to play professional football.

Jim Parker

Born: 4-3-34
Macon, Georgia
Ohio State
Offensive Guard/Tackle

6′ 3″, 275 lbs.
Drafted: #1, 1957
Colts: 1957–1967
Hall of Fame, 1973

"That piece of pie cost me a thousand bucks."

I left Macon, Georgia, when I was in the eleventh grade and went to Toledo, Ohio, to live with my uncle, go to school for one year, and join the army.

One morning in Toledo I got up at 5:30 and started walking. I came to Scott High School and went in. Somebody in the hall thought I was what they called a hallwalker—somebody just hanging around looking at the girls—and they carried me to the principal's office. I sat there for about an hour trying to convince a lady that I was not a student there. She kept insisting that I was, said she had caught me a dozen times herself. I tried to tell her that she hadn't, that I was a new student and hadn't even enrolled.

I went there for one year and played football. One night I was working parking cars across the street from where a big football banquet was going on. Woody Hayes, the coach at Ohio State, was there because they were honoring their football captain, George Jacoby, who came from Toledo. Somebody told Woody, "You're wasting your time over here. The best football player in this area is across the street parking cars."

Woody came over and introduced himself to me, and that's how I got to Ohio State. I stayed with Woody for two years. He didn't want me out of his sight. He met me at the bus station when I got to Columbus, and I stayed at his home during the entrance exams. I weighed 220 pounds, and wanted to gain some weight, but food portions on campus were small, so I had to pick up a couple jobs to fill my stomach.

Woody gave me a job as his chauffeur. I had to pick up the new players and show them the campus, get the game films, and take Woody wherever he wanted to go. If Woody liked you, he liked you. If he didn't, you caught hell for the four years of your time there. One time he wanted me to go fishing with him, but I told him I wouldn't go with anybody as nervous as he was; he'd overturn the boat. But he was as close to my father as any man I ever met.

Jim Parker. Photograph © 1995 TADDER/Baltimore

I played both ways at Ohio State, tackle and guard and linebacker. Woody had a theory: from tackle to tackle, a fullback and quarterback was all you needed. Everything else was dead. We ran the ball 60 to 70 offensive plays a game. The only time I ever carried the ball there was when I intercepted a pass against Indiana and ran it back 70 yards for a touchdown.

We had a quarterback, John Boynton, number one high school quarterback in the nation. Woody didn't like the passing game. In four years we threw the ball only twenty-one times. He said when you throw the ball in the air, anybody can catch it. He told Boynton not to throw the ball, but Boynton did one time against Illinois, and J.C. Caroline picked it off and carried it 90 yards for a touchdown. That was the end of John Boynton; he never played another game for OSU.

It hurt Boynton so bad he wound up over at Sheppard Pratt mental institution. I got a call one day years later from Ohio State, asking me to go over there and see him. He was president of Timken Steel, and the thing that bugged him was why Woody Hayes had benched him. I told him, "It was obvious; he told you not to throw the ball, and you threw it. Everybody on the team knew it."

We didn't really need a quarterback except to hand off the ball to Howard Cassady, the halfback. Cassady won the Heisman my junior year, and I thought I should have won it my senior year. I had my speech all ready to go to New York, and they gave it to Paul Hornung at Notre Dame. They only won a few games that year. The reason I didn't win it is that they didn't want to give it to an Ohio State player two years in a row.

At the time, John Brodie from Stanford, Lou Michaels from Kentucky, and I were the leading candidates. All the newspapers were backing me. I was on the team that beat USC in the Rose Bowl, I had made All-American, and won the Outland Trophy as the most outstanding lineman. When it was over, I felt a little bit hurt because I had worked for it. I wanted it more than anything else in college and didn't get it. I went back to Ohio State in 1994 for a homecoming game, and they honored me as the best offensive lineman who ever played there.

Before teams use a draft pick on you, they inquire about your interest in playing for them. They don't want to waste one if a guy says he won't play for them. I could have been Cleveland's first draft pick in 1957, but I didn't like Paul Brown because of what he did to Marion Motley. After all those years playing for him, Motley asked him for a job, and Brown said he was no employment agency.

I went to Washington with a friend, Harry Stroebel, to see George Preston Marshall. When Marshall saw I was black, he said, "Get your black ass out of here." Harry wanted to make an uproar, but I told him to let it die, and we went back to Columbus.

I was drafted the same time as Jim Brown and John Brodie. That night, after the Colts drafted me number one, we all went to Sardi's in New York for dinner.

I was reluctant to come to Baltimore. Buddy Young and Carroll Rosenbloom came to Columbus to get me to sign a contract, but I hesitated. I didn't visit the city until January. Big Daddy Lipscomb picked me up and showed me around, and I didn't like what I saw. I couldn't go to a movie. I couldn't go to the Hecht Company. But I told Rosenbloom, "You find me a decent place to stay in this city, and I'll come."

He found me an apartment and now I've been here thirty-eight years. I like Baltimore almost as much as Macon, Georgia, my first love. All my twelve kids were born here. I've seen this city turned upside down since I've been here, through the riots and all.

But I almost didn't stay. When I showed up at Westminster training camp, I went to get my pads and helmet, and they were lying on the floor in the gymnasium. I wasn't accustomed to picking up my helmet off the floor and putting it on my head. At Ohio State, the man from Riddell came down from Chicago and measured my head and made my helmet to custom. My pads were custom made. When I left there, they gave them to me.

So I went over to the window in that gym and said to the equipment man, "Mr. Schubach, I need a helmet."

He said, "Right there on the floor, son."

I said, "I can't wear that. It won't fit. I want a custom-made helmet."

He looked at me and said, "Listen, rookie, you ain't made the damn team yet. When you make the team, we'll buy you one." He got a big kick out of that.

So I walked out of the locker room, got in my car and drove back to Ohio. After three days Carroll Rosenbloom called and asked me what was wrong. I told him about the man making a joke about my equipment. I said I wanted a custom-made hat. I came back and the guy from Chi came down and made two hats for me. And the whole team rode me over that for three, four days.

We had one trainer, Eddie Block, and an assistant, Dimitri Spassoff, at Westminster. At Ohio State we had sixty—one for each guy. They taped you up before a game and cut the tape off afterwards. At Westminster we had one whirlpool. If the offensive backs were using it, you had to wait your turn till after dark to use it. Later, when they moved to Owings Mills, it was better.

We had hand-me-down uniforms and socks. Every day at practice they'd throw forty-five pairs of socks on the floor. If some guy wore two, you didn't get any. You had to go out there with your damn skin. Five dollar jocks in the middle of the floor. That was it.

The team had a quota: seven blacks. There were seven of us for eight years. At Westminster, the eighth black come, don't give a damn how good he was, they'd ship him out at midnight. We had a big fullback from Virginia. I thought he was better than Ameche. They cut him at two o'clock in the morning. Next morning we got up looking for him and he was gone. We asked around what happened to him. They said, "He wasn't good enough."

So for the eleven years I played here I had a chip on my shoulder.

I got along with my teammates because that was a close-knit family. It was outsiders. When the coaches had their annual picnic at Westminster the local people didn't like mixing with us, so we had to rent the entire hall at the country club for our Colt Night. We had an amateur night and we all participated.

Carroll Rosenbloom came to me and Big Daddy and Lenny and asked us if we wanted to leave Westminster and go to Philadelphia or Canada.

He said he would move the training site because of the conditions there. We sat down and had a meeting and decided we'd stay at Westminster because we could visit our families at least three times a week. Rosenbloom brought first-run movies to the camp for us, because we couldn't go to the movies in town. One time we had a light dude from North Carolina in camp, a big red kid. We sent him to the movie one night, paid his way, and we sat outside and ate popcorn and roared because they let him in. We got a kick out of that.

I didn't think anybody at training camp could whip me. It was an attitude I carried from Ohio State. I played against Marchetti and Don Joyce.

Marchetti was the quickest and fastest person that I've ever seen. I studied him, and tried to figure out how to block in case I got traded and had to come back and play against him. I was here eleven years with him, and he's the only guy I didn't figure out. Anybody else I could whip. But he was so quick and agile, you couldn't figure him out. I really appreciated the great honor of being selected with Gino on the all-time NFL team.

Don Joyce was a dirty player in practice. Before practice he was a different person. He'd go in his locker and take a pill of some kind and his eyeballs would get small and get large. I said, "That SOB is going crazy." Somebody warned me: don't take your eyes off him or he'll take you out.

Big Daddy Lipscomb could have been a great coach. He took me under his wing from the start and taught me everything I know about offensive tackle. You wouldn't think a defense man would know as much as he did about offense. When I came to Baltimore to sign a contract, before I went to the College All-Star game, we worked out together. One day I said to him, "You want to race for a hundred dollars?" I challenged him to 40 yards. I had spent the money before I won it. We lined up, and he left me 3 yards on the 40.

I figured this must be an accident. "Let's do it again for another hundred."

He beat me again. I said, "Look, I got a problem with this leg. I'll see you at training camp."

I never could beat him. Nobody could.

I signed a two-year contract for $12,500. The contract was basic; everybody got the same one. On the back they would type in the incentive "ifs": if you made the Pro Bowl, etc. I had a lot of jobs during the off-season. I sold embalming fluid, worked at Sparrows Point. Artie Donovan helped me get a job with Morris Kasoff's liquor distributorship. I sold cemetery plots for $95; now they are $1,400. I should have bought the cemetery.

One year I went to the office on Charles Street to sign. The general manager, Don Kellett, picks up the telephone and pretends to be talking with Carroll Rosenbloom, and Carroll was no more on that telephone than the man in the moon. Kellett went over the contract with me and my wife, Mae; then he went upstairs and left us alone, with the speaker on so he could hear what we were saying.

He came back in a little bit and put 1,500 one-dollar bills on the desk and said, "Are you ready to sign?"

"No, I'm not," I said.

Mae had her foot under the table and almost broke my leg kicking me to sign. She was looking at all that money, and it looked like all the money in the world. So I signed and we took the money and went to the Belvedere Hotel. At that time no blacks could stay there, but Rosenbloom had rented a whole floor, and put champagne in every room. Mae put all those dollar bills in the bathtub and said, "I'm going to take a bath in one-dollar bills."

When I was a rookie at Westminster in 1957 the public never heard anything about offensive linemen. We had good talent but no big names. The Colts had a depth chart and I was listed as the number four or five offensive left tackle. I went to coach Weeb Ewbank and said, "I thought I was an offensive guard or defensive linebacker. That's where I want to play."

He said, "This is the team, and this is where you're going to play—offensive tackle."

I told the rest of the guys that when the season started, that would be my position. They laughed and had a good time over that. But I went out to master it. When I walked on a football field, I went out there to play. I didn't go out there to loaf or make the time pass. I went out there to do a job for sixty minutes.

In a couple weeks I was number three, then two, then number one. On opening day at Memorial Stadium, Weeb came to me and said, "You and Don Shinnick are starting as rookies. Don't let the crowd upset you."

I looked at Weeb and said, "How many you having today?"

He said, "Forty thousand."

I said, "We had forty thousand at practice every day at Ohio State. So forty thousand here ain't going to excite me."

Weeb was an organizer. He had everything in sequence. Practice started at two o'clock. Before you went out there, he told you what you were going to do: fifteen minutes offense, fifteen minutes defense, fifteen minutes total offense, fifteen minutes kicking game, practice is over. If he said one hour and a half, he'd bring you out after one hour and a half.

On game days he had everything planned down to the last minute before we went out on the field. Three minutes for the prayer meeting. Two minutes to get taped. When the ref knocked on the door, you got one minute to go to the bathroom and be on the field. Everything was organized. Weeb was the best at that, better than all of them put together.

Don Shula was the kind of guy who could look you square in the eye and call you an asshole, but Weeb wasn't built that way. Whatever he was feeling, he always communicated it through somebody else. He would tell Artie Donovan or Big Daddy to tell me something.

On the practice field, the only thing Weeb was afraid of was lightning. If we were practicing and there was any lightning, practice was over. Everybody prayed for lightning every day. Rain didn't stop anything, but lightning did.

And Weeb was big on missing meals and watching your weight and fines. Sherman Plunkett had an eating problem. He had gained 30 pounds, so he was exempt from all the meals. If I missed a lunch, it would cost me $500. If Donovan missed a lunch, that was $500. Not Plunkett. But he was still gaining weight. So they sent him to Johns Hopkins to be evaluated, and they couldn't find anything wrong with him.

I was rooming with Sherman. One night I woke up about 3:30. I heard somebody or something munching in the room. I thought it was one of those Westminster rats or snakes in the room. If you turned on a light after eleven o'clock, you're talking about $500. I lay there listening, and then I took a chance and flicked on the light, and there's Plunkett, sitting up in bed with a whole foot-long piece of liverwurst and another foot of cheese, and crackers, eating away.

I told him, "Sherman, I'm going to go get the coach and put the man on your ass because I don't want to be around you eating like that. You're hurting me and the team and you're going to eat yourself right out of the league."

I went and got Weeb and he came up and chewed his ass out and we went back to sleep.

I have a picture on the wall of my son bringing me a cup of lemonade that cost me $500. It was at Westminster, hot, 104 degrees in the shade. My boy, Jimmy, was four years old and he brought it to me. Weeb looked over and saw it and it cost me $500. He didn't want you having anything on the bench. No ice. No water. Nothing.

Weeb put me on the kickoff team, kickoff receiving team, and place kick team. He wanted you in the game on every play, even when you were sitting on the bench. If you turned your back, you'd miss something. He'd say, "Offensive team," and if you didn't pop up. . ."kicking team" boom, you be there or you get fined for that. One day in Chicago I was sitting on the bench talking to somebody, and I missed the call for the place kick team, and it cost me 500 bucks.

I ran the ball once for Weeb Ewbank. On the kickoff receiving team, I was part of a four-man wedge formation around the 10 or 15 yard line. The halfback would catch the ball and we would lead him down the field. One day at Memorial Stadium the ball was kicked to me. I should have moved up and let one of the backs catch the ball, but something told me to catch it and take it down the field. So I caught it and carried it across the 50 and the crowd stood up and roared. I thought I was really doing something. I got to the 45 and they still roared, and then I coughed up the ball and everybody in that stadium booed the hell out of me.

When I came off the field, the coach kicked my ass, and there's Lenny Moore stretched out laughing.

Later, Don Shula begged me, "Please don't touch the football," but from that point on, I never wanted to carry another football.

Weeb let me know that my main job was to protect John Unitas. They blamed me whenever somebody got to him. Weeb would say to me, "If you lose the quarterback, you'll be in the unemployment line for the rest of the year." We had to protect the quarterback or we didn't eat. We sat down with the man and said, "To set up the pocket, we'll start back 7 yards behind the line of scrimmage, come up at 5 and guarantee you nobody will put a hand on you." We had to do that.

One day we were playing the Bears. Joe Fortunato was the linebacker and Doug Atkins the end. They would switch positions, and that meant L.G. Dupre would wind up blocking the big man and me the little man. They would beat us every time. At half-time I said to Weeb, "Why don't you let me stay with the big man, and let L.G. block the linebacker? If not that, leave him back there to pick him up."

Weeb said, "I get paid to coach the team. Let me coach the team." He didn't take my suggestion. And everybody in the stands thought it was me getting beat, but it was L.G.

For my first two years, I led the 100-yard dash in practice. After that, I refused to run it. Weeb and then Shula raised hell about it, but I told them I wasn't being paid to run sprints. I might pull a muscle.

Playing the Giants in the 1958 championship game, I was up against Andy Robustelli. He scared the hell out of me because of his name and reputation. I dreamt about him for two weeks before the game. My main job was to keep him away from Unitas. How was I going to attack him? Each play is like a chess play. Am I going to beat him head-on? Am I going to sit this way or that way?

After the first three plays, I found that I could get into his head; he was a team player. He played a total defense, responsible for draws and sweeps, and he played soft because of it. That made it easy for me. After staying up for two weeks looking at films, wondering if he drank, what time he went to bed—everything about him—and come to find out he was a team player.

Sam Huff was the same way. They were playing the way they were coached, the way we were trying to get to with our defense. With us, Lipscomb was responsible for the screens and draws, Donovan for the middle from tackle to tackle. You could help out if you didn't have anything coming your way. The Giants played a team defense.

I got beat once in that game, by Jim Katcavage. When Robustelli went out, Katcavage came over to my side. He was a tackle, not an end, and I didn't know how to handle him.

Beating the Giants was my biggest thrill in football, but the biggest kick I got on the field came one time when we were in Dallas. Steve Myhra kicked off into a strong wind. The ball went straight up in the air and made a U-turn and went back the other direction. We're running down the field and had to put on the brakes and go back the other way. They got the ball on our 10 yard line. I never laughed so hard on the football field.

All this time I was a left tackle. I had to learn everything about every defensive end I played against. I knew every mole on every one of them. Then Shula came in as our coach in 1963. Woody Hayes called him and said, "You want to win the championship? Move Parker to guard and let Bob Vogel play tackle." The Colts had just drafted Vogel number one from Ohio State.

Shula went for it. He asked me to move to guard and I agreed. Now I had to learn a new position. I'd have to play against guys like Roger Brown at Detroit. He weighed 400 pounds. I'm used to doing things one way; now I had to do them another way.

When we played the Rams, Shula moved me to right end to block on Deacon Jones. Deacon was in a class by himself, one of the toughest I ever played against. I wound up playing every position but right guard.

As a guard, I had to pull more, and cheat sometimes. Pulling and blocking for Lenny Moore was fun, because you didn't have to do it a specific way. You could do it any way and he could adjust to it and make the change. But Lenny was so much quicker than I was, I never went on the count. So when the ball went on hut, I left before the hut. That's the only way I could get there. And the ref could never catch it.

Pound for pound, Lenny Moore was the best football player I've ever seen. I was his roommate, and I can tell you, he was weird. He had to have ice cream and cake or pie the night before every game. If he didn't get it, he wouldn't play. It was just that simple.

We're in Milwaukee one time the night before a game and Lenny called room service. It was closed. We went down to the lobby and Lenny saw a guy in a pretty uniform and gave him $50 to bring back some ice cream and pie. I said, "Lenny, that guy's not a bellman. He's a marine."

Lenny said, "He's the bell captain."

We waited till two o' clock. No pie and ice cream. I said, "The man was a marine. He got the money and was gone."

Lenny couldn't sleep. "Come on," he said. "Let's go across the street and get some pie and ice cream."

"I don't want no pie," I said. "But I'll go with you."

We started down the hall. Don Shula got off the elevator and we're out there at two o' clock in the morning. That's a thousand dollars apiece.

Lenny said, "Don't worry about a thing. I can handle him." He walked down the hall with his hands outstretched. Shula looked at him and said, "What are you doing?"

"He's sleepwalking," I said.

Shula said, "When he wakes up, that'll be a thousand for him, and a thousand for you for going with him."

That piece of pie cost me a thousand bucks.

Lenny could laugh all night, but he was the best football player I ever played with.

We looked like we were the best team in football when we went to Cleveland for that championship game in 1964. Every game you have to be motivated to a certain level. You have to start at eight o'clock in the morning getting ready for the game. We just never got ready that day. You could ask your legs to do this or that, but they just wouldn't do it.

When Raymond Berry had first gone to Weeb Ewbank, and then to Shula, and told them he wanted to have a Sunday service before every game, everybody thought he was crazy. But it became a regular thing. We started at 6:30 or 6:45 in the morning with the service at the hotel. That morning in Cleveland we had a guest speaker in, we had Governor Mandel in, we had Miss America in, we had all these people to come in. That started your day. Then we had the pregame meal and went to the stadium. We started getting ready early in the morning, but that day we never really got started.

For myself, after the services, I would start thinking about my opponent, thinking about the first five offensive plays we got in advance. What would they do on defense? Sometimes I'd try to guess the first five plays before we got them. I'd dream about how bad my opponent was going to get beat that day. I never thought that I was going to get beat. And I had no butterflies.

But once in a while I did get beat. I remember Tommy Nobis in Atlanta. I looked at that guy and thought I could whip him. During the game I went to Unitas and said, "John, give me 32 trap." I trapped Nobis like he was in a box.

John said to me, "You want it again?"

I said, "Yes."

He gave it to me again. This time Nobis threw us for a 2-yard loss. My neck went down in my body about six inches. I was six feet three when I started; I was five feet tall now, and I'm mad.

Back in the huddle, John said, "You want it again?"

I said, "Hell, no."

Played the whole game, never could block Nobis. Now I see he's been nominated for the Hall of Fame. I would vote for him. You never forget the name of anybody who beat you.

I have a bad memory of a kid I beat bad in a game: Jess Arnelle, one of Lenny Moore's friends from Penn State. He played defensive end for the Colts, then left and went to the Steelers. We were playing in Pittsburgh and I beat that kid so bad, sometimes I have nightmares about the beating I put on him. He'd be lying on the ground and I'd start thumping him on the face, and I didn't have any reason to do that.

He looked at me and said, "Why?"

I said, " 'Cause you ought to get off the field."

Now he's a big lawyer, and I just want to tell him before I die that I was sorry I put a whipping on him.

Shula was a genius. But when he came to Baltimore, he was nervous. Before he got here, he'd call my house every night: "I want you to be my offensive captain."

I said, "No. You wait till you get here and make that decision. I'm not going to accept that responsibility."

When he arrived, he got rid of the network of little cliques. When I was a rookie, Marchetti had me taken into his clique. We had a phone down in the basement at training camp. When the phone rang in the coaches' office, we monitored it twenty-four hours a day. We would know who was going to get cut. When somebody was going to go, we'd go to the guy and tell him to get ready, 'cause his ass was out the door.

One day Marchetti asked me to bring in three half-gallons of vodka from my store. I thought he wanted it for his house, but he put it in the lemonade for after practice. So after practice, everybody's drinking lemonade, and by seven o'clock everybody's drunk. Now he's scared. He'll have to face Shula wanting to know who put the vodka in the lemonade. And I'm on the hot seat because I brought it in and gave it to him. But nobody ever said anything, and it died down.

Shula covered every phase of football: short yardage, short short yardage, special teams, down and distance. If the ball was on the 18 yard line, we had four or five plays that we could use to get it in. We had plays for the 4 yard line, the 2 yard line; we knew what we were going to do, and if you didn't get the ball in from the 2 or 4, that was your ass when you came off the field. He would get in your face no matter who you were.

He and I got into a big fight one time in training camp. On weigh-in day I went in and preweighed myself: 280. Then I went in and ate breakfast— a dozen eggs, fourteen pieces of sausage. I'm looking at Shula and he's looking at me, because I don't usually eat on weigh-in day. I knew I was overweight.

I went into the locker room and got dressed, and everybody weighed in but Marchetti and Berry and someone else. I knew when they called their names, it would just go on the chart.

"Marchetti."

"Two seventy-five."

"Berry."

"One ninety."

"Parker."

"Two seventy-five."

"Wait a minute," the trainer said. "Who said that?"

"I did," I said.

"Get over here and get on the scale."

"No way, not unless you put Raymond and those other guys on the scale, too."

The trainer goes and tells Shula I didn't get on the scale. Shula comes out. "Get on the scale."

"Not unless the others get on. What's good for the gander's good for the goose."

He took me into his office and we had a long talk. He told me if I didn't get on the scale, the others would never have any respect for him. I told him, "If you don't put those other guys on the scale, *they'll* never have any respect for you."

"The hell with them," he said. "It's going to cost you $100 a day."

I was so glad he did that, because I was 5 pounds over my prescribed weight before I ate breakfast, so I was probably 10 pounds over after I ate, and that would have cost me $1,000, and we didn't make all that much money in those days.

Raymond Berry was a self-made player. I made a mistake one day. He asked me to stay after practice and throw him a few passes. I must have thrown him a thousand passes. My arm swelled up so, I had two arms on the right side. I said, "Never again." He went out and hired a local college athlete to throw to him. He'd work on all his weaknesses. Low passes? He'd catch them two inches from the ground a thousand times. I never saw a guy work as hard as he did.

Artie Donovan was my locker mate for eleven years. Alex Sandusky would go out in the woods and shoot a groundhog or a skunk or something and hang it in Artie's locker. Every morning Arthur would sit down in front of his locker for twenty minutes before he'd open it. One morning he opened it and all this blood was coming out of that groundhog. He saw that and passed out right there on the floor. We had to call the paramedics.

Shula came over and raised all kinds of hell. "He could have had a heart attack," he yelled.

One of the guys said, "Who cares?"

It took me two days to get my composure back; it was so funny.

John Mackey came to Baltimore with an agent when nobody had ever heard of one. I thought Mackey was a better player than Mike Ditka. He did more things. When he got the ball he was the toughest to bring down.

Among guys I played against, I mentioned that Deacon Jones was the toughest for me. Doug Atkins, who came from Tennessee to the Bears, didn't have but one objective: to break John Unitas's arms and legs. He didn't have any other responsibility, and didn't care how he got there.

Rosey Grier was tough.

Willie Davis of the Packers knew Vince Lombardi's program, knew where to go, what to do. Lombardi coached everything on the field. And Davis knew everything he wanted and gave it to him. Davis never did anything for himself to make an outstanding play, like some players do. He was a team player.

Henry Jordan was on that team, too. A crazy, baldheaded guy, he never got the recognition he should have received.

Jim Parker. Photograph by Vince Bagli

Every Sunday you had a day's work cut out for you. But after so many years, I could look at a Sunday going to work and know whether the guy was easy pickings. You'd start rating how much energy you'd have to use each Sunday on the schedule.

The dirtiest player I ever played against was Les Richter, a middle linebacker for the Rams. He would hook a back in the neck running through, and try to break his neck. If your leg was on the ground, he'd step on it and try to break it. One day I was walking off the field and I was about 2 yards from the sidelines when he took off his helmet and hit me across the head—bam! Knocked me silly. I pretended to be really out of it, because I wanted to retaliate. Carroll Rosenbloom was sitting there, and I went through the motions like I was dying. I wanted him to speak up for me if I retaliated and got thrown out of the game.

I went back on the field and about four plays later there was some action that left Richter down on the ground. He was getting up with his fingers on the ground and I stomped his hands for about twenty minutes.

We both went to the Pro Bowl that year, and guys were talking about dirty players in the locker room. I said I never did anything like that, and Richter jumped up and said, "You're a damn liar. You stomped my hands. They're still raw."

There were also some very sportsmanlike guys; a few who come to mind are Ricky Williams and Paul Wiggin at Cleveland, and John Brodie at San Francisco.

Among the Colts' assistant coaches, John Sandusky was a good offensive line coach, but he had to satisfy the head coaches. Herman Ball did what he wanted to do. If he thought you needed work on pass protection, he would give it to you during the fifteen-minute offensive drills, regardless of what the other coaches thought.

I never heard a word about gambling or fixing point spreads in all my time in football. If anybody ever approached anybody on my team, I never heard any talk of it. The only person who could throw a game would be the quarterback. Bert Bell, the old commissioner, used to come to camp and tell you what places to stay away from: The Block, places on Greenmount. If you were caught in those places, they put a rubber stamp on you and sent you back home.

I read where somebody said that Carroll Rosenbloom would bet against his team, but I never believed that.

The commissioner also came around once a year and gave us the bubble-gum card money and the Coca-Cola money off the caps with the players' pictures on them. Out of that, we formed a players' association. Then we began to collect a pension, and today I get more from the pension than I did when I was playing. Recently, we took in the old-time players who were finished before that started.

Today I own a lounge and a liquor store in Baltimore, but I don't drink anymore, since I had a stroke a few years ago.

I believe today's game is a bunch of overpaid guys who believe they can play football. A few could have played then: Bruce Smith, Lawrence Taylor, Troy Aikman. It's a different game now, all specialists who can do one thing.

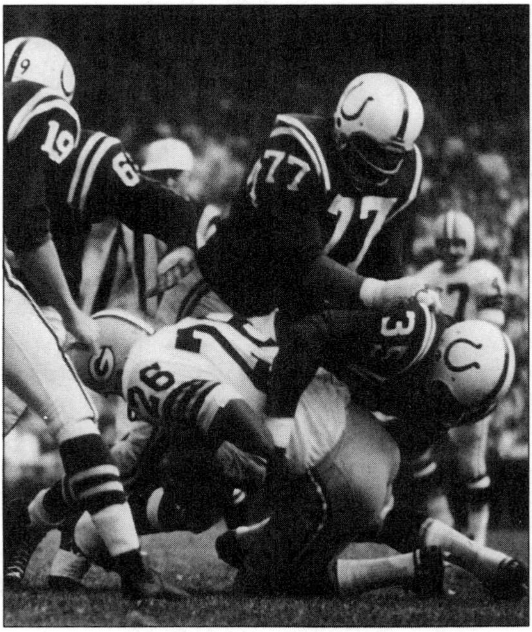

Jim Parker, one of five Colts on All-Time NFL team.
Photograph © 1995 TADDER/Baltimore

Gino Marchetti

Born: 1-2-27
Antioch, California
University of San Francisco
Defensive End

6′ 4″, 245 lbs.
Drafted: #2
(New York Yankees)
Colts: 1953–1964, 1966
Hall of Fame: 1972

"To me, running on that field, hearing that Baltimore Colts song. . . gave me such a thrill. I heard it for fifteen years; from the first day I heard it to the last, it jumped me up a little bit."

We had nine guys off my team at USF who played professional football. Three of them—Bob St. Clair, Ollie Matson, and me—are in the Hall of Fame. The shame of it was that the best of us all, Burl Tolar, tore up his knee in the college All-Star Game and never played again. He became an NFL official.

In my senior year we were undefeated and uninvited. Our last game was against College of the Pacific, who was also undefeated. There was a rumor that the winner would go to one of the major bowls. We beat them, 47–14; they went to a bowl and we didn't. I don't know why we didn't get invited.

I had no intention of playing professional football. I guess it was pride. I thought I might not be big enough; I was only 6-4 and weighed 220. I come from a very small town—Antioch, California—population three thousand. I was afraid that because I wasn't that big I would go to a pro team and not make it and have to go home and face everybody.

Even when I was drafted pretty high by the New York Yankees, who became the Dallas Texans for the 1952 season, I really wasn't looking forward to it. I told them, "There's only one way I'll ever sign, and that's if I get a non-release contract."

The coach, Jimmy Phelan, said, "We don't do that."

"Then I'm not going to sign."

Finally they agreed, and I went to training camp. Within the first week I was there, I was ready to quit and go home. I was very lonely. I was the only player who went there from the college all-stars, and everybody else was already in a clique, so I had nobody to hang around with. I called my brother and told him I might come home. He said, "Stay there and give 'em hell. Once you quit, you'll always wonder about it."

Gino Marchetti (89) and Bill Pellington, all-pro defenders.
Photograph © 1995 TADDER/Baltimore

So I stayed. That team folded and I got the big break when they transferred it to Baltimore in 1953. I came over with Buddy Young, George Taliaferro, Art Donovan, Sisto Averno, and Joe Campanella.

Weeb Ewbank was the best coach I ever played for as far as being organized. His biggest asset was that he really knew talent. I was an offensive tackle and he moved me to defensive end. Alex Sandusky was a defensive end; Weeb moved him to offensive guard. He made all kinds of moves like that.

Weeb had his peculiarities. One problem was that his team would die on him, mainly because he wasn't strong enough or didn't take strong stances against the strong personalities. Example: Big Daddy Lipscomb was a great tackle, who should be in the Hall of Fame (Fatso Donovan may not think so, but I do). He was not a pass rusher, but he was reliable, and probably made more tackles than our linebackers. But Weeb was not strong enough to handle that type of personality.

Playing alongside Donovan all those years gave me a lot of confidence to do more with my ability, because my speed sometimes would get me in trouble, and Fatso would always be there. Sometimes his quickness would get him in trouble, too, by overrunning the play or maybe getting off quick and some guy would come and trap, and I'd be there for him.

I thought he was a better football player than a lot of people might have given him credit for, even though he is in the Hall of Fame. We used to laugh about him running the 40-yard dash, telling him we'd have to time him with an hourglass. He was very slow running, but on the line moving laterally he was probably as quick as any lineman we had. And he could diagnose a play in a hurry.

I worked with Ordell Braase a lot in training camp, and sometimes I felt bad because I got more publicity than he did. I thought he was all-pro material and should have had more pro bowls. I had the greatest respect for his ability.

To me, the biggest game we played and the one I'll always remember most was not the '58 championship game, but the one on November 30 that year at Memorial Stadium when we clinched the western conference against the 49ers. We were behind, 27–7, at half-time, and I can remember walking into the locker room and Weeb had written on the blackboard: "Must score 4 touchdowns and stop their offense." I looked at that and thought, "That's almost impossible, the way they're running at us." But we did just what he wrote.

I think there's more pressure getting to the big game than in the big game itself. The '58 championship game is known as the greatest game, because it was played in New York City. To be honest, I don't think that was the best game ever played. Frank Gifford fumbled a few times for them, and if we had scored when we were down there and leading 14–3, it would have been 21–3. Alan Ameche was supposed to throw the ball, and he decided to run, or he didn't see the receiver, or something.

The best offensive tackles I played against were Bob St. Clair of the 49ers and Forrest Gregg of the Green Bay Packers. St. Clair was the biggest tackle I ever saw. We had been teammates at USF, had scrimmaged against each other, but I didn't think of him on the field as a friend of mine. We never talked prior to the game, never said hello or anything, just walked by each other. After the game we'd go out.

I was always nervous prior to a game against him, especially the first year. But after the first series in a game, he was just a number to me. And if he held me, I'd cuss him out like anybody else.

Forrest Gregg wasn't the biggest, but he gave me trouble because he was very quick, which neutralized my quickness. He had great balance and strength. I had some sleepless nights before facing him in a game.

Frannie O'Brien from the Redskins was notorious for holding. Once after a game Freddie Schubach asked me, "Gino, what happened to your jersey?" O'Brien had held me so much he actually tore the numbers from the front of my jersey. He couldn't stop my inside move, so after he held me a couple times I told the ref, "I'm going to do an inside on this guy and he can't block me, so he'll hold me." I'd make that inside move, he'd hold me—15 yards. That day I got him for five holding penalties—75 yards.

Gino Marchetti menaces Fran Tarkington.
Photograph © TADDER/Baltimore

I made all-pro when I was almost forty in 1964, then retired. I laid out a year, then the line got hurt in '66 and Don Shula asked me to come back in case somebody else got hurt. I really didn't want to. Then Carroll Rosenbloom called me. I guess I did it because the organization was always so good to me. Then there was so much negative press about bringing me back: "Why did they let me retire" and all that malarkey.

I played in a few games and Shula said, "We're not going to play you anymore." They were afraid I might get hurt and the press would come down on them.

I think Don Shula is a great coach. Has he changed over the years? Maybe. He was a disciplinarian then; I hope he still is today. He says the players have changed, but I don't know if he has. I think you have to be a disciplinarian. They say today the players won't take it. But if you're fair, honest and strong, a player needs it. You think of us; even though we were thirty or thirty-five or thirty-eight, you're a kid, living in a kid's world, playing a kid's game, so you still do kiddish things, like putting a groundhog in Artie's locker or a bat in his room—all those things that kids do, and we're grown men doing them. So you do need discipline.

I look at some of today's linemen and they look fat, not solid. They got a gut hanging over. I often wonder how a quick guy would do against them.

There's a lot of things I don't like about today's football. I don't think they act professionally, doing flips, dancing into the end zone, spiking the ball, trash talking and all that. I just don't think it's good for the game.

The best thing about being inducted into the Hall of Fame was going to Canton and how well they treat you and your family, and the people you meet. I met a couple from Iowa; I never knew them. They told me, "We've been following your career ever since you got into pro football, and we just had to spend the day with you here."

How did they know me? They didn't have national television in those days. Things like that mean a lot to me.

What meant even more to me was being named to the NFL's seventy-fifth anniversary all-time team. You're in there with some pretty good company. But most of all, the amazing thing is that thirty years after taking off the pads, people still talk about you. It makes you think that somewhere along the line you got lucky enough to do something like that.

I love two things in my life. I loved the people end of our business—we opened our first hamburger place in 1959, and I retired in 1972. It gave me an opportunity to be a leader for the people who worked for me. They all called me coach.

But I love football probably more than anything else. To me, running on that field, hearing that Baltimore Colts song—greatest song in the NFL—gave me such a thrill. I heard it for fifteen years; from the first day I heard it to the last, it jumped me up a little bit.

Our team was close-knit, and we had a city that we loved. I'd come in and find a note in my locker: "Appear at such and such a place Wednesday night at 7:30." And you went. I really felt that by the time I ended my career in Baltimore, I had met every fan in that stadium, all 57,000 of them. We had become their college football team.

Above, left to right: The Colts coaching staff—Offensive Line Coach Herman Ball, Defensive Line Coach John Sandusky, Head Coach Weeb Ewbank, End Coach Don McCafferty, and Backfield Coach Charlie Winner.
Below: Weeb Ewbank, Big Daddy Lipscomb, and Gino Marchetti in 1958.
Courtesy of Transcendental Graphics

Weeb Ewbank

Born: 5-6-07
Richmond, Indiana
Miami of Ohio

Coach
Colts: 1954–1962
Hall of Fame: 1978

"In 1958 my theme was: 'Know your football and we'll be known.'"

I got the name Weeb because my kid brother couldn't say Wilbur, and I'm glad of it.

Paul Brown taught me a lot about professional football, but I learned from all my coaches beginning in high school. My high school coach said, "No smoking," and I never smoked. It was a matter of training in those days.

I was a quarterback, but baseball was probably my better sport. I was a contact hitter, rarely struck out. I played semipro ball three nights a week, and I think I could have made it as a professional outfielder or catcher. Once a scout recommended me to the Indians, but I would have had to drop out of college to go to spring training, and I decided not to go.

When I was a senior at Miami of Ohio, Paul Brown was a junior. He had switched from Ohio State, so he had to sit out a year. He was a quarterback, same as I was, and I knew him there, but we never played on the same team. I graduated in 1928, then worked at Van Wert, Ohio, for two years, and the athletic director at Miami brought me back.

There was a McGuffey School—you remember the old McGuffey Reader—in Oxford, where the Miami School of Education did their practice teaching. I taught health and phys ed there, and as head coach of the football team, I taught the assistant coaches who wanted to become coaches. My ambition was to become a college coach.

I was at Miami from 1930 to 1943, when I went into the navy. I was stationed at Great Lakes Naval Training Station near Chicago when Paul Brown came there as the football coach. He asked me to help him, and I wound up coaching the basketball team, too.

When I got out of the navy I went to Brown University as a backfield and basketball coach. Joe Paterno was my freshman quarterback. After a year there, I got the head coaching job at Washington University in St. Louis. We had no athletic scholarships, but we won seventeen games and lost four in two years. One night my wife, Lucy, and I were sitting at home when the telephone rang. It was Paul Brown in Cleveland. He had lost one of his coaches and he wanted me to join his staff as a tackle coach. I said, "Paul, you know what position you and I played. I know the backfield. I can do anything there. I know about the line, but I don't have any experience coaching linemen since high school."

He said, "Let me worry about that."

It was the best thing that ever happened to me. I coached offensive and defensive tackles for him for five years. By doing that, when I became a head coach, one of the strengths of my teams was their line play. As a player, I hadn't realized how many variations linemen had to learn to adjust to different plays and situations. There are very few exceptions. You can take a new play and put it in with another group of plays and it will fit right in and be easy for the backfield to run. It was harder for the linemen. As a head coach, I had to favor the linemen more than the backs.

I learned pro football working with Paul Brown, but I never tried to mimic him. I've seen a lot of coaches try to do that. People are better off to be themselves. But I took everything I liked about organization and plays with me when I left Cleveland.

We were at the 1953 Senior Bowl in Miami when Colts general manager Don Kellett asked to interview me for the Colts job. I had to get Brown's okay. Paul said, "You're not going to be satisfied unless I let you do it, so go ahead."

Kellett and I talked down there, and they hired me. Somebody said they had been talking to Blanton Collier, too, but I knew nothing about that.

At my first press conference at the Belvedere Hotel in Baltimore, I said it would take five years to build a winner. I was just whistling Dixie in a way. I knew the team wasn't there yet to win in the first three years. I could have said four or six. I just happened to pick five. As it turned out, it took five years and eight minutes.

On the first play of the first game I ever coached as a head coach in the pros, the Rams pulled that sleeper play on Don Shula. It was tough, a real letdown. I still kid Shula about that, telling him, "You tried to get my job early." Later he got that sleeper play outlawed. We lost that game, 48–0, and I was very disappointed. I just told the team, "We got to know our stuff and be alert."

I always thought Shula would make a fine coach, but he didn't have the speed as a defensive back. But I wasn't going to give up on him. He was all we had.

At the end of the first year, when we looked over our team, we thought we had fourteen guys altogether who belonged in the NFL. We knew we had to replace all the others. We went into the draft aiming to pick the best players, and then make them into whatever we wanted them to be.

In judging players, I tried to stay away from the so-called characters as much as I could. (I inherited Artie Donovan.) A lot of times, when I made some player change positions, it was because we needed a man to fill another position. Gino Marchetti was an offensive tackle, and Joe Campanella was on the offense. We needed Gino at defensive end and Joe at defensive tackle. We had two ends—Art Spinney and Alex Sandusky—I made guards. We had a lot of teaching to do on their running and footwork to get out and run interference. Except for Gino, they weren't Hall of Famers, but they were good, solid people and team players, and they worked hard. Occasionally I could see somebody who was in the wrong position, but most of the changes were to fill a need.

To size up a player as a person—what's inside him—before drafting him, I tried to get as much information as I could. A lot of times a player's head coach is not the best guy to give you a recommendation. An assistant coach or a trainer is a better source. I'd take a guy who may not be as good a player if his teamwork was better. For example, years later, after I left the New York Jets, somebody said to me, "Too bad you never had Mark Gastineau. He made all those sacks."

I said, "I'd rather have Gerry Philbin."

"But Gastineau was all-pro," they said.

"I don't care. I knew where Philbin was on every play. Gastineau was only going to go where he might look good getting a sack."

I preferred a guy out there who was playing where we wanted him to be. And I think that's the way we won championships. It's tough to get teamwork nowadays. I coached in the best time, no question about it. I had teams that won because of fine teamwork. The only advantage those Cleveland teams had in the early 1950s over my Colts teams was that, if they got somebody hurt, they might put somebody in to replace him who was better than the other guy. I didn't have that depth. I was lucky to have enough guys to go. One time we were playing the Redskins in a game we needed. Our left guard got hurt, but fortunately the guy who played opposite him wasn't worth a damn. If it had been our right guard who got hurt, their left tackle would have killed us.

I look for people who are attentive, who want to grab all they can and learn and work. Like Raymond Berry. He had one leg shorter than the other, wore a corset for a back injury, wore contact lenses, even tried goggles for a while. You had to run him and John Unitas off the practice field.

If a guy was giving me trouble, I'd call him in and say, "Just so you understand; you know you're not doing what you're supposed to do. Unless you change, I'm going to get rid of you. But I'm not going to get rid of you till I get somebody else, so when you look around and see somebody new in here, you can just bet he's here trying to get your job."

They'd generally straighten out.

The black players had some problems at Westminster in the 1950s with the segregation. And in Dallas they had to stay at a black hotel. But Carroll Rosenbloom announced that we wouldn't go back there unless they changed that.

Our players selected their own roommates, and Buddy Young roomed with a white player. But I had one player that nobody wanted to stay with. At one time I tried to put players together who played the same position, so they could talk about it. I told them, "Get your book out once in a while and use it." But it got to the point where they weren't studying anyway, so I let them select their own roommates.

I was a stickler for weight. Donovan gave me the most problems. Many years later, I introduced him at a dinner one night and I said, "Arthur was a great football player. He made the Hall of Fame. I think about as good a thing for me to do is just tell you what the Hall of Fame said about Arthur, and I think that'll be enough. They say he's 6-foot-4, from Boston College, and he weighed 280 pounds. That had to be at birth."

Then Donovan got up and told them about my fiendish routine of weighing them all every Friday. He said, "Every Friday I'd go out there and Weeb would say, 'Arthur, what did you weigh?' I knew damn well he knew what I weighed. Whenever I get to thinking about old Weeb and about those days when he was weighing us every Friday, every time I see a pair of scales I just turn and piss on them."

I tried to get Sherm Plunkett to report under 300 pounds, told him I'd give him $1,000 if he could do it. He couldn't make it. One year I told his wife I'd give her the thousand if she'd help him make it. But he couldn't. I told him, "You're not a bad trainer. It's just that you eat too much. Your legs aren't built to carry 350 pounds for very long."

Later I had him on the Jets, but then he got cancer. We were in Baltimore when he went into the hospital for the last time. Just before he died, I went with two black players to see him. We went into his room and he had all kinds of tubes coming out of him. It was sad. I hung back while the other two guys went up to him and shook hands. They were calling him some black names they used to call him; I didn't even know what they were talking about. Then finally little old Weeb came along and I put out my hand and he said to me, "Man, hug me."

Goddamn, [I was so moved,] I had to get out of there.

I used fines a lot. It was common in those days. We were in California one time for the last game of the season and Alex Hawkins missed bed check. I had the assistant coach who did the checking tell the house detective to watch for Hawkins, and tell him when he came in to be in my room at seven o'clock in the morning.

Hawkins was at my door at seven. I said, "If this was training camp, I'd send you home. But we'll take you back to Baltimore and you can get home the best you can."

He said, "I was wrong, coach. What are you going to do about it?"

I said, "It's going to cost you $500."

"Oh," he said, "I'm not making that much money. That's a lot. I don't know what my wife is going to say."

"There's the telephone," I said. "You call your wife, and if you can convince her that you had a good reason to be out until three o'clock in the morning, it'll be all right."

He said, "I'll take the fine."

It's also true that I was concerned about spies watching us practice. That was another common thing in those days. We got an end from the Rams once who told us that they would put a guy up on a hill overlooking the Coliseum, and he'd watch the other teams practice, using binoculars. About the only thing they'd see is maybe a new formation or something like that. Later I had a guy tell me he worked for the Raiders for years, and he'd watch us practice in Memorial Stadium. I know every time I saw a helicopter go over the field, I'd say, "There's George Halas of the Bears."

I was not a drive, drive, drive guy. I let my players go out there and show me some things. Any time that you have to pump 'em up every week, why, they're no good. And I never believed that anybody did well when they had people hanging right over their head, watching everything they did. Some people get results that way because guys are scared of them. Vince Lombardi was a screamer; his players knew he'd be screaming at them. That was his makeup. I just believe you get more teamwork by not hanging over them.

But we graded every player on every play and they knew they were getting graded. If their grades weren't good enough, they'd be told by an assistant coach.

I would get on the officials during a game, but the only penalty I ever drew was with the Jets, when an assistant coach got on a guy and I got into it and it cost me 15 yards. That's the only time in twenty-five years. I would get mad at them—you have to get after them—but I never once swore at them. There was a guy who always talked to me, a fraternity brother who went to Lafayette. He was a great baseball umpire, and he would miss the early games until the baseball season was over. One time he was rusty and he missed three plays where the player had to have both feet inside the sideline when he caught a pass. The third time I told him he missed it, and he said, "Weeb, you don't know the rules." So I bet him a steak dinner I was right. Later he admitted that he had gotten it mixed up with the college rules, where you only needed to get one foot down. But I never got the steak dinner.

We were playing the Bears one day. Bill Pellington was our captain. The Bears received, and they were very, very close to a first down on fourth and inches at the 40 yard line. Halas decided to go for it. They vroomed into the line and it was close. The referee was an old guy from Chicago who had no business working a Bears game. Pellington was standing there when Halas went right out onto the field and said to the ref, "You better give me that first down." I saw him do it.

The ref said, "George, I can't give it to you unless you made it."

Pellington told me, "I couldn't believe it."

I don't think there's any question that the pass that bounced off Norb Hecker's shoulder into Jim Mutscheller's hands in the last game of the 1956 season saved my job. After he made the catch, Jim just dragged the defender into the end zone. The preceding two weeks we had lost two games on the West Coast when Donovan had a bad leg and couldn't play.

After we beat the Redskins, 19–17, on that freak play, Carroll went to every player and asked them if they thought I should be fired. There was only one against me.

Carroll said to me, "We had a disappointing season."

"I was disappointed, too," I said.

There was a lot of talk about Rosenbloom betting on games. I could never say that he bet on a game, because I never talked to him about it. But he had some friends who were big gamblers. All they thought about was the point spread. One year I was the coach of the South team in the Senior Bowl. I got a call from Rosenbloom; he had some friends in New York who wanted to know what the game looked like. I said, "Carroll, I never see the other team play until the game itself, but my friends are telling me they have a good passer and we haven't got a chance."

He said, "Don't you have any idea?"

"I have no way to know. They haven't played a game. I haven't played a game."

Well, we had them, 26–0, at the half, and the woman connected with the Senior Bowl who gave us our checks at half-time said to me, "Slow it down. Don't beat them so bad."

Carroll's friends told him, "I can't understand how you have a coach who didn't know he was going to win. We could have cleaned up on that game."

Carroll would listen to those friends, who didn't know what they were talking about. Having played some, he knew just a little bit, but a little bit of knowledge is dangerous. He didn't really know anything.

We were a good team in 1957, just unlucky. Dealing with the emotional ups and downs of a game and a season, I would spend a sleepless night sometimes after some of those tough losses. I could be hard to live with after a loss, but I never took the game home with me. My wife loves football and knows the game. After sixty-eight years with me, she deserves a medal.

Still, when you know you did nothing wrong and they blame you, anyhow, that's tough to take. Like in the Detroit game that year; all we had to do was run the clock out. We put the ball in Lenny Moore's hands. We probably should have given it to Ameche. The ball bounced out of Lenny's hands. Had it bounced out of bounds, no harm done. But it didn't. They recovered and hit that little guy, Hopalong Cassady, in the end zone and won.

That kind of stuff can get to a lot of guys, but I managed to stay on an even keel. I had no set routine to unwind. You have to be realistic;

there's no way you're going to win them all. I used to drink some milk before a game. I don't know if it helped, but I never had an ulcer. Never had any headaches. I would feel disappointed, but I tried not to show it. I wouldn't get all over the players if they made a mistake.

Every year I tried to pick a theme. On one of my championship rings, it says "Poise" on one side and "Execution" on the other. Don't lose your poise and execute your offense well. I saw teams lose their poise and go downhill from there. In 1958 my theme was, "Know your football and we'll be known." I borrowed it from a minister who said, "Know your Bible and you'll be known."

In the game against the 49ers at home when we clinched the western conference, they had us 20–7 with two minutes to go in the first half. During a time-out, John Unitas came over to the side and I said, "We're playing terrible. Keep it on the ground and we'll go in and straighten this out." John went back out there and threw one, somebody hit his arm, and the ball caromed into the linebacker's hands and he went in and scored. Now it's 27–7.

At the half-time I said, "The defense hasn't played that poorly. Seven of their points was John. We've got to go out there and beat them this half more than they beat us in the first half." The defense went out and shut them out and John got hot and we won.

The championship game in New York was an emotional wringer. John Unitas and I worked all week on the plays and what we wanted to do. I let him call the plays. I told him I would never question him if he had a reason. I don't think a quarterback can call a game if he's always wondering if the old so-and-so is going to like it. Both Unitas and, later, Joe Namath, would think if they got down to the 20 yard line, boom, they'd get a touchdown right away. They used to think they could throw anything and get it between two or three defenders. And a lot of times you end up having to go for a field goal, or you don't get anything. I kept reminding him: "From the 20, two times 10 is a touchdown. Sometimes you've got to go for a first down. You can't always go for it all."

In the locker room just before the game, I said to the team, "Nobody knows you. We're in a good place–New York City–to be known, but we're going to have to win this game." Then I took out my notes and started down the roster, naming each player and how I got him. For example, I got to Alan Ameche and I said, "Ameche, I caught hell for taking you in the draft. There was a guy at Maryland [Ron Waller] they wanted me to take. I didn't take him and that made a lot of people mad." On the first play for the Colts he had gone 79 yards for a touchdown against the Bears and they got off my back quick. So I went down the list and said how I'd picked each man up. Some had been released by other teams, and I reminded them how we had taken them on. I still have my notes from that talk.

In the game I would have gone for a field goal and won it earlier in the overtime, but I had no confidence in my kicker, Steve Myhra. We were glad that we had gotten the one kick near the end of regular time to tie it and get us into overtime. We weren't going to press our luck and ask him to make another one. Myhra was just a bad place kicker, a straight-on kicker. I had coached Lou Groza at Cleveland. If Lou kicked ten times, his steps would leave the same marks in the dirt each time. If Myhra kicked twice, it looked like the chickens had been scratching in the dirt. He never did the same thing twice.

Well, as I said, we had gotten that field goal to tie it at 17. Now we were down there again. I don't remember what the point spread was, but later I heard that one of Carroll's gambler friends complained that a touchdown meant he lost his bet. He couldn't understand why I didn't go for the field goal, but he didn't know the kicker I had.

So John came over to the sidelines and asked, "What do you want?"

I said, "John, we were lucky to get the one field goal. Try to keep the ball in front of the goal posts, but give it to a guy who can run well. Give it to Ameche. He rarely fumbles. Just keep it on the ground."

He said, "Okay," and went back out.

First play, Mutscheller went out on a slant out on the right side and John threw the ball. I liked to have crapped in my pants. Mutscheller did a good job catching the pass. If he had known where he was and turned the right way, he'd have been in the end zone.

The next play, John gave the ball to Ameche and he went in and scored.

First thing the press did after the game was grab me and ask, "Why did you call that pass down there? You were lucky to get it through there."

I said, "I didn't call it. Ask John."

And John said, "I wouldn't have let them get an interception. If it wasn't there, I'd have thrown it away."

But I knew what could happen—the same thing that had happened four weeks earlier in the 49ers game. Somebody could have hit his arm from behind as he's throwing the ball, or the ball's dropped, or something.

I had been on a championship team with Cleveland, but it wasn't mine. This was mine, and it was great. They didn't dump a bucket or water or anything on the coach in those days.

It had taken five years and eight minutes to get there from when I had come to Baltimore. At least, that's what somebody wrote.

The next year all we had to do was keep from going to sleep to win our second in a row.

Dealing with a game like the one against the Lions at Memorial Stadium in 1960 is tough. Lenny Moore beat Night Train Lane and caught a pass to give us the lead, 15–13, with fourteen seconds to play. Lenny came over to the sidelines and everybody thought, "The game's over. We won."

I said, "It's not over. We got to stop them."

After they ran back the kickoff they didn't have any time-outs left, so they started a fight to stop the clock. We learned something from that; we had never used that ploy. But we added it to our list of things to do with two minutes to play. It went in the book: start a fight to stop the clock. I don't recall if we ever actually used it.

Anyhow, I'm looking for Lenny and I can't find him. He was supposed to be on the field as the safety, because he could run and he could tackle, when he had to. So I sent in Carl Taseff.

"Don't go for the interception," we told Carl. "Let the guy catch the ball and everybody be around him, and don't let him get out of there."

Earl Morrall threw it and Carl went for the interception and the ball caromed off him and Jim Gibbons caught it and went all the way for a 65-yard touchdown and they beat us, 20–15.

How do you deal with that? That's the kind of business you're in.

We had a lot of bad luck and injuries in 1962, and a lot of guys were getting old. But they didn't want to retire. Art Donovan would have played on and on forever if they let him.

Carroll Rosenbloom hung around with the Kennedys down in Palm Beach, and the big theme was youth in those days. He thought that youth was the thing, and we had hung on to some of our guys too long because we thought they had more in them. But they didn't play as well, and some got hurt, and they could not come back as fast as when they were younger. In addition, our drafts had not done too well, and the newspapers were full of stories about that stuff.

I tried to maintain good relations with the press. I tried to treat them all alike, not giving any scoops to anybody. I thought I was treated fairly in most cases, but not all.

Before I went down to coach in the Senior Bowl, I told Carroll, "I have a lot of responsibility to those people as well as to myself."

He said, "I'm not thinking about doing anything this year."

When I came back, I got a phone call early one morning from a newspaperman, telling me there was going to be a meeting at ten that morning, and I was going to get fired.

"I don't know anything about it," I told him.

I went down to the office and that's what happened.

Later, Rosenbloom's wife told me that he said many times during the following year that he had made a mistake in letting me go.

Standing on the sidelines is not the greatest place to watch a game. You can't see the wide perimeter of the field, but you learn to look through there and you can see more than you'd think. Here are some observations on some of the Colts that I coached from the sidelines:

Jim Mutscheller: One of the best blockers I ever had. He had perfect technique. I had a friend who was a coach; he built a two-pad spring with a big pan for practicing blocking. Two guys could use it at one time. He asked us to make a film demonstrating it, and I used Jim. The guy who made the device said he had never seen anybody demonstrate better technique of setting that shoulder and driving.

Jim had good hands but lacked speed. We used a lot of pop passes to him, or short hooks, and he was always open.

Carl Taseff: A fine athlete. Could play halfback, fullback, corner back, or safety. A good guy for a team. Going for that interception against Detroit in 1960 is the only thing I have against him.

Art DeCarlo: Not a speed artist, but he had good hands and could run good patterns and get open. A fine person, part of our close-knit Colts family.

Dick Szymanski: Good training at Notre Dame. A good athlete who could play offense or defense.

Buddy Young: A wonderful individual. I met him when he was at the University of Illinois and I was in the navy. I liked Buddy very much. He was not a very good receiver. He would try to go up with his arms to catch the ball and bring it against his body. His arms were in his eyes so he couldn't watch the ball. I tried to get him to square around and make the catch, but I could never get him to do it that way.

Lenny Moore: A great runner and receiver, Lenny could also play good defense, especially as an extra safety man protecting a lead late in a game. But a lot of times he'd get lazy. We graded the players zero to five; five was the tops, and zero was no effort. Lenny had more fives than anybody and more zeroes than anybody. He could have been a good blocker because he did it at times. But if Lenny could get by without doing it, he'd rather not do it. A fine person, he was not serious enough. Things came to him so easily, he did not have to put so much into it. Other guys were not nearly as good athletes, but they put a lot into it.

Artie Donovan: Every team needs a guy like Artie. He kept them loose. There was always a big group in Artie's room in the hotels. He was our best beer drinker—a two-case guy. If anybody got beat by Artie in a race, the guy was automatically cut, because Arthur was the slowest one on the team. But on defense, there's nobody could play a trap better than Arthur and take care of his responsibility on the line.

Donovan was one of the first in the locker room on game days, and he'd start right in with the dry heaves, just thinking about the game. Then he'd give everything he had on the field.

Gino Marchetti: Gino is the best defensive end in the past seventy-five years. He deserves his place on the all-time team. He gave you everything he had, all-out, and was completely spent at the end of a game. He was the same in practice; no loafing with him.

At USF, Gino played on the same team with Bob St. Clair, who became an offensive right tackle for the 49ers. When we played San Francisco, Gino played opposite him. St. Clair told me this story:

"We were playing the Colts one day and at the end of the first quarter we had given up the ball, so as we're coming off the field I went over to Gino and tapped him on the back. He turned and said, 'What the hell's wrong with you?' I said, 'I just wanted to touch you. I haven't touched you the whole first quarter.' "

Gino was great on helping young kids coming in. We were having trouble once with a young player from Kent State. He just wasn't good enough. He was lining up against Gino in practice, and Gino was just going boom, boom—right by him. He told the kid, "You're up too high. Get lower." The guy got lower and Gino, with that powerful torso of his, gave him a fake and a shove and knocked the kid down and went by him.

The coach told the guy to get down still lower. This time Gino went straight at him, put his hands on the kid's shoulders and leap-frogged over him. The kid looked at the coach and said, "Now what do I do?"

John Unitas was standing there watching. He said, "You just applaud, that's all."

John Unitas: In my prayers sometimes I thank the Good Lord for some decisions I made that I'm sure someone else made for me. Signing John was one of them.

I first saw Unitas when my Washington University team played Louisville twice. Then he went to Pittsburgh. The Steelers had two quarterbacks, neither one very good, but their offense was tough to learn. I had an assistant coach who had been there when John was there. He told me the Steelers' offense was so complicated, John just couldn't learn it.

After Pittsburgh let John go, he was playing sandlot ball. Then somebody wrote us a letter and said we should take a look at him. I had a lot of respect for Frank Camp, John's coach at Louisville. So I called him and asked about John. We didn't have any movies, just some still photos to show his setup and follow-through. We liked what we heard about him, and signed him.

We knew from the start that John had the arm. He was one who could pass the ball 70 yards, not throw it. A lot of guys can throw it that far, but there's a difference between throwing it and passing it. He could hit a man open at 70 yards.

John worked hard and studied the films. And he had a mind of his own and lots of confidence. He'd give the guys hell in the huddle if they didn't do something the way he wanted. He'd tell them, "I need more time. We're going to go long on this one." Or, if somebody missed a block, "Goddammit, this is no fun back here. You should try throwing that ball, the way you're letting them through."

Joe Namath was the opposite. He'd buy 'em a beer if they protected him. He'd rarely give anybody hell.

Milt Davis: We were lucky to get him. Somebody made a mistake and let him float and he was a free agent and they didn't know it.

Alan Ameche: Alan was the kind of guy who didn't put as much into it because he was so gifted he didn't have to. He didn't reach the level he could have if he had just given it a little bit more. He was a fine athlete, an amateur boxer, and basketball player. When I was thinking of drafting him, I called his coach at Wisconsin and asked how Alan was at catching the ball. He said, "I don't know; we don't throw the ball much. We just run over people and Alan can do that. He catches screen passes okay." Well, he caught everything we threw to him. And he was much faster than he looked.

Big Daddy Lipscomb: We picked him up when the Rams let him go. He was the fastest big man I ever saw: 6-foot-7, 290 pounds. But Donovan and the two ends would get on him because he might not get any farther into the backfield than just past those guys. He didn't get to the quarterback on pass rush, although he'd block an average of at least one pass a game with his long arms covering the center area. But if he got to chase the quarterback, he'd get him. Except for Marchetti, Lipscomb was the fastest on the chase, and one of the greatest tacklers I've ever seen. When he made a tackle he bent the guy backwards.

One game day we had a pregame meal of steak and baked potato four hours before the game. The theory was that the meat would give you energy and the potato was digestible. Nowadays they have a variety of food for the players. Big Daddy didn't like red meat rare; it had to be well-done. One day we were on the West Coast and Donovan got Lipscomb's steak by mistake and Big Daddy got a rare one, and he just sat there looking at it and pouting.

Jim Parker: The greatest offensive tackle I've ever seen. Did what he was supposed to do and did it well. He didn't seem to be working hard at it, but it was getting done. I saw him pick up a defensive tackle for the 49ers one time, carry him back about 6 yards and dump him.

Parker was a great guy, and funny. We were on our way to the West Coast for two games one year and he came to me and said, "Coach, would you lend me $3.00? We're going to be out there for two weeks and my wife won't give me any money."

Alex Sandusky: We moved him from end to guard, and it took him about a year to get adjusted, but he did it all and was very reliable. Same with *Art Spinney.* They did everything they were supposed to do.

Bill Pellington: A Hall of Famer all the way. I could never understand why he is not in there. Tough as he could be. We were playing Detroit, and they had a tight end—you let him get out, he'd get open. I told the guys to go inside and rough him up a little bit; don't let him out too quick so he can't get deep. Well, before I knew it, there's a play and the whistle blew and I saw that tight end's legs just wilt. Down he went in a heap.

Pellington came out and I said to him, "God, Bill, I didn't say kill him. Just rough him up a little, push him around, and don't let him get through there clean."

Bill said, "Coach, my fist didn't move but a few inches."

I first met Pellington at the draft when I was with Cleveland. We were down near the end of the line, and we picked him from Rutgers. But the Browns didn't need another linebacker, so we traded him to the Colts in a big trade in 1953. He and Donovan claimed I put them both on the trading block so I would have them when I got to Baltimore.

Andy Nelson: Steady, reliable, never a rah rah guy. No problems.

Buzz Nutter: Old reliable. Never said much, but he had a personality that everybody loved. I hated it when I had to let him go. It was tough telling guys you thought they were through.

Don Shinnick: He and Raymond Berry were the most religious players we had. We drafted him out of UCLA. When I asked him about signing a contract, he said he didn't know if he wanted to play or not. I reminded him that he had told the scouts he wanted to play, but now he said he was going to wait until Jesus Christ told him what to do. When that happened, he would let me know.

Since high school and college, I always had a minute or two of prayer before a game. One day Raymond Berry came to me and said, "Coach, I think we should have a time for prayer after a game, too." After that, I did. I would ask different players to lead it.

When Shinnick had his first child, instead of passing out cigars, he took a pack of cigarettes around and shook one out for each guy. A studious player, he would take movies home and watch them. In practice he would correct guys like an assistant coach.

Don Shula: A very smart student of the game. I knew he would become a coach. He was at Cleveland when I was there, and any time there was a discussion on pass defense, Don was always in there. I didn't cut him because of that sleeper play. It was his lack of speed.

Ordell Braase: A good person and steady player. One of the things we looked for was people who would fit in. Braase was the kind of person we looked for.

Sherm Plunkett: Sherm weighed about 240 when we brought him in. One of the fastest guys on the team, he was one of the first guys downfield on kickoff returns. His pass protection was almost flawless. He didn't pick guys up and drive them like Jim Parker did. Sherman might turn a guy and smother him, keeping his body between the guy and the quarterback. And if they ran around him, he was so big it was too late by the time they got to the quarterback.

In training camp Sherman would look at me like I was the meanest guy that ever was. I had incentive payments in his contract if he made a certain weight, which he never made. If he thought I was watching him, he wouldn't eat anything, then he'd send a rookie out to get him some hot dogs or something. But I wasn't watching him eat. I just kept telling him he was kidding himself because his legs couldn't take it. Sherm was very quiet, wouldn't hurt a flea.

George Preas: A steady, reliable guy who did his job, Preas would rarely be the cause of a play not working.

Don Joyce: Don was a defensive tackle for the Chicago Cardinals. Late in a game in Chicago he hit John Unitas near our bench. I hollered at him, "You're the dirtiest player in the NFL."

The following Tuesday he was put on waivers and we picked him up. He told somebody that he thought I was going to get even with him, and he wouldn't have a job. But I made an end out of him and he stayed in the league a long while and was good at it. He was not really dirty, just rough and tough.

Joe Perry: I put him down as one of the Hall of Famers I coached, but he really had his best years with the 49ers. I picked him up near the end of his career. He was tough. Had a knee operation during the season and wanted to come back after three weeks. But the doctor told him to wait another week. Anybody else would have been out six weeks.

Eddie Block: I have to say something about Eddie Block. Eddie is the guy who brought good medical practices into professional football. He knew anatomy, was a physiotherapist at Washington University when I was there. When I came to Baltimore, I asked him to join us. He organized the training room and equipment for the first time. I loved the guy.

I watch games today, with two TV sets going at once. It's a different game. I don't like today's rules. When Raymond Berry played, they would put a guy in front of him and one on either side of him, and they'd knock the hell out of him. Now you can go one hit on a guy and let him go. That's a big difference. They put these guys like Jerry Rice on a pedestal. He can run faster than Raymond, but that's all.

On pass protection, we had to keep our hands in front of us. Now they are grabbing guys and end up tackling them. (Runners should have better blocking, because blockers can practically tackle a guy on offense now.)

I don't think you can compare the teams. We had big players, but there are more of them today. They're all big now. I am all for anything they've done to take the violence out of football, because the game is contact, good hard tackles. It's not to kill guys. When anybody hits a guy in the face, he should be out of the game.

When I retired I was both physically and mentally tired. But I was coach and general manager with the Jets at the end, and you can't do both.

We had a lot of spirit in Baltimore, and the Colts' Band was part of it. There were about ten organizations in different parts of the city—Colt Corrals—and they were all a part of the organization.

I still think of those players as family. I lost three of them in the past year—Art Spinney, Bill Pellington, and Steve Myhra. I try to keep in touch with their wives and families, but I don't always know how to reach them.

Raymond Berry

Born: 2-27-33
Paris, Texas
Southern Methodist
University (SMU)
End

6′ 2″, 190 lbs.
Drafted: #20, 1954
Colts: 1955–1967
Hall of Fame: 1973

"I was born with two great gifts: great hands and an inner desire, a tremendous driving force that was going on inside of me."

My dad was a high school football coach, but he never pushed me into playing. From the time I could walk, I had a tremendous love for the game and desire to play. Had he been in some other business, I'm not sure that would have happened. He was an excellent coach, and he did so many things that molded and directed me; he was the biggest influence in my life.

I grew up in Paris, Texas, and went to a very small high school. I was very slow developing and didn't play much until my senior year, when I weighed 150 pounds. My first big thrill in football was when we beat Gainesville High School for the district championship.

I wanted to play in the Southwest Conference, but I wasn't big enough. Still, I went over to TCU to see the coach, Dutch Meyer. But when he put me on the scales I knew the interview was over.

Shriner Institute, a junior college in south Texas, was the only place that offered me a scholarship, so I went there. The coach had been at Paris Junior College and had seen me play, but he probably felt sorry for me and wanted to help my dad. I played there one year, caught a lot of passes, and got up to 155 pounds.

So I went up to Southern Methodist, where the coach, Rusty Russell, told me, "I'll give you a scholarship for the first semester. You're not eligible to play, so I'll put you on our redshirt team and watch you, and if I think you can play Southwest Conference football, I'll give you a full scholarship. If not, it might be better for you to go to a smaller college."

So it was like a tryout, and every time I went out to practice, it was like a game to me. I was nervous and uptight and getting all keyed up every day for three months. I was running pass plays against the varsity pass defense, and I had the best quarterback in the country, Fred Benners, throwing to me, so I was making catches all over the place.

After practice one day near the end of the season, coach Russell got the whole team together before they went into the showers, and he said

Raymond Berry, who with Lance Alworth, Don Hutson and Jerry Rice, was named to All-Time NFL team.
Courtesy Transcendental Graphics

something like this: "Hey, you see that little broomstick kid over there? If all you guys could catch the ball like he does, we'd have a heck of a team." Soon as he said that, I knew I had a scholarship.

I never started a game at SMU. They had a lot of good football players; the two guys ahead of me both made it to the pros. My junior year I played about a third of the time. I made some great catches, and I was getting a reputation as somebody who could catch the football.

I don't know who recommended me to the Colts, but they drafted me in the twentieth round in 1954. They took a big risk, didn't they?

My first two years in pro football were two of the hardest years of my life. I really didn't know anything about being a pro receiver. In college, we played offense and defense in those days, so we had a very basic type of offense and I had no training for the pro game. I had a real battle just surviving the cut.

Weeb Ewbank was responsible for my making the team, because he saw something in me when I was a very raw talent. His ability to spot potential was critical, because it took me those two years before I really began to play, and in a lot of cases I would have been out of the game by then.

The other crucial thing Weeb did was hire Bob Shaw, who was absolutely the most influential coach in my pro career. I only had him for two years, but during those two years he influenced my career for the remaining ten. He taught me the concept of running pass routes, and the ability to fake that I never would have had in the absence of Bob Shaw.

I started to have some success in the tail end of my second year. But after the first three games in 1957, I had only one catch for two yards. That's all. Then I wound up leading the league in yardage gained for a receiver and had a very good year.

I was born with two great gifts: great hands and an inner desire, a tremendous driving force that was going on inside of me. Like a Pavarotti, who had to be born with a great voice. He wouldn't have reached the performing level he did without adding tremendous training and discipline. When I came into professional football, I took my gift and started learning how to develop it.

Stretching out to catch the ball in the middle of a bunch of linebackers touches on that inner desire. Everybody is aware of how high a guy can jump, how fast he can run—the obvious physical skills, but I think the makeup of an individual that gives him a good motor inside is often overlooked and is equally important.

The post-practice drills that Unitas and I did long after regular practice was over was just a natural development of that inner desire to succeed. It was just there, and it manifested itself inside me so that I wanted that football. I didn't pay any attention to anything that would keep me from getting it. I was obsessed with catching it; to drop one really made me mad. That was the motivation for me to work: I just hated a dropped football.

Another thing that I had going for me was a physical body that could bend and bounce and very seldom ever broke. My durable physique allowed me to dive, jump, roll, hit the ground, and get hit all over by people, and never get hurt. If you don't get hurt, you don't really think about it. I don't call it courage; why should I worry about getting hurt when I do all those things and don't get hurt?

Our success in the last two minutes of games was due to Weeb and John Unitas. Weeb was a sound coach in preparing his team for a game and practicing the two-minute drills. Being a receiver, I just had my little part of the whole picture. I had no real awareness of the strategy involved or what the quarterback was doing in the two-minute operation. But I knew Unitas had the natural ability and an instinct for the game.

The greatest thrill I had was beating the Giants in New York for the championship in 1958. You can't describe what that first world championship is like. I scored the first touchdown in that game, and years later a man from the Eastern Shore gave me the football I had when I scored. He was in the stands in the end zone and caught the extra point kick.

There's no question in my mind that we blew a great opportunity to blow the Giants off the field when we were ahead, 14–3, inside the 5 yard line, and didn't score. The third down play was a miscommunication. It was supposed to be a flip to Alan Ameche and he would toss a little pass to Jim Mutscheller, who was wide open for a touchdown. The calls for those plays were: 28 for a toss and run, and 428 was the fake toss and pass. When the play was called in the huddle, Alan heard the 28, and not the 428. Jim heard the 428, so he did not block, but turned the linebacker loose to go out and get open. Alan thought it was a run and didn't throw the ball. That's what happened.

The momentum change at that point was awful. The Giants took over, 95 yards out, and a few plays later they scored. Somebody gave me a recording of the radio broadcast of that game. When I listened to it a few years ago, I didn't realize that we had jumped out and scored 14 points in the first half, and for the rest of the next three quarters we don't do a thing on offense. Good grief. It was an absolute shutdown. People say why did Jim Lee Howell punt so much for the Giants? Why shouldn't he? They stopped us with their defense, and we don't do a thing in the second half until the last two minutes. During that long drought the Giants had to be very confident.

Then the last two times we had the ball we scored.

In my opinion, the great strength of our championship teams was the defense. As a player, I knew the offense got a whole lot of ink, but the defense was the backbone of our team. They were always getting us the ball.

I had 631 receptions in my career, but even with the bump and run, I could have caught the ball in any era. Records don't mean anything anymore, with the changes in the rules and the schedules.

I faced a lot of defensive backs in my thirteen years. Our offensive system had me lining up on the left side only. Consequently I never had to face people like Night Train Lane or Herb Adderley. The first really tough corner that I remember playing against was Dick Lynch of the Giants. Very smart, good size and speed, he could read your mail.

Jesse Whittenton of the great Packers defenses of the 1960s was extremely hard to get away from. Later on I had a lot of problems with Irv Cross of the Eagles. Abe Woodson with the 49ers was always tough. He broke in the bump and run on me, and he was a Big 10 sprint champion, so he could outrun me 10 yards in a 100-yard dash. He gave me some difficult times.

Rating the quarterbacks I saw is tough. If I'm a head coach I could list twenty or twenty-five of them and say, "Give me any one of them." You can win a world championship with Terry Bradshaw. Joe Montana—four Super Bowls and didn't throw an interception; that's unbelievable. Roger Staubach. That's enough for openers. Dan Marino has never had a chance to play with a dominating defensive team like the 1958–59 Colts, or Montana's teams.

One of the main factors that puts guys like Unitas and the others I've named in this category is the organizations they played for. They played for very good owners who provided stability, the right people, and total commitment to winning. Carroll Rosenbloom had the right people in place.

As for runners, Jim Brown was at a level by himself. And Jerry Rice is the Jim Brown of receivers, the best I've ever seen.

I enjoyed coaching professional football more than college [at Arkansas]. In pro football, if you're fortunate enough to get an owner with commitment and judgment, you can win a world championship. In college football, there are so many programs with no chance of winning a national title.

When I coached the New England Patriots, we had a real good team in 1985, with everybody healthy. Late in the year we went on a roll and became a wild card team, then went on the road and won three playoff games. We beat Miami for the AFC championship, 31–14, the first time New England had beaten them in nineteen games.

Then we played the Bears in Super Bowl XX. They were a superior team, and we didn't play very well in that game. But looking back, I could see that we had had to win for two months to get there. There's a good chance that we expended most of our emotional energy getting there, and just weren't very sharp that day.

Coaching that year was an unbelievable experience.

Lenny Moore adding six vs. the Redskins.
Photograph © 1995 TADDER/Baltimore

Lenny Moore

Born: 11-25-33
Reading, Pennsylvania
Penn State
Halfback

6′ 1″, 190 lbs.
Drafted: #1, 1956
Colts: 1956–1967
Hall of Fame: 1975

"I never went into a game thinking individually . . . as long as we won, it was a collective effort."

Andy Stopper, my high school coach in Reading, Pennsylvania, was my mentor all through my college and pro years. When I went into the Hall of Fame in Canton, there was never any question that he was the one I wanted to present me with my plaque.

When I went to Penn State in 1952, Rip Engle was the coach. We were independents, not part of any league, and didn't get any publicity. We played top teams, even beat the Rose Bowl champions, Illinois, but the Harrisburg *Patriot-News* was about the extent of any publicity we got outside of that game. So when the Colts made me their number one draft pick in 1956, it wasn't important to me that they were a struggling team. Being picked was the important thing, and to be number one was overwhelming. I was in awe of Buddy Young, so when he came to Reading to see me, I was completely sold on coming to Baltimore.

My thing was just making the team. There was a question in my mind as to whether I was good enough. I knew I was up against top-caliber competition, beginning with Young himself. But when he retired that year, I became a starter.

My first exposure to the professional game was in the College All-Star game against the Cleveland Browns. I only got into the game for the last few minutes, but one time I saw the Browns hit Alan Ameche and drive him into a table by the sidelines, and that table splintered. I said to myself, "Man, what goes on here? Is this the way these guys hit?"

The Colts put me on the kickoff return team, and my real initiation was when we played the Philadelphia Eagles in a preseason game in Hershey. I was nervous as I could be when I took that first kickoff. I don't even remember what happened on the play.

It's amazing, but the older I get, the more appreciative I am of Weeb Ewbank and his tactics. We came up at a time when there was real racial discontent. We were immature guys facing a lot of obstacles, outside of football as well as inside. The tactics that Weeb used were unbelievable, silly schoolboy things. We'd go to the movies in twos, coaches in the front and on the sides and behind us, lined up just like grade school kids going to a museum. We'd start out at the hotel. He'd say, "All right, pair off in twos and line up at the door." Here's all these big men lining up and marching down to the movies. When we got there, we would stand in the lobby in pairs while they took care of the tickets, then they'd check us off as we went in—by twos.

He would waste time, like the Saturday night before a Sunday game. He would hold an impromptu meeting at seven o'clock, knowing we'd barely have time to get to a movie and be back in the hotel by ten o'clock curfew. So he would lengthen the meeting: "Okay, fellows, let's go over it again. What are we going to have for breakfast? How many guys want eggs?" And you would raise your hand and they'd count them. "Okay, who wants them scrambled?" And you'd raise your hand. "Who wants them over light?" He'd count the hands and jot it down. I'm serious. Then it was, "Okay, how many steaks?" Raise the hands. "Well done?" Hands up. "Medium?" And it would just go on that way. He'd do it every road trip. Time we got out it would be like twenty minutes of eight. We'd just have time to get to the movie and get back for bed check. He had it all set up.

With all of his idiosyncrasies and things we thought were silly and childish, he was doing them to create fun and get your mind off other things. We had guys who had problems, whose emotions would get the better of them, and all these things were meant to put that in check. We used to laugh about Weeb because he treated us like little boys. But he knew when to do it and when to stop it and get firm.

I think Weeb's greatest attribute was preparing a team for a game. We had the best scouting reports that any team could possibly have. We knew what each team was going to do, and where they were going to do it: from 20 yards out to the end zone, or 30 or 40 yards out, or anywhere on the field. The game is based on percentages: what are they likely to do inside the 20 if it's first and long, or second and short? Then he based the defenses on those percentages. On offense, where was the weak spot? And if Plan A didn't work, Weeb always had Plan B, a backup list of alternative plays.

When we went on that field, we were ready.

Weeb sent in plays, but the difference with our team from others was that if Unitas didn't like the play, he didn't call it. Sometimes Weeb might think we were a little flat and send in a play to pick us up. If Unitas liked it, he'd go with it.

Give you another example. In 1958, we were playing the Packers, and John had his ribs stove in by John Symank. John was out two games; then he came back against the Rams and first series of the game he threw one 60 yards to me. That was to show the Rams that John was okay. The message was: "Get it out of your mind if you want to come after him." That was Weeb's idea. He knew what to do. Even if it hadn't hooked up, that was the message. Raymond Berry and I still talk about that. Raymond says, "We didn't realize that Weeb was a genius."

On the field it was our responsibility to be always scouting. I'd come back to the huddle and tell Unitas, "Hey, John, if I line up outside wide, the slant is there," meaning if we can get the slant, that automatically kicks in the slant takeoff, slant takeoff sideline, and slant in. So we would establish the slant early in the game, then we'd know we got these other derivatives off of it.

Same with Raymond Berry. He'd say, "John, I can do a Q," which was a sort of post corner kind of thing called a Q. We were always bringing things back. But even if I knew I had something, if we were in tight straits at that particular time, he might not call it then. He'd call it when he felt the timing was right, and more often than not the time he chose to call it was the right time. He'd say to me, "You still got it?" "Yeah." He may call another play, still waiting. I'd come back, "John, it's still there." "Okay." Maybe call another play.

People say I was fast and had good instincts. I never felt I had blinding speed, but I had good speed. I had the God-given ability to regulate and shift speeds and make moves.

I thought the best game we ever played as a team in my years with the Colts was the one when we were down 27–7 to the 49ers in '58 and came back to win. San Francisco was power-packed: Hugh McElhenny, Joe Perry, Leo Nomellini, Y.A. Tittle, Billy Wilson. Big playmakers.

At half-time, I remember exactly what Weeb said: "Defense, you shut 'em down. And Johnny, we're going to score and score again. We're going to be in the game and we're going to win this game."

We thought: "Shut 'em down, that's an impossibility. We can't come back from this. But we're going to go out and do the best we can." Weeb kept us positive. He would say the right thing at the right time to psychologically keep you right where you needed to be.

I made a 73-yard run in that game and we won, 35–27.

Same thing before the championship game in New York. He stood up there and read out each guy's name and took us down this whole litany of things:

"So-and-so, Green Bay didn't want you. They kicked you out. But we thought enough of you to bring you to us. And you became a Baltimore Colt."

He named somebody else. "You're a guy from a small town, didn't have much. Your family brought you up the best way they could. . . ."

He went down everybody on the roster and gave a little personal background on them. Man, we were ready to tear the door down. He had guys almost spouting fire.

A lot of people mention to me the catch I made against the Bears in Wrigley Field in 1960. It was a physical battle that day. John had been beaten to a pulp by Doug Atkins and others. Near the end of the game we were behind 20–17. We were going toward the outfield wall end of the field, not the dugout end.

During that game, we had run what we called 66, which was me going down about 15 yards and angling in, or I could break it off and do a short post. This time John called 66 and I said, "Fine." Then he said, "Lenny, what I want you to give me is that break-in, then plant and break back to the outside. I want a 66 takeoff to you, but I want that move to the inside."

Now, we hadn't done anything like this before. It was a new play. We hadn't worked on it; we hadn't timed it. With all the other things going on in his mind, he thinks of this new move at this second, and he had the confidence in me to do it.

So when I went down and made my break, J.C. Caroline comes up to me, then I plant and make my break, which puts Caroline automatically on the inside, which is exactly what Unitas wanted. As I was doing this, Caroline fell into the back of my legs. Halas screamed that I pushed Caroline, but how am I going to push him when I'm ahead of him? I had him beat.

We won that game, 24–20, then lost the next four. I would say that most of what we had was left on Wrigley Field that day. We didn't have much after that, and didn't execute well. I think the physical battles leading up to that game and then that one took its toll, especially on the linemen.

Tom Matte came in in 1961 and backed me up. Matte was a multiple player, a good defensive back with unlimited talents, which fit very well into our scheme of things. I think people tend to downplay Matte's overall ability.

But nobody can downplay Jim Parker's ability. When he came from Ohio State, he couldn't pass block, because they never threw the ball at Ohio State. He knew he had to learn that, and he became the best at his craft. He worked after practice with Ordell Braase, and he'd talk to Gino, and who knew better than Gino how to go against a defensive end? It molded Parker into a guy who could handle the Doug Atkinses of football.

We moved Jim around to go against the other teams' all-pro guys. They moved him to guard because we had nobody to handle Roger Brown. Then we had to put him on Leo Nomellini as an offensive tackle. He not only played those guys to a standoff, he mauled them. First play of the game, he'd knock Roger Brown down, all 300 pounds of him. One time he drove Nomellini 10 yards off the line. Unbelievable.

But we were concerned when Jim's legs were giving him some problems. Would he be able to pull at pulling guard? You know what happened; he became the best pulling guard in history.

I was well into my career when Don Shula arrived in 1963. You had to respect him as a football man. He knew football. But I didn't respect him initially because he lied to me. He asked me where I wanted to play. I said, "I'd like to continue what I'm doing," which was both slot back going out as a receiver and running back.

Shula said, "We're looking at some other things, but you'll stay where you are."

Then he made me primarily a running back. I can understand his thinking. It gave us more weapons. We'd get into double wing formations and short flood formations, and he'd have all his best receivers on the field at the same time. It bothered other people more than it bothered me that my role had changed. I could maybe say in hindsight I could have played a couple more years, but not really. Who's to say? I was a team man, and whatever he wanted me to do was okay. People made it out that I was primarily a running back, but I was back there for basic heavy duty.

The Friday before we opened against the Giants at home in 1963, I went into the hospital for an appendicitis operation. I was out for ten days and came back and played against Green Bay in the third game. About midway through the season we were playing Detroit at home, and my helmet came off and I got kicked in the side of the head. I had a contusion and a slight concussion.

I went out to practice the next week and I couldn't get on it, couldn't sight the ball. When we went out to Los Angeles, the Colts sent me to a doctor out there. He checked me and advised me to sit out the last few games of the season. I told him to call Dr. McDonnell at the hotel and tell him. He said he would do that.

I got back to the hotel and Dr. McDonnell said, "You got a clean bill of health."

"What?"

"The doctor said you can suit up and go."

I said, "You better talk to him again. He told me to hang it up for this year, and on his advice, that's exactly what I am going to do."

"That's not what he told me," the doc said.

"Well," I said, "you guys let me know what's going on. I'm not suiting up."

And I went to my room.

The last few games, I was getting these stares, like I had rebelled against something. I took offense to that. I went to my own physician in Baltimore, and I had him get hold of the general manager, Don Kellett. Kellett told him they'd go along with whatever he said. But I was getting a feeling of being ostracized from the Colts. Everybody wasn't on the same page.

The season was over and I was getting that cold shoulder treatment, and that hurt tremendously. Then I started hearing all these trade rumors, and that bothered me.

Why did I want to stay after reading all the negative stuff about me in '63? I guess I'm the kind of guy who, once I'm in, I'm settled. I'm not one to move around. I don't know if being traded would have been for the better or worse. As I look back, I know it would have been devastating. I wanted to stay here, but that was not the way things were pointing, and it bothered me immensely.

Then Carroll Rosenbloom called me and said, "I want you to come into the office and you, me, and Shula will sit down and talk."

When we met, Rosenbloom asked me one question. "Lenny, do you want to play for the Baltimore Colts in 1964?"

I said, "Carroll, I do."

"Fine," he said, and that was it.

But that didn't satisfy me, because I still didn't feel I was getting what was due me. I hadn't been healed emotionally. I thought I was being misjudged. As it got close to the 1964 season, I made a vow to myself, and that's something I've never done: "I'm going to have the best year that I've ever had; I'm going to show some of these folks."

I had to literally come out of myself, which was the most difficult thing that I've ever had to do. I'm normally kind of loose, like to laugh and do the jokes and that kind of stuff. Now I removed myself totally from all that. I said to myself, "I'm here. I'm going to play, and that's all I'm going to do, so that Shula will not have to say anything to me at any time about anything. That's the way it's going to be."

Sometimes you need a letdown from the stress, just by laughing to get it out. But during practice, when I finished running the ball, I'd do my 20–30 yards and come on back—boom—and I'd get off to the side and just stand. I did that for the entire year.

I don't know if anybody noticed, but it didn't bother me at all how anybody felt or what anybody thought. This was something that I had to do to satisfy me, knowing that if I was doing what I was doing in this matter, even coming out of myself like I did—not being the real me, putting on this other kind of personality—everything else will fall into place. And that's what happened. I had a great year, was voted Comeback Player of the Year.

I did it for my own satisfaction, to quiet those who said that I was washed up. To this day I've never understood why this happened, why they did that to me. But I was satisfied with the kind of year I had. I figured I had shut up some of those mouths who said that Lenny Moore was through.

That '64 season ended with the disaster in the playoff game in Cleveland. We had watched the films and seen all these gaping holes that we knew we could attack. But we got out of our game plan and were horrible, did absolutely nothing the first half, but it was still 0–0. Then we figured we'd go out there and take care of business, but we were just as bad the second half. We knew the wind was a factor, but we just weren't executing. Cleveland beat us, 27–0.

I didn't feel as disappointed as I would have if I felt there was something else I could have done. In my self-evaluations, there had been some games where I felt there were some things I could have done better, or where I thought I had done my job to my level, but when I looked at the films I saw that I hadn't, and I'd kick myself in the butt. But not in that game.

My gratification was that in just about every game I thought my level was where it was supposed to be. In that 1964 season particularly, I felt good about myself.

I never went into a game thinking individually. If the other team wanted to stack up against me, that would leave somebody else free. As long as we won—it was a collective effort. I always made it a point to congratulate my linemen any time I scored a touchdown. I'd go down to every one of them and thank them. I had God-given talents, but in order for those talents to flourish, some other things had to happen for me to be in position.

There have been great backs with great abilities that you never heard very much about. Two examples: Paul Lowe at San Diego and Abner Haynes at Dallas in the AFL. Those two guys had everything that an offensive running back could possess. And yet you don't hear their names ever brought into the package. They could play in any era.

The first three years O.J. Simpson was in the league, you didn't hear anything about Juice, because they didn't have a line up there in Buffalo. I don't care who you are, you can't do it by yourself. As great as Barry Sanders is, if he had had the Dallas line in front of him in 1994, he'd have made 3,000 yards.

I could not understand what was happening in 1965. Physically and mentally I felt the same as always. I was making my break; the thought patterns and reactions were the same. But they weren't. Watching the films, I started noticing that those defensive backs were getting one leg where before they hadn't been getting any leg. I couldn't understand this. I saw that I was making my break farther away from the guy and that gave him time to react, while in my mind I thought I was doing the same thing I had always done. It took quite a few games before it set in that I must be slowing up, because this is what was happening.

The Charlie Joiners and Charley Taylors and Art Monks keep going doing the same thing for so long because they stayed in one area. They weren't running the ball out of the backfield, so they were only being hit by guys their own size. They're not getting hit by linebackers, who will give you more physical wear and tear, and that takes its toll over the years.

I played my last game in 1967.

Without a doubt, the defensive back I most respected was Night Train Lane. It wasn't that I couldn't beat him; it was that he was so intelligent. He never lined up the same way on you twice. He'd be up on my nose, then he'd line up maybe 3 yards inside. I'd see where he was and say, "What's he doing? I got all that outside." But on the snap of the ball he'd be facing me. I thought I had something, but he'd take it away from me. He was very difficult to figure out.

One time we were watching the films of Detroit games and Raymond Berry came over to me and said, "Here's a couple things I wrote down that I think you can do on Night Train Lane."

He had drawn some patterns that I didn't have in my arsenal. One was sort of a quick post square out. I'd go down maybe 4 or 5 yards, drive two or three steps to the inside, plant my foot, spin around and go out toward the sideline. We worked on it and we got Lane with it. He had to bite on the inside move, and any time I had a step, I had him.

The first time I put that move on him in a game, he came up to me and said, "Hey, Spats, where'd you get that move from? You must've been working with Raymond Berry."

They called me Spats because I put white tape on my shoes and it looked like I was wearing spats.

Lane was a ferocious tackler. He had a habit of tackling you high, from the chest up, and you paid the price. If you had to reach out for the ball, you knew you'd have that clothesline coming at you.

One of my unforgettable catches against Lane was in that Detroit game where I scored late in the game and then they beat us a couple seconds later. Lane had speed and he was tall with enormously long arms. We were about 40 yards out when we called the play. I had him beat, but he made it up. He knew where that goal line was. I broke to his outside, which kept him inside of me. He kind of spun around, which meant that when Unitas throws the ball, he'd be throwing over Lane. That was the only way we could beat him, because he took away the inside. So I broke to the outside and went down, and John laid it out there. To this day I don't know how that ball stuck, because Lane was in the way and I couldn't sight the ball into my hands. I just dove and stuck my hands out, and the ball stuck as I went into the end zone.

I watch those films and I see that ball stick and I pull it into my stomach. You can't practice anything like that. The timing was there for it to hit and stick. Every time I watch it, I just say, "There's another one of God's great plans for me."

The game was tougher in my time than it is today, just because of the mechanics of it. They have tailor-made rules to fit more scoring and make the game more exciting. It's hands-off in many areas. You can't even touch the quarterback. What could Unitas do in today's game?

Players today are bigger, stronger, and faster. But there are some who could not play in our era, with the slow whistle (when defenders had more time to wrack you up before the ball was whistled dead). The qualified guys who played in our time could play in any era.

A guy like Jerry Rice wouldn't be doing near what he is doing if he played in our time, because of the bump and run. What did Deion Sanders do when he got to play Jerry Rice? He got right up in his face and rode him, so they kept the ball away from him. What I'm saying is that the Night Train Lanes and Herb Adderleys and all those guys who were solid defensive backs would have given Rice plenty of trouble.

When you shift into what you call pitch and catch—and that's all it is today—you don't have to run patterns. All you have to do is run down and get into an area and go across the field. If they don't hit you with the ball in this lane, they pick you up in that lane. And if the linebacker goes in there, they catch you in the third lane.

Today I think Barry Sanders is in a class by himself among running backs. You can't compare him with past players; there are too many variables. Are we looking at a complete back, a running back, a back who can do a couple things, or one who can do many things? Just in carrying the ball, Sanders has every natural technique, plus new ones he keeps adding on. The Lord has blessed him; you can't practice any of that. You can't orchestrate it. You can't teach what he does. It's all instinctive. And everything he does, he does better than anybody at this time.

I never thought of anything that happened on the football field as giving me a personal thrill, because I knew that it wasn't just me making it happen. When I was inducted into the Pro Football Hall of Fame in 1975, I had mixed feelings, because at the time my second wife was dying of cancer. So the true meaning of it didn't have the velocity that it should have had. I was overwhelmed by it, but at the same time I was deflated by what was happening to her. She made it to the induction ceremony; they had a nurse there and a cot for her to lie down when she needed to. Right after that she went downhill. She was up and down until she died October 16. So the significance of what was supposed to be an important time in my life was insignificant at the time.

Ten years later I went back for an induction ceremony. I put myself up there on the stage in my mind and went through the same thing that the new guys up there were going through, and I got the feeling. You talk about fairy tales; the few times I've been up there and I see my bust there, that's not real to me. It's me but it's not me. I can't believe it. As I sit here in Baltimore and that bust is in Canton, Ohio, I can't really accept that it's real, an actuality, unless somebody brings it to me. It's like a dream.

Today I work in juvenile services, in the street, from elementary schools to high schools. I have seen some horror stories. Every time you think you've seen it all, something else happens that surpasses it. People whose lives are so traumatic every day, they have no social life, worrying will they get shot on the way to school. I've been in those areas where you hear the gunshots. I'm ducking behind a car and they don't even flinch. You can't explain that to people who haven't been out there.

These little kids don't know who Lenny Moore is, but what's important to them is that I'm honest with them. I'm there when they reject me, and I work through the spirit of rejection so they can learn to trust me.

Ernie Harwell. Courtesy Baltimore Orioles

ERNIE HARWELL

Born: 1-25-18
Washington, Georgia

Emory University
Colts Broadcaster, 1956

"In the early days of my career I was just as fond of football as I was baseball."

In the 1950s, when I was the radio announcer for the Baltimore Orioles, there was fierce competition between National Beer and Gunther's. If one had the baseball rights, the other had the football. So that's why I didn't do more Colts games than I did.

The two breweries' rivalry was so intense, one year Gunther had an advertising slogan: "It's good like Gunther!" So when National Boh was sponsoring the football games, and a guy kicked an extra point or a field goal, you couldn't say on the air, "It's good!" because that was Gunther's promotion. You had to say, "It's through the uprights," or "He executes the extra point."

In the early days of my career I was just as fond of football as I was baseball. I loved to work football. I had done Georgia Tech games in Atlanta, and was on the old CBS football roundup on Saturday afternoons. Red Barber was in the studio in New York, and several of us were stationed at different games.

The only year I did the Colts games was 1955, when National Brewing had the rights to both baseball and football. Chuck Thompson would do the first half on TV and I would do the radio, then we'd switch. No analysts, no color guys. You worked alone.

George Shaw was the quarterback. I remember my first game was the opener, the Chicago Bears at Memorial Stadium. On the first play Alan Ameche ran 78 or 79 yards for a touchdown. That was a big kick. I doubt if I remember any other single play the whole season.

Weeb Ewbank was great to me. He would give me the movies of the next opponent on Tuesdays and I would run them during the week to get to know the teams. He'd tell me the tendencies, like how many times they threw to the left end, that kind of stuff. He even let me look at his play book. I don't think a coach would do that today. He'd tell me what they were going to do on the first play if they received the kickoff. That first play in football is the toughest of all, when you're not really quite ready and they pull some kind of surprise on you and you're left with your jaw hanging. But I was pretty well prepared when I went into those games.

One funny incident I recall: Chuck and I were at a dinner of some sort for the Colts. After the banquet, some guy comes up to Chuck and says, "You guys are doing a good job, but you're not pronouncing Szymanski's name correctly. And tell that to Ernie 'Hartwell' too."

Photograph by Bob Miller

JOHN UNITAS

Born: 5-7-33
Pittsburgh, Pennsylvania
University of Louisville
Quarterback

6′ 1″, 194 lbs.
Drafted: #9, 1955
Pittsburgh
Colts: 1956–1972
Hall of Fame: 1979

"Raymond Berry had a lot to do with my success, because both our successes were hand in hand."

When I played at the University of Louisville, I used every formation I would later use in professional football, which was a break for me.

In 1955 I went in the ninth round of the draft to the Pittsburgh Steelers. Cleveland had expressed interest in me, but as a lower pick in the draft. They were the 1954 champions; Otto Graham had retired, but they had Babe Parilli and George Ratterman and Tommy O'Connell at quarterback.

My introduction to professional football at Pittsburgh was deflating. I walked into their training camp at St. Bonaventure's in Olean, New York, and the first thing I asked was, "Where do you get the whites?" meaning socks, T-shirts, shorts maybe, and athletic supporter. The guy pointed to this big conglomeration of socks and jocks and shirts sitting on the floor.

"Help yourself," he said.

So you had to dig through all that to pick out what you needed. After practice you took your stuff off and hung it on a hanger in your locker. They had a big fan blowing, and you hoped your stuff would dry by the time of the next workout that day.

Then I asked a guy, "Where do you get taped?" and they started laughing. I said, "What are you laughing at? Don't people get taped ankles around here?"

They said, "You don't get taped unless you get hurt."

So I just used ankle wraps.

Those were the first two things that were a big surprise to me.

They didn't seem to put a whole lot of time and effort into things. Most of the guys weren't very friendly. Nobody tried to work with you and help you. For example, they had a receiver, Lynn Chandnois. We were working out on a 7-on-7 passing scrimmage one day, where he would go out and hook up. On one play he hooked up behind a linebacker and I couldn't see him, so I passed to somebody else. When he came back to the

Second and short, what'll he do?
Photograph © 1995 TADDER/Baltimore

huddle, I said, "Lynn, if you're going to hook up, slide one way or the other so I can have a target and find you."

He said, "If you can't throw it, you shouldn't be here."

I felt if I had the opportunity, I could play. But I scrimmaged all the time and never got into a game. When they cut me, my expectations were bleak. My high school coach, James "Max" Carey, advised me to send a telegram to Paul Brown, who had shown some interest in me. So I did. Brown wrote back that they had just talked Otto Graham into coming out of retirement, but if I was interested, they'd have me in camp the next year. So I just played sandlot ball the remainder of that year to keep my hand in the game, intending to go to Cleveland in the spring.

In February 1956 Baltimore general manager Don Kellett called and asked if I was interested in playing professional football. I told him I was. "We are looking for a backup quarterback for George Shaw," he said. I looked at their roster and the only other quarterback they had besides Shaw was another rookie, so I thought I'd have a better chance with the Colts than at Cleveland. Kellett sent me a contract for $6,000; that was $1,000 more than I would have gotten at Pittsburgh.

When I came to Baltimore, I expected the same kind of reception as I had gotten with the Steelers. I flew in from Pittsburgh with a kid named Dickie Nyers, who ran back kickoffs for the Colts for a few years. Somebody picked us up at the airport and drove us to the Colts office at 2023 North Charles Street. Then somebody else drove us to the camp at Westminster. I thought: "Well, first-class treatment so far."

We got into the locker room and wondered where the whites were and, lo and behold, there they were in the top of the locker all rolled up neatly, whatever you needed. When you came in after practice, you just threw those on the floor, and when you went out for the next practice, you had a whole new set waiting for you there.

The rookies were the only ones in camp at the time, but when the veterans showed up, I had another surprise. The camaraderie and social atmosphere between the younger and older players was fantastic. These guys would take you aside and try to work with you and help you. George Shaw was happy to help me with anything I asked of him. You could see Gino Marchetti taking a defensive end and showing him how to work. You never got any of that kind of treatment in Pittsburgh.

One of Weeb Ewbank's greatest assets was that he was a tremendous judge of talent. He could see what talent people had for which positions and move them around. Alex Sandusky was a receiver at Clarion; Weeb moved him to guard. Jim Parker could play tackle or guard. Szymanski played center and middle linebacker. All those guys had played both ways in college.

But on game day you could have left Weeb in the closet most of the time. He got too nervous. Weeb always called the first three plays to start the game, using different formations. But most of the time your offensive coach would take care of the offensive line, and your offensive backfield coach would make whatever changes were needed. They might call down from the booth to put somebody in, and Weeb would put them in. The bench is the worst place in the world to watch a game anyhow.

The play changes would come from upstairs. But they didn't control the play-calling like they do now. Innovative plays, like throwing deep on first down, were my calls. They would send me down a suggestion, and when you came off the field you could talk to them. Most of the time all I wanted to know was whether they had an idea on blitzing. Sometimes teams get into habits, like always blitzing on third down no matter what. So I would say, "If you can get any kind of indication that they are keying on something, let me know." That's all I wanted to know.

Most defenses were predictable. Defenses fall into habits. If they win by playing zone defense two games in a row, they're not going to change. So when you're calling a play, you know this is what they're going to do, and you do what you need to do to beat that defense. The down, the yardage, and the position on the field dictated how they were going to play defense. Then it was up to me to get them to do what I wanted them to do.

The coaches who gave you the most trouble were ones like Vince Lombardi, who didn't give you much time to throw. Their defensive linemen and the linebacker and secondary were so well coordinated, you didn't always get a second look. You had to look fast and decide where you were going to go, because the rush was going to be there. We always predicated everything on two and a half seconds. If I got two and a half seconds to throw, I'm going to get rid of the football. The patterns were based and run on that timing.

Raymond Berry had a lot to do with my success, because both our successes were hand in hand. Raymond was the type of guy who would never leave anything to guesswork. When we went into a game, we knew exactly what we were going to do to that defensive back. It was just a matter of when and how it was going to happen, depending on how the defense played.

On Mondays he would watch game films of the next opponent. Tuesday mornings he would come in with his yellow pad and come over to my locker and say, "This is what I want to run on this guy this week: five-step inside outside move . . . a three-step inside . . . a corner position. . . . that's all I want to run." Whatever it was each week, that's all we would work on. He'd say, "What you call is your problem, but this is what I can do."

It was up to me to set the blocking up, the linebacker control, and all that stuff. And I'd say to him, "You just let me know what you want, how you want it, and when you want it." And during the game, he would come back into the huddle and say something like, "Five-step inside move 15 yards." Then it was up to me to do the formation, and get the ball to him.

The 49er game in '58 that clinched the western conference was really a bigger and better game than the championship game. After Weeb's half-time talk, our defense played tremendously. When you held those guys to no points for thirty minutes, you gotta be doing a hell of a job. There was no stopping Lenny Moore that afternoon. He ran one in backwards from 20 yards out.

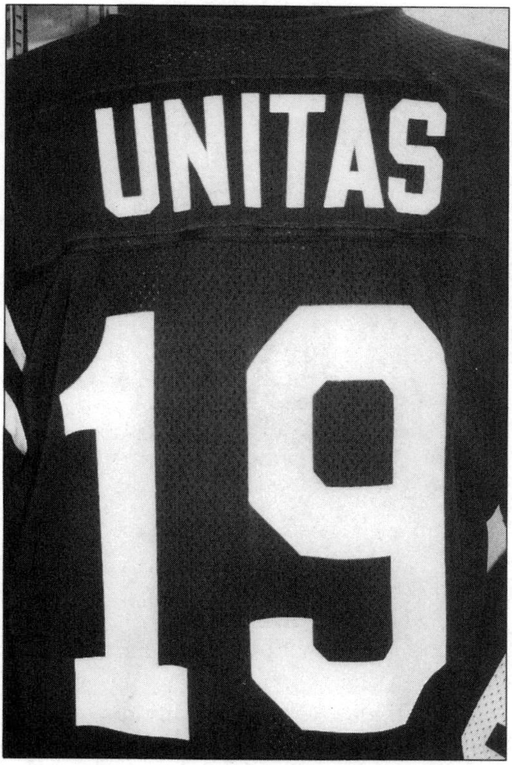

John Unitas's uniform, 1972.
Photograph by Bob Miller

Lenny was something that comes along once in a lifetime. He had so much natural ability; the way he ran the football, his movements, his judgments—he didn't have to work at it. As an outside receiver, he was good, but he wasn't as good as when he came back into the backfield. One year as a receiver, he caught only 25 percent of what was thrown at him, but coming out of the backfield his percentage went up to 75. He had the ability to go any distance any time he got the ball, and never seemed to get tired.

Our team was great for coming back. Sometimes we devoted an entire practice to working on the two-minute drill. It was fun. It was all planned out, so we were able to do it in games a lot of times.

Game after game, Gino Marchetti did things to amaze me. Forrest Gregg gave Gino fits, but Gino ate up Hall of Famers like Bob St. Clair. Gino wasn't a weightlifter. He probably couldn't bench press 150 pounds. He was a football player. I always get a kick out of these announcers who talk about linemen who can bench press 450. Maybe they can, but they can't play the game. They're big and strong, but they're not football players. They're pushers. They're out there dancing. Gino played the game.

My worst nightmare in eighteen years was the 1964 championship game in Cleveland. We should have beaten them. They played an outstanding defensive game against us. They were so well coordinated, by the time I looked for my second choice, I had to duck or get out of the

John Unitas's 1970 Super Bowl championship ring. Photograph by Bob Miller

pocket. John Mackey dropped a ball coming across the middle, probably would have gone for a touchdown. After he caught it, he was running and his knee came up and knocked the ball out of his arm, and they recovered it. Lenny Moore had Galen Fiss on a screen play, clear sailing to the goal line, and Fiss reaches up and just touches his foot and Lenny goes down.

In Super Bowl III against the Jets in the Orange Bowl I firmly believe if I had gotten in the game earlier, I would have turned it around. Tom Matte's open one time on a flea-flicker and Jimmy Orr is waving his hands, and he's the first man you go to. But Earl Morrall just doesn't see Jimmy down in the corner, I suppose. I don't know. But that's where you go with the ball. He elected to go down the middle to Jerry Hill, down the seam, and it's intercepted.

Then he hits Tommy Mitchell in the end zone and, instead of the ball coming into Tommy's hands, it comes into his chest, hits the pad, and bounces up in the air, and they intercept it.

Another time Matte fumbles after running it 60 or 70 yards, and they recover it.

Yet the game is never out of reach, because the Jets don't score a lot. Their strategy was to run at Don Shinnick and Ordell Braase—the left side—all day and stay away from Bubba Smith. That way Joe Namath maintained control of the football and ate the clock up on us.

Bubba Smith? Could have been as good as he wanted to be, but he was lazy.

I thought Bert Jones had a lot of ability, but when he got to Baltimore, I think they pampered him, didn't use him as well as they should have. They should have controlled him more.

You can blame Bob Irsay and Joe Thomas for my winding up in San Diego. You can also blame Carroll Rosenbloom for selling the team. All he wanted to do was get out of Baltimore. And he sells it to a guy who is a jerk at best. But the biggest jerk is Joe Thomas for treating the players and the people of this town the way he did.

I wanted to play longer and he didn't want me. That's all there was to it. Here's how it happened. I was at the Super Bowl in Los Angeles—Miami against Washington. So we had a meeting out there: Thomas and a guy named Pfeiffer, Irsay's lawyer at the time, and me. We're having a discussion and in walks Irsay and says, "What seems to be the problem?"

"I don't know," I said. "Joe Thomas doesn't want me with this football team anymore."

Irsay says, "Oh, well, then suppose we trade you?"

"That's your prerogative," I said. "If you're going to do that, I would like to know who's interested in having me. You find that out and then I'll tell you, 'Yes, I'll go there,' or 'No, I won't.' Then you can make the best deal for yourself."

Irsay says, "That sounds fair."

Three weeks go by. Then one morning at seven o'clock I get a call from Larry Harris of the *Morning Sun.* He says to me, "What are you doing going to San Diego?"

I said, "Larry, all I know is I'm going to Tallahassee to speak at the Touchdown Club tomorrow."

He said, "They've sold you to San Diego for $150,000 and future considerations."

I said, "Well, I don't know anything about it."

He hangs up, and the phone rings. It's Ernie Accorsi. "Joe Thomas wants to talk to you," he says.

"Fine. Put him on."

"No, no, he just wanted to know if you'd talk to him."

I said, "Ernie, what is this?"

"I'm just doing what I was asked to do."

"Sure, I'll talk to him."

He hangs up. I take a shower. Phone rings. It's Ernie again.

"Joe says he'll call you at nine o'clock."

"Too late. I'll be on an airplane. If he wants to talk to me, you tell him to pick up the phone and call me now."

A few minutes later the phone rings.

"John?"

"Yep."

"Joe Thomas."

"Yep."

"I just wanted to let you know we traded you to San Diego. Good luck."

Bang. He hung up.

So now they got all this crap in the papers. And Commissioner Pete Rozelle calls me, asks me to come to New York to meet with him. So I go. There's Bob Pfeiffer the lawyer and Joe Thomas sitting there.

Rozelle says, "What's going on in Baltimore? What's the problem?"

So I told him the story just like I've told you. Pfeiffer stands up and says, "Wait a minute. There must be some mistake. You were supposed to find out who was interested in you and let us know, and we'd make the deal."

I said to Rozelle, "If I'm not mistaken, if you look at paragraph three in your NFL contracts, it states that a player who is under contract to a football team does not have the right to talk to any other football team in the National Football League. Is that not right?"

Rozelle says, "That's right."

I said, "Case closed. They're both a bunch of jerks."

Rozelle got rid of them, then said to me, "What do you want to resolve the contract?" I had a ten-year deal for $300,000 with Rosenbloom which they had to pick up.

I said, "I'll take $200,000 and you'll never hear from me again."

This is one time that Pete Rozelle could have been very helpful. He called me a week later and said, "They offered you $50,000."

They got $150,000 from San Diego just for the rights to talk to me. If they had wanted to do something right, they'd have given me that 150 plus the 50 they offered me. The whole thing would have been closed out. But Rozelle never interceded, never told them they should do that.

I said, "Tell 'em to go to hell." They just lied through their teeth one time after another.

San Diego had the rights to me now, so I had to negotiate with them. I could have refused to go, which I probably should have done. But I wanted to play another couple years.

Harland Svare was the coach there. Couldn't coach little leaguers.

Before I left the Colts, I worked with some young quarterbacks. They had one guy who looked good setting up and throwing and running, but he knew nothing about the game and the defenses. Coach Don McCafferty told me to work with him. First thing I did was ask the kid, "What do you want to get out of playing professional football."

He said, "A Corvette and a German shepherd dog."

That was the end of that. He didn't make it.

The quarterback position in the NFL is the weakest position in the whole game. They're not there. I think the kids who have the best chance of standing out are Drew Bledsoe of New England and Seattle's Rick Mirer.

It's a matter of discipline and self-discipline, and I don't think it's out there anymore. You don't allow quarterbacks to wear fatigue hats during practice when everybody else has a helmet on. Who says it has to be different from our days? Why is it Mike Ditka is not coaching anymore? Because he's tired of putting up with that crap.

Vince Lombardi didn't have any earrings or long-haired guys on his team. He wouldn't put up with it. My motto is: You play the way I want you to, or you don't play here.

Another reason the quarterbacks aren't there today is that all the way down to high school and little league, the coaches have taken control of the game. Coaches call all the plays.

Another factor is the players don't play both ways; they are all specialists. I played both offense and defense, so I understood defense. If I called a play and my coach asked me why I called it, I better have an answer. Today quarterbacks have no idea of why you run a draw screen, why you run a trap, why you do whatever it is you do. The plays come in from the bench and that's it.

There's no secret about calling plays. Bobby Layne once told me, "You just run when they think you're going to pass, and pass when they think you're going to run."

You have to study the game, know when to call certain plays. The coaches upstairs don't have the same information the quarterback has from the people in the huddle. If I had to wait for the coach upstairs to send a play down so Raymond Berry could run a square out or a turn-in or a corner pattern, it would take five or six plays. Instead, Raymond would come back and say, "I got this guy—18 yards."

I'd say, "Okay, 18 yards sideline, you got it."

John Unitas.
Photograph © 1995
TADDER/Baltimore

I made those decisions, and I was capable of doing it because I knew the game inside out. I don't think these guys do today. They are not permitted to learn the game. Kids should play both ways through high school. They should play defense to learn how to beat a defense. If it's a two-man zone, put three guys into the two-man zone, or overload the situation; go back weak side, flare-control the linebacker, work one on one the outside. It's not that difficult. But you have to work at it, study it, be involved in it, and I don't think they are.

Modern coaches call a meeting to find out what time the next meeting's going to be. Those coaches who say they have to sleep in the locker room to get the job done—how many plays are there in a game on offense? Seventy? Maybe seventy-five? How many times does first and 10, second and 3, or third and 7 come up?

It's the performance, the attitude of the players on the field, and playing with no mistakes that wins games.

Today's game is interesting, but boring for those who like defense. I never watch one all the way through.

Ordell Braase (81) slashes to the ball.

Ordell Braase

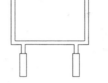

Born: 3-13-32
Mitchell, South Dakota
University of South Dakota
Defensive End

6′ 4″, 242 lbs.
Drafted: #14, 1954
Colts: 1957–1968

"I was one of five guys who were involved in both the 1958 championship game and the 1969 Super Bowl against the Jets."

I came out of Mitchell, South Dakota, and went to the University of South Dakota. In the early 1950s, we used the two-platoon system, and I played offensive and defensive tackle, which in college was almost like a defensive end in the pros. In my senior year, they went back to restricted substitution, so you had to play both ways. But I was used to that.

We had a P.R. guy, Dean Belvis, who cranked out a lot of publicity about me and pushed me hard. I had the height—6-foot-4—and the speed to be a pro lineman, but at 210 pounds I did not have the weight. But the Colts drafted me ahead of Alex Sandusky and Raymond Berry in 1954.

After graduation, I had a military obligation and went to Ft. Lewis, Washington, for summer camp. I got a two-week leave and came to the Colts camp in Westminster. They worked on me as an offensive tackle, but I didn't have the bulk to deal with guys like Tom Finnin, who weighed 275. It looked like an overmatch situation to me, so I decided to put in my two years in the army and then come back and see if I could make it.

After I came back from Korea in '56, I played football at Ft. Ord, where Don Coryell was the coach. I'll never forget watching that game when Jim Mutscheller caught that pass against Washington that saved Weeb's job.

When I rejoined the Colts in 1957, I took a look at Don Joyce, the regular defensive right end, and Gino Marchetti on the left side. It didn't take long to decide that my best shot was on the right side. It's a left-handed position—you put your left hand down in the set position—so it was a little awkward at first. But there are more right-handers than left-handers, so it automatically reduces your competition for the job. It's also usually the weak side; most teams are right-oriented and will run to their right side. The Raiders were an exception; they ran to the left. Al Davis believed that teams usually put their best players on the left side defensively, so they took advantage of that and ran the other way. And right-handed quarterbacks are going to roll out to their right.

Jim Parker had been the number one pick in the draft, but he was in the College All-Star game and came in two weeks late. I decided I'm going to test him in practice. The first time I hit him a hell of a shot and I got his attention. The next time I thought I was going to do the same, but he hit me and knocked me 5 yards down the field. I learned right then that I couldn't take that guy head-on. He was just too powerful.

I played against Parker only in practice, but he was the best I ever lined up against. He weighed around 280, but he was quick. They put weight limits on us; they didn't want so much weight as mobility. Most of the 300-pounders are not that good at pass protection because they are slow setting up. That's why you see linebackers beating them today. But not Parker. He could set up quick. He was like a boxer, using his hands. You couldn't overpower him.

I remember one time in a preseason scrimmage, Colt Night at Memorial Stadium. It was a short yardage situation, and Parker comes up to the line of scrimmage, his butt sticking way up in the air, his head way down. I'm looking across at him and thinking, "There's no way I'm going to get underneath this guy. I can't handle that."

So as soon as the ball is snapped, I just jump straight up in the air. Parker's looking all over; where did that guy go?

I don't see anybody today who can compare with him.

You can't let the big guys come at you and uncork and really hit you. You have to get them off balance. Set on his shoulder and give him a little bit of a fake or hesitation, so he has to adjust in his momentum. You can't let them tee off on you.

I learned how to do that by watching Bobby Boyd. He was a small, squatty guy, but powerful. As soon as he saw that sweep coming, with that tackle or guard coming at him with 10 or 15 yards of momentum—if you try to bury yourself in that, you're going to lose that battle. Bobby would sit there, and just about the time they were ready to make contact with him, he'd give them a little bit of a movement one way or the other, and that slight adjustment slowed down their momentum and took them off balance. I used to see him knock some of those big guys right on their butt. That's what you have to do in the interior line play. But you can get caught on that little fake, if you fake one way and they're running the other way.

Weeb Ewbank would have both the offensive and defensive teams in there together, and we'd write down all the plays. Position by position, we wrote them all down. The defensive players were there to learn offense. He gave us a basic football education. He was very methodical and knew what he was doing.

Weeb had some eccentricities, some quirky habits. Sometimes it seemed that he was more interested in getting a good price on a case of toilet paper than you'd be buying a new car. He was a very frugal guy.

He was also very suspicious. You had to be careful what you said in front of him. He'd be wondering what your ulterior motives were. He also suspected opposing teams were spying on us. He had the equipment man, Freddie Schubach, looking up in the trees all the time and surveying the stadium for spies. And rightly so; he had coached under Paul Brown and he knew Brown did it. George Halas, too. They'd have guys pose as newspaper reporters to pick up whatever they could.

Charlie Winner was a scout for the Browns when Weeb was there. They put him through a course in climbing telephone poles, then they outfitted him and he'd go up a pole with those spikes on, or up in a tree with binoculars and a notebook.

Sometimes you pick up something that way. The 49ers came in with their shotgun formation in 1960. They were staying near Washington, and the end of the week we got word about what they were doing. But they beat us anyhow.

One day Weeb sees a guy walk into Memorial Stadium with all these cameras hanging on him. He stops practice and yells, "Get that S.O.B. with the cameras out of here. Who let him in?" He's yelling and swearing, and finally he says, "Who is that guy?" And Ken Jackson, one of our guards, says, "Weeb, that's my daddy."

We'd be in the locker room at Wrigley Field, and Weeb swore that Halas had the room bugged, and he's looking all over, behind the pictures, looking for bugs. Before the game he always told us the first four plays, but he'd whisper so you almost had to lip-read.

I always got a kick out of the fans at Wrigley Field. When you came off the field and went up some steps to the locker room, there was nothing but a chain link fence between the players and the fans. If we won, all the guys who had bet on us would be out there cheering us on—"Way to go, Colts"—and if we lost, they'd be cussing and screaming at us.

One of Weeb's defensive coaches was John Bridgers from Johns Hopkins. He had Marchetti, Donovan, Big Daddy, Joyce, and me. Now, who do you think got overcoached? I was the only guy who would listen to him. Artie Donovan said, "I think I've seen everything. I've been on a team that got bought back by the league, and another club that went broke in mid-season. But I never thought I'd be coached by some guy from Johns Hopkins."

A lot of guys didn't know what to think of Bridgers. But you could see that he had a lot of depth to him. He was a good, solid, dedicated guy. Carroll Rosenbloom put in a curfew at camp, and Bridgers had the job of making the room check. So one night in comes Gino and Bill Pellington and a couple other guys about five minutes late. Bridgers turned them in. Their first reaction was, "That lousy so-and-so." They played tricks on him, like putting shaving cream on the doorknob when he went to open the door, stuff like that. Later Gino wrote him a letter of apology.

Weeb brought Otto Graham to camp to work with Unitas. Otto liked the flat stuff (throwing to the backfield guy in the flat) but I'm sure John would say he learned something from Graham.

At that time, George Shaw was the starting quarterback. We had a trainer, Dimitri Spassoff, who had been a gymnast in the 1928 Olympics.

We played a few preseason games, just experimenting, and Spassoff, in his Bulgarian accent, would say, "You just vait, when Georgia Shaw get ready to play football, then ve really go."

We had Lenny Moore and Jim Mutscheller and Raymond Berry as receivers, but John Unitas had one of the most important ingredients for a quarterback: the mental toughness to focus and concentrate in critical situations. A lot of guys can throw the ball far and hard, but they don't have that extra quality. You see some quarterbacks with nervous feet. John just stayed in there and kept looking. He was oblivious to what was happening around him, who was near him, who was getting ready to lower the boom on him. He just kept scanning and waiting until that last split-second when his receiver would come open and he'd hit him.

Today I see teams give their quarterbacks much less protection than we gave John. They send everybody out. I see mental errors and guys giving blitzers a free ride. I've always said that if a quarterback gets rushed, half the time it's his own fault. There are things he can do to slow down the rush: play-action passes, screens and draws, and how they use their tight ends.

We should have won in 1957. The day we led, 27–3, in Detroit and then lost it, Jug Girard, a guy we had cut, had a big game against us.

But to me the most memorable event of that season was the locker room speech before the game at Washington. We knew we were a good team, but after the Detroit loss we had lost the next two to Green Bay and Pittsburgh, two lousy clubs. This was the year Weeb had to win or be a contender, and it didn't look like we were going anywhere. We were 3–3 after six games.

So, just before game time at Griffith Stadium, Weeb stands up and says, "We're not out of it yet. But we've got to have this game. Just before I came up here, Gino Marchetti asked if he could say something to the team."

Gino's sitting way in the back. He says, "Who in the hell told him that?"

Weeb says, "Everybody else out—coaches, trainers, equipment guys—just the players. Gino's going to say something to the team."

Gino knows nothing about all this. He walks up in front of the team, looks around, and says, "Everybody know the party after the game's at my house?"

"Yeah, Gino."

"Ten dollars a couple. Everybody know how to get there?"

"Yeah."

"Well, let's go out and win this game. We'll have a lot more fun if we win it."

We went out and won it, 21–17. Next day in the newspapers, "Colts spurred on by inspirational speech by Marchetti."

We won four in a row and then got robbed out in San Francisco. Of all the bad calls in that game, the most atrocious was when they threw a Hail Mary pass and the official called defensive interference on Andy Nelson on the goal line. In the college game now, they have a maximum 15-yard penalty on that play, and that's okay. But when they put the ball on the one that day, it was a 45-yard penalty.

We finished 7 and 5, and you could see that the team was beginning to solidify.

I was one of five guys who were involved in both the 1958 championship game and the 1969 Super Bowl against the Jets. [The others: Don Shinnick, John Unitas, Lenny Lyles, and Johnny Sample.] In '58 I was the swing end between Marchetti and Joyce. During the game in New York, I was in for a couple series. Then, with about two and a half minutes to go in regulation time, Gino got hurt on a second down play. Big Daddy piled on him and broke his ankle, around the Giants' 40.

Frank Gifford maintains to this day that when the official went to place the ball after that play, he was so concerned about Marchetti lying on the ground with that broken ankle, he placed it with his left foot instead of his right foot, and that took away the first down Gifford thought they had made. Later, when I read that somewhere, I wrote to the author and said, "If that is true, that official had to have the greatest peripheral vision known to man, because Marchetti was 60 yards down the field lying on a stretcher."

We were down 17–14 at the time. It was third down and less than a yard when I went in for Gino at left end. The Giants had Alex Webster, a big 230-pound fullback who ran like he was trying to get through a brick wall. I thought they'd be better off sending him straight ahead to pick up that yard, but I knew they'd be coming at me with Marchetti out.

I got down in position. Bob Schnelker was the Giants' end, and he's blocking down on me. Any time you see a tight end setting down like that, you have to respect him. Bill Pellington, the outside linebacker, said, "Look out, here they come." He was right. Here came Frank Gifford on that power sweep. I got out and forced the play in, and Artie Donovan was right inside of me, and we both hit Gifford before he got to the line of scrimmage.

That was one of the biggest plays of my career. If they control the ball at that point, we might never get it back and have a chance to tie it. But the play-by-play accounts have Marchetti making that tackle on Gifford, and he was in the locker room on a stretcher.

The play ended up very close to the sidelines right in front of their bench. Jim Lee Howell was the coach. He was standing there in his hat and coat with his arms folded. I'm standing in the middle of a bunch of Giants—Rosey Brown, Jack Stroud—and they're yelling they want to go for it. "We can make it!" somebody hollered. But Howell sent in the kicker, Don Chandler, and he got off a beautiful punt down around the 14.

You know the rest of the story.

In 1968, Unitas had been hurt, and Earl Morrall came in and did a great job to get us to Miami. I used to kid Earl, because he played for so many teams: "Every town we go to to play a game, it's like a homecoming to you."

Once we got off a plane at Newark airport, and we're getting on the buses when some guy comes running up.

"Where's my boy Oil?"

I looked at him. "Who are you talking about?"

"My boy Oil."

"Who's that?"

"My boy, Oil Moyall."

For years the NFL wanted to change the name Super Bowl to something else, but they never managed it. We were 17-point favorites amid all that hoorah and hoopla in Miami. We had been playing good defense all year, but we tried to take our game another level or two beyond what we had been playing, and we got out of sync and screwed it up.

The other thing that happened—and I really believe this—is that the first two Super Bowls had been real blowouts, and the third one had all the markings of being another blowout. I think the NFL was not really getting the play on this game that they wanted. I know the NFL well enough to know that if they wanted to pull a game, they'd do it one way—through their officials.

When I look back, I know that you couldn't get an official to call a holding call at all that day. Winston Hill was playing opposite me. He was a good tackle, but you know when you're being held, and when a guy's being obnoxious about it. Finally I decided if that official isn't going to call it, I'm going to put Hill out of commission. One time he fell down, and I started jumping on his hands, trying to break them.

I know if I had that problem, other guys did, too. After the game, Don Shula said to me, "Didn't you ever say anything to the official about that guy holding you?"

I said, "I yelled and screamed at him so much, I got tired of it."

We drove up and down the field all day, and ended up with interceptions or missed field goals. That's the way it went.

The worst I was ever injured was when I broke my jaw December 9, 1961. We were playing the Rams out there in the next to last game of the season. That's the game where Unitas was stopped after forty-seven consecutive games throwing at least one touchdown pass.

Roy Hord was a pulling guard for Los Angeles. They were doing a sweep our way and the play was strung out to the sideline. The corner back, Lenny Lyles, came up and made the tackle. The play was over, and I turned around and saw Hord still roaring at me, so I just put my arm up to ward him off. He threw an elbow at me and clipped my jaw and snapped it.

Doc McDonnell liked to set broken bones right out there on the field. So he comes out and starts cranking on my jaw. I was in shock, didn't really feel any pain. I said, "Jesus, Doc, what the hell you trying to do?"

He opens my mouth and reaches in and finds a wisdom tooth that got knocked out right there at the break in the jaw, and he pops that out with his hand. Then he starts cranking on me again, but he just couldn't set it, because it was broken right at the angle. So he tied something around my jaw and head, and I got up and walked back to the bench. I'm standing there spitting blood all over in front of all those fans in the seats right back of the bench, and they're getting disgusted. They start hollering for me to go someplace else and do that.

The league rules said there had to be an ambulance at the field. But they didn't have one. So Ben Small, the business manager, who had about a two-inch fuse, starts yelling for an ambulance. He had to see that I got to a hospital. He's screaming and swearing at everybody, and a few minutes later here comes two little guys running across the field with one of those army stretchers, looking like two characters out of M*A*S*H. They want me to get on the thing and they're going to carry me out.

First of all, I didn't think they could lift and carry me. Secondly, I'm spitting blood, and the last thing I want to do is lie down. So I told them I'd walk.

Meanwhile, Ben Small is yelling, "Where's that ambulance? League rules say an ambulance supposed to be here. . . ." And on and on he's raving, all the way up the exit ramp. Still no ambulance.

Small runs out into the six-lane highway looking for a car or something. Finally a guy in a pickup stops. Ben says, "We got to get this guy to a hospital," and waves me over. I said, "Ben, where we going? What hospital?"

"I don't know," he says, and asks the guy in the truck, "What hospital?"

I guess the guy noticed my uniform or something, 'cause he says, "Go to hell. I wouldn't tell you if you were the last guy in the world," and drives away.

Finally the ambulance comes. When we get to the emergency room, Ben says to me, "Stay here," and he runs in. We're waiting and waiting, and he's not coming out. The driver says he has to go, and he leaves me standing out there.

Ben Small was inside trying to locate a doctor to fix me up. But it was a Saturday afternoon, and the guy he got hold of was at a cocktail party or something, and he told Ben, "Just shoot him up and I'll be there tomorrow." So that's what they did.

The next morning the doc came in and set it, but that night, when he came back to check it, he discovered that it had slipped. He had to set it again. Then I flew back to Baltimore, and the doctor there didn't like the way it looked, so he rebroke it and set it again. When he checked it a few days later, he still wasn't satisfied, so he stuck some pins in it, and that didn't work. Eventually they fixed it with wires and did an open reduction. That was a long ordeal.

I never heard from Hord, that cheap shot artist. I've never spoken to him since. The next year, when it came time to play against the Rams, my wife, Jan, said, "Don't do anything silly when you play against Roy Hord this afternoon." I never got the opportunity that day to take a shot at him.

The two guys who gave me the most trouble on opposing teams were two birds with the Packers, Bob Skoronski and Norm Masters. The Packers were the team to beat in the 1960s. You knew you had to be at your best against them. You didn't have to get yourself psyched up, unlike facing an expansion team, when you had a hard time getting excited.

In football, the defensive line is kind of give and take. You try to set things up. They take the outside away from you, they give you the inside. They take the inside away, and you try to make something happen on the outside. But when you get one guy set up on one series, and they send in the other guy on the next series of plays, you had a hard time keeping up with what you had set up with whom. That's the way it was with those two guys.

I played against Forrest Gregg when he was on the left side early in his career, and I didn't think he was that good. He made his reputation by having great games against Marchetti. He wouldn't let Gino get hold of him, just kept backing up with him. He had good footwork, but if he had to stand up and take Gino head-on, he couldn't handle it.

I never had much respect for blocking backs. I took the approach of just going in and kicking the hell out of them; go in as hard as you can and make them respect you. The next time you went at them, they'd try to dive and clip you, knock your feet out from under you. Then all you had to do was jump over them, once they committed to trying to hit you low.

I'd say Jim Taylor of the Packers was the most punishing running back for a lineman. Taylor was strong and powerful; he would plow right in. But he was also shifty. Once, on a draw play, the tackle stood up like it was a pass, but I recognized it as a draw and got inside Skoronski. Here came Taylor, and when he saw me, he put on the brakes, stopped, and jumped outside Skoronski. So I got outside Skoronski, and I'm right with him, getting ready to hit him, and that sucker bounced back into the original hole. By that time, Skoronski had recovered enough to seal me off. It takes a hell of a back to do what Taylor did.

Paul Hornung was a hard driver; so was Bill Brown of the Vikings, Gale Sayers, and John Henry Johnson. Alex Webster was an old-time, hard-nosed, hard-running back, a real load and a half.

Alan Ameche belongs up there, too. A tough, tough runner. I've seen him go through there and get into the secondary running straight up and down with that high knee action. He punished some backs. Yeah, Horse belongs up there.

Hugh McElhenny was a dancer, one of these guys who would start out the other way, then start running back this way. When a back starts doing that, you've got to look around, because that's when you get blind-sided.

We had a lot of little scat backs then: Jon Arnett, Dickie Bass, Ronnie Waller, Howie Ferguson. But Lenny Moore was the best running back of all that I saw. He could do so many things well. That diving catch he made against Night Train Lane was the greatest I ever saw.

A lot of people think Jim Brown was a punishing runner, but not to a lineman. Brown would just trot up toward the line, looking for that hole. Once he found it, then he put on the big acceleration. But you never saw him pile into a line.

Brown was a horrible blocker, and I think I have the distinction of being the only guy he ever blocked. We were playing in Cleveland in '62. Jim Ninowski was their quarterback. There was a play where he rolled out to the right, which was away from me, and Brown sealed off his back side. I came running by Brown, and he's setting there like he's counting the crowd. So as I'm going by, I thought, "I'll give him a little shot." I nailed him hard in the head with my elbow.

About two plays later, they're lined up for the same play, Ninowski rolling to the right. Brown set up real casual, and I'm going by him, and I'm about ready to unload on him a second time when he nailed me. I mean he really hit me. That may be the only block he ever threw.

Halfway through the 1968 season, I saw that what had happened to other players was happening to me. The Colts were edging me out. I began to realize that they were making a big issue out of things I had gotten by with before. Physically it was becoming harder. The resiliency of the body wasn't there as it once had been. I was ready to retire.

It took me two years after I quit playing to where I could take my arm and raise it above my head.

I'm sixty-three now, and I have hip problems, arthritis, but you can't get a surgeon to say it's from football. I had a doctor tell me that every time you take a step, just walking, it's like putting three times your weight on that hip from the impact. I believe football accelerates the wear on it. I never played on artificial turf, but I have to believe that it, and the extra weight of today's players, have got to take a toll.

Ordell Braase.
Photograph by Vince Bagli

Art DeCarlo. Photograph courtesy of Art DeCarlo

Art DeCarlo

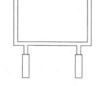

Born: 3-23-31
Youngstown, Ohio
Georgia
Defensive Back

6′ 2″, 202 lbs.
Drafted: #6, 1953
Chicago Bears
Colts: 1957–1960

"As soon as I arrived in Baltimore, it seemed like this was where I should be."

I was a center and linebacker in high school in Youngstown, Ohio. I was only second or third All-Youngstown, and was not heavily recruited. The University of Georgia had a scout who lived in Youngstown and he sent me down there on a tryout. My father had died when I was thirteen, my mother when I was seventeen, and my brother played an important part in my life.

Wally Butts was the coach at Georgia. Bill Harman, who played a few years with the Redskins, was one of the coaches who took to me. The freshman coach, Quinton Lumpkin, gave me my start. Butts said I had the ability to play a lot of positions, so I played defensive back and offensive end. Even when the platoon system came in in my senior year, I still played both ways. That helped me later with the Colts.

Butts wanted to create tough teams, and I guess he succeeded. Later I ran into guys in the NFL who had played against the Bulldogs in college. They told me that playing Georgia was the worst game, because they got beat up more than with any other team.

In those days players like me did not really follow the pro game closely because it was not what we intended to do. I never thought about playing professional football. Then the Chicago Bears drafted me in 1953. But before I went to the All-Star camp to prepare for the College All-Star game, they traded me to Pittsburgh. I just decided to follow my nose, play for the Steelers, and see what happens. Jim Finks was the quarterback there, and Ted Marchibroda was the backup; we had played against each other in the Blue-Gray game that year.

Then I was drafted into the army and spent two years at Ft. Belvoir, Virginia. I was a left-handed quarterback on the service team. In the meantime the Steelers had traded me to Washington. Redskins' owner George Preston Marshall saw me in an army game and got upset, because I was playing quarterback and they wanted me to be practicing as a defensive back.

Then the Redskins cut me, and Charlie Trippi, an ex-Bulldog who was a coach with the Chicago Cardinals, invited me to practice with them. My wife, Mary, and I went up there and we were looking for an apartment, but each one we looked at was more depressing than the one before. I hadn't signed a contract, and Mary kept saying, "We can't stay here."

Meanwhile, in a game at Detroit on October 20, Carl Taseff of the Colts got his nose broken by John Henry Johnson while blocking an extra point kick. Johnson was noted for swinging his elbow in such a way that if he hit you in the face he could break your nose. Carl could have been killed by it; they couldn't stop the bleeding for a while.

The next day Don Kellett was on the phone to me. I didn't care for the Cardinals because they didn't seem to be going anywhere, and Mary didn't care for Chicago because we couldn't find a decent place to live, so we talked it over and decided to go. We packed up the car and drove over to the stadium to tell Trippi I was leaving, and took off from there.

The next Sunday I was wearing Carl's number 23 and playing his left cornerback position, which I did for the rest of the 1957 season.

As soon as I arrived in Baltimore, it seemed like this was where I should be. I don't know why; it just hit me like that. One of the things I picked up on was the greatness of the guys—Lenny Moore, Raymond Berry, Mutscheller, Ameche. Playing against them, I was always impressed at how well they would get their jobs done. I had noticed that Unitas was a natural leader on the field, and could do a lot of things that other quarterbacks just couldn't do.

The treatment of the players by the Colts management was by far the best in the league, as far as I was concerned. Compared to them, the Steelers and Redskins were like pickup teams off the street. They didn't have the proper support and medical treatment like they had at Baltimore.

Everybody on the Colts' first team played all the time because Eddie Block knew what he was doing and kept them healthy. I think he was one of the main reasons they were able to be so successful. They stressed good physical condition and health, and they knew how to handle minor physical problems that would come up in a game or in practice.

I brought a shoulder injury with me from the Redskins. I knew there was something wrong with the muscle in my right shoulder, but they didn't treat it in Washington or even tell me what it was. When I got to Baltimore, right away Eddie Block said it was a dislocated shoulder. I played with it all year in 1957. In the Rams game, I made a play and knocked it out of place. I was lying on the field and Dr. McDonnell came out and grabbed it and pulled it back in place. They had cut the TV coverage when I went down, and Mary was at home watching and wondering what happened to me. The next year Dr. McDonnell operated on the shoulder, and it never went out again.

Of all the heartbreaking losses we had in 1957, the one I remember most was in San Francisco. They got away with a lot of fouling. Their receivers would come at you and hit you in the chest, and you'd back away a few steps. By the time you could recover, they had turned around and caught the ball. The referees didn't call it much.

In 1958 Weeb had other ideas for me. He felt he had a good enough defensive team, and he could use me best as an extra player who could play a lot of positions. I can thank Wally Butts for giving me that diversity.

Ewbank did not make the team lose in practice. He was better than Butts at putting together an offensive and defensive program that would prepare them to do the best they could against their next opponent.

Winning the 1958 championship stands out. I was on all the special teams, and I felt all along we were going to win that game. When they took the lead, 17–14, that's when I got nervous. Then when Steve Myhra went out there to kick the field goal to tie it, I said, "Steve, be lucky this one time." When he made it, I couldn't believe it. That was the most momentous event to me.

One of the things that made it difficult playing the Giants was that they made it hard for you to try to cover punts. There weren't that many in the game, but when we did punt, they had two guys on defense trying to keep you from getting downfield. Kyle Rote was the punt returner, and I was an end on the outside, trying to get down fast and press him inside toward the rest of the team.

In 1983 the Giants invited us up for the twenty-fifth anniversary of that game, and we saw a lot of the Giants we had played against. That was great.

As I got near the end of my playing career, I realized that I was on a team with a lot of great athletes, and the two I was most in awe of were John Unitas and Raymond Berry.

I played for Jim Mutscheller in two games in 1960, and caught six or seven passes from Unitas in each game. But the only Unitas pass I ever caught for a touchdown was when I was with the Redskins in 1957. In an exhibition game I intercepted one of his sideline passes and ran 80 yards for a touchdown. I bring that up to him once in a while.

Berry was not more than an average-sized person, but he was exceptional because of the attitude he had toward what he was bound to do, and he did it with such tenacity. He was never satisfied. Once I volunteered to throw for him after practice, but he chased me out of there in a hurry because I was throwing left-handed, and the ball was spinning the wrong way. I offered to throw right-handed, but he said I wasn't good enough with my right hand.

One factor that made the 1958–1959 Colts winners was guys like Jim Parker and Artie Donovan, not just as players, but as the comedians who kept the team loose. I don't think the Colts, with all the talent they had, would have won without that. They had the ability to say things that would break up everybody without even thinking. It wasn't planned. And they'd do it any time.

Art DeCarlo.
Photograph by Vince Bagli

We were playing the Rams in Los Angeles after we had clinched the conference. Near the end of the game Donovan walked right into the Rams' huddle and said to their quarterback, Frank Ryan, who was trying to make a name for himself, "Will you stop this crap and running around, and let's get this game over with."

Parker was a huge guy and a great athlete, but he was afraid of needles from the doctor.

Donovan was always overweight; you'd look at him and think he couldn't do anything. But he protected his area and that was his job. We used to play basketball during the off-season, and Donovan was as quick as anybody on the court.

Bert Rechichar was another guy who could crack us up and keep us loose, even though he was a surly guy. I think part of that surliness may have been an act.

The better you got to know guys on the Colts, the more you realized how great they were. To this day, a bunch of us get together for dinner every few months.

Tough runners? Jim Brown was not a punishing runner, but if you didn't get him with a good tackle—wrapping your arms around him—you wouldn't bring him down. Watching the films, we'd see Brown run right through some guy's arms like you'd think there was something wrong with the tacklers.

Jimmy Taylor at Green Bay was the same way. You couldn't just block those guys down.

You had to tackle Leon Hart a certain way, or they'd be carrying you off the field.

In scrimmages, Alan Ameche was hard to tackle because his hips were about as wide as his shoulders. You had a hard time wrapping your arms around him.

I was in awe of all those guys.

An injury in training camp in 1961 put me out of football. I tore the anterior cruciate ligament in my left knee. I was in agony until they gave me a shot to knock me out. They rushed me to Union Memorial Hospital and Dr. McDonnell operated that day. Donovan and Mutscheller came to see me. Artie says, "You looked like you were dead."

I had opportunities to make a comeback. Bob Shaw had gone to Canada to coach, and he asked me if I wanted to play there. But I decided not to.

Today my shoulders ache all the time. I exercise two or three times a week to help overcome the pain.

My three sons played high school football and lacrosse. Two of them still play lacrosse. My son, Artie, is a dentist in Birmingham, Alabama. He has started a lacrosse little league and has a high school team there.

The best thing about football for me was that it opened a lot of doors. I could do almost anything I wanted to do in business, and did a lot of different things.

If certain things had turned out differently, our whole lives would have changed. I coached at Loyola High School after my playing days were over. One day Don Shula called me and asked if I wanted to be an assistant coach with him on the Colts. "But," he said, "I can't offer you the job yet, until the other guy gives me an answer."

The other guy was Chuck Noll, who was at San Diego. He took the job with Shula. Who knows what would have happened if Noll had said no and stayed out at San Diego? I would have had a different life.

This banner, made by F. W. Haxel Flag Co., flew from the big flagpole behind the center field bleachers at every home game from 1959 to 1970, when a new one replaced it. Photograph by Bob Miller

Tom Matte, tough, resourceful competitor.
Photograph by Hugh B. McNally, Jr.

Tom Matte

Born: 6-14-39
Cleveland, Ohio
Ohio State
Halfback

6′ 0″, 195 lbs.
Drafted: #1, 1961
Colts: 1961–1972

"Let me tell you something about the Baltimore Colts. . . We were always concerned about each other, and about the people of Baltimore."

I grew up in inner city Cleveland at 93rd and Hough, the number one crime district in the city. It was that way in the 1950s, and it still is.

We were making zip guns in machine shop in the seventh grade. They raided our lockers and found brass knuckles, sawed-off shotguns, chains. You had to fight your way to school, and if you didn't have a push-button knife, you didn't get there. If you saw a gang walking down one side of the street and you didn't cross over to the other side, you were going to have a broken jaw. They worked over my brother once. It was really tough. It wasn't racist; it was school against school. Later it started to become more racist.

My father was a professional hockey player; he played seventeen years in the NHL with Detroit, Chicago, and St. Louis. He made two or three thousand a year, and had to work three jobs, so I didn't get to see him very often, and my mom was sick. My main outlet was the YMCA. I was a swimmer, gymnast, and ran track. But my main game was hockey. I played from midget league up.

Then we moved to East Cleveland, where football was the game. My father didn't want me to play football. The first time I ever picked up a ball I was in the ninth grade. I got clipped on the first play, and they had to operate on my knee. The cartilage was so smashed, the doctor didn't get all of it the first time. It drifted to the other side and locked my knee, so they had to cut it again. Ninth grade, and I had two knee operations already.

When I got to high school, I never started a game until I was a senior. I was sort of a pudgy tailback, but I could run the 100-yard dash in 9.9, and the quarter mile in 47 flat. When I was with the Colts, everybody thought I was the slowest guy in the world, but I had offers of track scholarships all over the country as a quarter-miler and decathlete. I did a lot of things good, nothing great, which was the way I played football.

Our coach, Leo Strange, was a real disciplinarian, and we had good teams, number one or two in the state.

Woody Hayes wanted me for a defensive back at Ohio State. He knew I could run, so he played me at offensive and defensive halfback. I also did the punting and kickoffs. When our quarterback got hurt, Woody's idea was to convert the best athlete to quarterback. I wanted to play halfback, and I really liked playing defense best, so I could hit other guys.

Our game plan at Ohio State really was 3 yards and a cloud of dust. I didn't understand what a pass pattern was until I came to Baltimore and John Unitas explained it to me.

I thought I was being drafted as a defensive back when the Colts made me their first pick in 1961. But when I got here they started me at halfback. It was difficult for Weeb Ewbank to find a place for me at that time. I played different positions, including backup defensive back.

At that time, halfbacks were the outside receivers. I was not an outside receiver like Lenny Moore was. I didn't have the burning speed or the maneuvers. But I could catch the ball. If I couldn't, I would never have made the team. Even with that, I never thought I'd make it.

I was an illiterate when it came to the pro system; it took me two years to learn the Colts' offense. It didn't help that I got hurt in the second game of the 1961 season and missed eight games. We were playing Detroit at Memorial Stadium. Wayne Walker, a linebacker, came in on a blitz. I picked him up. I ducked my head down and he tried to jump over me. His thigh hit me in the head and crushed two vertebrae in my back. When I came back, it didn't bother me, but since I've retired, those vertebrae deteriorated and popped out a disc and I have a real problem with my back now.

While I was out that first year, I went back to Ohio State and got my degree. I started some pre-law courses in the spring, intending to go to law school. I still didn't think I'd make it with the Colts.

When I went back to school after my rookie season, a guy named Jack Nicklaus recruited me into his fraternity, Phi Gam. I didn't know who he was. He showed me how to play golf, and we'd play twenty-seven holes a day practicing. Within three months I was down to a seven handicap.

When he turned pro that year, he got a $100,000 check from McGregor. When I had signed with the Colts, I got a $4,000 bonus and $11,000 salary. He gave me a set of McGregor clubs he had used. Later I traded them for $50 to upgrade. They'd probably be worth at least $20,000 today.

Nicklaus was built like a round ball; we used to call him Blobber the Whale. But he was a great athlete. They wanted him to play on Ohio State's 1960 championship basketball team, and I saw him kick a 43-yard field goal wearing tennis shoes in an intramural football game. He's a great guy and a good friend.

I mentioned that, as halfbacks, we were the outside receivers. Lenny Moore was probably the greatest, most versatile halfback that ever played. Outside and inside, the guy had more raw talent, and he was faster than anybody who ever chased him.

Out in San Francisco one day, Lenny Lyles, Bobby Harrison, and Lenny each put up $100 to see who was the fastest. They raced 100 yards—goal line to goal line. Lenny had enough time to bend down and pick up the money and head into the locker room before the other guys finished. That's how fast Lenny Moore was.

The only thing that upset me about Moore was that he didn't like to practice. He'd always take a dive near the end of a game—get hurt, pull a hamstring or something—so he wouldn't have to practice the following week. Late in the game, if it wasn't close, I'd go up to Don Shula on the sidelines and say, "It's time for me to go in."

He'd say, "What are you talking about?"

"Watch."

A few plays later, Lenny'd come limping off.

We only had two halfbacks. That meant that I had to run every play in practice all week. Then all of a sudden on Saturday mornings, Lenny'd come bouncing out of the locker room, claiming the trainers had fixed him up. He used to piss me off so bad. He had more talent in one little finger than I had in my whole body. I was so competitive, if I had that much ability, they couldn't keep me off the field.

That's the kind of inner fighting we had going on.

When Lenny was hurt in 1963, I led the team in total offense. Then he came back and was Comeback Player of the Year in '64.

In Don Shula's first year as coach, 1963, we started staying down at the Belvedere Hotel the night before a game. Shula wanted us to stay together as a team, or with our families. I was rooming with Jimmy Orr. The night before a Redskins game, Jimmy wanted to go out. I said, "We've got to play tomorrow. I need some sleep."

"Aw, you'll be all right," he said.

I stayed in. He went out. About two o'clock in the morning he rolls in, knocks on the door, wakes me up. I open the door and he falls in, drunk as a skunk, a bottle of Cutty Sark in his hands. I put him to bed, clothes and all.

In the morning I wake him up and he's still drunk. Never took his clothes off. Still got the bottle in his arms. It's five hours to kickoff.

I get him up, take him over to the training room, and throw him in the whirlpool. He's sleeping away when Shula comes in, so I drag Jimmy into the bathroom and hide him until Shula gets dressed and out of there. Then Jimmy Welsh helps me get Orr into his uniform.

We won the game, and afterward we come into the locker room. Jimmy's still hammered. He comes up to me and whispers, "How'd I play?"

"Jimmy, you had a great day. You caught 10 balls, over 200 yards, scored a couple of touchdowns."

He looks at me and says, "God, I can't wait to watch the movies."

This was Jimmy Orr.

Jimmy Orr had the best hands in the world. I look back at all the players who were here: Raymond Berry, Willie Richardson, Eddie Hinton, John Mackey—he had boards for hands—Lenny Moore, and I think the guy who had the softest pair of hands was Jimmy Orr. He ran that corner pattern down there in Orrsville as well as anybody.

And Unitas had confidence in him. He'd look at Jimmy in the huddle and say, "Whata you got, Jimmy?" And Jimmy would say, "I got the corner." He'd set the pattern and—boom—6 points. I don't know how he did it. Great players.

Jimmy didn't have the greatest speed, ran a 4.7 40-yard dash, but he would always win the quickness drills. He'd blow everybody out of the box making cuts. And he always waited until the last second to put his hands up. He'd be running full stride and just reach up and snatch the ball. That was his secret.

Jimmy was not physically tough; in fact, he was a mouse. He wouldn't block anybody. After the line ran over him a couple times, I'd say to him, "Jimmy, just get in the way of the defensive back." Then he'd do what we called the crab block—get down on all fours and jump around.

After we retired as players, I brought him to town once, let him stay in my house, use my car, a stick shift. One night he drives by my house, drunk as a skunk, puts the gear in reverse, drops the transmission, walks up the hill. I wake him up in the morning, he's still in the same clothes he wore the day before.

We used to talk mostly about women and gambling. He went through several wives, and loved to gamble, drink Cutty Sark, and smoke cigars. Hardly drinks at all now, and stopped smoking, but he still chews on a big unlit cigar all day. Last I heard he was taking junkets to the riverboats in Biloxi, going with somebody down there, having a good time, still living life one day at a time. Always did.

But when he put on a uniform, you always got 150 percent out of Jimmy Orr.

I set the record for the longest run by a Colt in a game at home against the Cardinals in 1964. I ran 80 yards on a 25 lag—a rollout draw. The old record was 79, set by Alan Ameche on his first carry.

On the 25 lag, John did a sort of semi-rollout and handed the ball off to me as he continued to roll out. I had great blocking; Parker opened the hole and I shot through. The outside receivers shot to the outside, and when they saw me take off they raced me to the goal line. Two 9.6 guys caught me at the goal line, and I fell in the end zone, exhausted.

Whenever we scored a touchdown, we never said anything, just handed the ball to the official. That was my job. What upsets me about coaches today is that they let the showboating go on, and the NFL promotes it. I think all the flips and dances and all that stuff detracts from the game.

I became the starting quarterback in 1965 when Unitas and his backup, Gary Cuozzo, both went down with injuries. Unitas tore up a knee in the twelfth game, and a week later Cuozzo dislocated his shoulder. We had one more game to play, in Los Angeles. We were 9–3–1, and Green Bay was 10–3 in the western conference.

It was between me and Bobby Boyd to play quarterback. Boyd had come from Oklahoma, where they had the same "3 yards and a cloud of dust" offense. The thing that helped me was that I had played on both sides of the line, offense and defense.

Shula asked Woody Hayes about me. Woody said, "He ain't pretty, but he'll get the job done for you."

Shula and Don McCafferty took advantage of my capabilities, and designed an offense totally around me. I could roll out, so they used a lot of diversionary tactics, where the backs would go one way, and I'd step back and pull a trap and go the other way.

The play that really screwed up the Rams' defense was the quarterback draw, which was the greatest play in the world for me. I'd set up about 5 yards, sit back there, let the backs flare out, get everybody out there. I'd have four guys blocking and four guys rushing, and I'd just take off up the middle. I think I averaged about 10 yards a carry on that play.

The Rams had a 4–3 defense, led by the Fearsome Foursome: Deacon Jones, Lamar Lundy, Merlin Olsen, and Roger Brown. I remember there was a lot of conversation across the line that day.

Just before half-time, we stopped them on a goal line stand at the 1 yard line. There's a time out, with thirty seconds left. What do I do now?

I'm talking to my linemen: "What do you think we ought to call?" And they're looking right through me, like I hadn't said a word. I punched Danny Sullivan and said, "I need some help. What play should I call here?"

He said, "I don't care what you call, but look at that babe in the first row."

I looked, and there's this gal with her boobs hanging out flopping all over the place.

So we get in the huddle and I say, "36 trap on one."

As we break, Lenny Moore comes over and taps me on the shoulder and says, "If we do that, I'm going to run into the goal posts."

This is when there were two poles on the goal line holding up the crossbar, and we're behind them in the end zone. I said, "Oh, my God."

Shula didn't let me have any automatics, but what else could I do? So I go up to the line of scrimmage and I say out loud, "Automatic. Quarterback sneak on one." The whole offensive line turned and looked up at me. Sully says, "Are you kidding?"

I yell again, "Automatic. Quarterback sneak on one." I get the ball, take off, pick up about 6 yards on the play, and the clock runs out.

As we're walking in the tunnel to the locker rooms, Deacon Jones comes up to me and says, "Matte, call that play again."

Back then they had a rule that you had to be on the active roster for the last three games of the season to be eligible to be in a playoff game. But we had picked up Ed Brown from Pittsburgh just for that last game. He threw one pass to Mackey for a touchdown. Near the end of the game we had the ball and a 20–17 lead and the clock was running out, and Tommy Bell, an official, comes running into the huddle as we're about to break and says, "Stay in here."

"What?"

"Stay in here. The clock'll run out," he says. "I don't know how you did it, but you did it."

I was the Player of the Game that week.

Green Bay was held to a tie by San Francisco, so we finished with identical records. That created a playoff against them the next week in Green Bay. It was the day after Christmas, and it was cold. They had to shovel snow off the tarps covering the field. When they took the tarps off, the field was real mushy. Then it froze up.

That game was unbelievable. We played our hearts out, and the defense played so great. On the first play from scrimmage, they knocked the ball loose from Green Bay tight end Bill Anderson, and Don Shinnick recovered it and ran it in 25 yards for a touchdown. Jimmy Welsh threw a block on Bart Starr at the goal line that knocked Starr out for most of the game. Zeke Bratkowski replaced him, which inspired this story TV sportscaster Scott Garceau likes to tell:

"Here I am a young kid. I got a ticket to the game in my Christmas stocking, and I'm all excited that I'm going to see Bart Starr and Johnny Unitas play in a playoff game. And who do I wind up watching? Zeke Bratkowski and Tom Matte. What a disappointment."

Once we had that 7-point lead, Shula played it ultraconservative. Too conservative. He sent in all the plays, and a field goal is all we scored the rest of the game. They scored once, and late in the game Don Chandler kicked a field goal, which we thought was wide, but they called good, and we went into overtime tied 10–10. We played almost fifteen minutes more without a score. Then there was a play where Billy Ray Smith hit Bratkowski in the head, and that cost us 15 yards and put them within field goal range. Chandler kicked it, and Green Bay won, 13–10.

That winter I was invited to a banquet in Minneapolis where they gave me an MVP award. Vince Lombardi, the Packers' coach, was there. Before I went, I made a miniature goal post out of wood, with one side extended farther out from the middle than the other side, above the crossbar. When I got up to speak, I said, "Back in Baltimore, we had duplicate goal posts made of what they are in Green Bay," and I pulled out this miniature and held it up, and the audience loved it.

When Vince Lombardi's turn came, he said, "Tom, I don't know if that field goal was good or bad, but when I went to the bank on Monday morning, my check said we were the champions."

Lombardi was a solid football coach. He knew the game inside and out, and he knew how to motivate his players. He knew what buttons to push on each player and he pushed to the *n*th degree. He turned average talent into good, even super, talent.

Shula had the same innate ability to motivate people; he knew what buttons to push, too. For example, if you yelled at Jerry Hill, who was one of the best blocking fullbacks who ever played the game, he was no good. If you yelled at me, kicked me in the butt like Woody used to do, that's fine.

I think both Lombardi and Shula could have been corporation heads.

In 1966 Shula told me I was going to play a lot more. But I didn't. I had a good month, but then I didn't play as much. So I told him I didn't like the situation and what was happening. "I'd like to get out of here," I said. "Here's a list of the teams that would like to have me. Please let me go." I was never a hot dog. I didn't have a swelled head. I just thought I should have been in there instead of somebody who wasn't doing the job.

Then we went down to Miami to play in that "Toilet Bowl" (runner-up playoff bowl) the second year in a row. Just before the game, Shula said to me, "You're going to play halfback today, and you're going to be my halfback next year."

That's when he retired Lenny Moore. I thought Lenny had lots left. I still think he could have played longer.

I picked up the nickname "Garbage Can" in a game at home against the Detroit Lions on November 19, 1967. We beat them 41–7.

Jim Parker was playing over Alex Karras on the line. There's always conversation at the line between offensive and defensive linemen. When I scored my third touchdown of the day, going right over the top of Parker and Karras, there was a big pileup, and I heard this conversation coming up from the bottom of the pile.

"Goddamn it, Jim."

"What's that, Alex?"

"A garbage can halfback like Matte can score three touchdowns over me!"

Parker bursts out laughing, runs to the sidelines. Everybody thinks he's hurt. Shula comes running. "Jimmy, you all right?"

Parker says, "Yeah, I'm all right. You ain't gonna believe what Karras called Matte. He called him a garbage can halfback."

Well, it wasn't three days later National Beer was having a big banquet, and they got this big old garbage can and banged it up and painted it gold and presented it to me as the garbage can runner of the Colts. I must have ten of those garbage cans from all over the country. It was a fun comment, nothing malicious, but the tag stayed with me.

I scored three touchdowns in the 1968 NFL championship game in Cleveland, and had a great Super Bowl against the Jets. It was the best game I ever played; 116 yards rushing, 30 receiving. But we made stupid mistakes in that game that we should never make. I had a 58-yard run, but then we threw an interception. In the second half, I broke one for 15 yards, and they stripped the ball away from me. Then the flea-flicker pass where Earl Morrall doesn't see Jimmy Orr standing open, waving his arms in the end zone. Why didn't Earl see him? Was the Colts band down there in their blue and white uniforms? Was the tuba waving too?

We were 17-point favorites, but I never figured anybody to be that much of a favorite. I don't think we were overconfident. To get to the Super Bowl you have to be a good football team. We had a great team, lost one game that year.

The Jets were a good sound defensive club, and they had Joe Namath at quarterback and some great receivers. Namath was sounding off about beating us, and Lou Michaels responded. Lou was a great competitor, and he would go off the deep end. You could pull his chain a little bit, and Namath did that. Lou didn't want to see some punk kid saying, "We're going to kick your ass." But I don't think any of us took them lightly.

People wondered what happened. Namath picked our defense apart pretty good. He had a quick release and knew how to read defenses. If we tried to blitz, he dumped it off to the backs. They just beat us that day.

Of all the things that have happened in my life, one of the all-time upsetting things to me was when Bubba Smith wrote in a book that we threw the game to the Jets. To this day, that upsets not just me but a lot of other guys.

Bubba was one of those guys you had to kick in the butt, and then he'd go for maybe two plays and rest anyway. He wrote something about if Shula had played him differently in that game, he could have done the job. Listen, he never touched the quarterback the whole game. Why didn't he do the job where he was supposed to, and maybe we would have gotten the ball. He did nothing all day.

And yet he has the audacity to say we threw the game. Why did he write that? I don't know. It's just outrageous.

I think the credit should go to the Jets' coach, Weeb Ewbank. He knew our team; he hadn't been gone from Baltimore that long. He knew what the players' weaknesses were.

And I think we made a mistake when Earl was not having a great day, and we had the greatest quarterback in the world sitting on the bench until late. I thought he should have started the second half.

That was the beginning of the demise of Don Shula here as far as Carroll Rosenbloom was concerned.

As slow as I was for a back, I was near the top of the league in total offense in 1968, and led in '69. Nobody remembers that about me.

All during my playing career, I suffered with stomach ulcers. I even played a game while they were bleeding. Outside of that, I'd only had one knee operation after the two I had back in the ninth grade.

The 1972 season was a crazy one. Unitas and I started off unbelievably. I was near the top in rushing and receiving. John was near the top in passing. But we lost four of our first five games. Then Bob Irsay and Joe Thomas fired Don McCafferty, and put John Sandusky in charge. I got so upset my ulcer started bleeding again. It never settled down until after that season, when I retired and went into the hospital and had my stomach cut out.

Irsay and Thomas said we had an old team and that's why we were losing. As well as John and I were playing, they said we were having a bad year and benched us. They put me on the injured reserve list for four weeks because of my ulcers, then extended it for another four weeks. So I said to them, "Why don't you just release me?" But they wouldn't. They suspected I had a deal to go to Minnesota.

When they reinstated me, they told Sandusky to put me on every special team—running kickoffs, punts—to embarrass me. I told John, "You make me the safety, because I'm going to be deeper than the deepest." It was ridiculous.

I never hated anybody as much as I hated Joe Thomas. I can remember, after a game in Miami, where Ted Hendricks picked Thomas up right off the ground and was ready to punch him out. I told Ted, "Don't. It's not worth it."

Thomas a great judge of talent? I think that's a myth. He destroyed the tradition of the Colts, where leadership was handed down. When Gino retired, Braase picked it up, Pellington picked it up, John Mackey and Bobby Boyd. The coaches didn't have to be disciplinarians—the team did its own. If you got out of line, the older guys jumped in your face.

All Thomas wanted was turmoil. He wanted to develop his own image, his own team, and gave away the franchise in trades. Irsay didn't know what was happening at the time; it was all Thomas.

At the end of the season they traded me and Unitas to San Diego. After putting in twelve hard years working our buns off for the Baltimore Colts, the way we found out we were traded was on the radio. They didn't even have the balls to call us and tell us we'd been traded. They had no class in the organization.

San Diego wanted us both to be sort of player-coaches. They offered me $125,000; the highest I ever made in Baltimore was $85,000. But I needed the ulcer operation. I went into the hospital weighing 236; twenty-eight days later I came out weighing 187. I didn't have the strength to lift a pencil, so I hung it up.

Later, when I was working Colts exhibition games on television, I learned about Irsay's tricks. He would come up to the booth and start telling me about all the trades they were working on, and the guys we were going to get, trying to get me to say something about it on the air. But I'd check with Ernie Accorsi or Dick Szymanski first, and they'd tell me, "Irsay been up there? Don't believe any of it." He was trying to embarrass me.

I don't blame Irsay for leaving Baltimore. It was just business. Indianapolis gave him an unbeatable offer. He went out there and has

Tom Matte.
Photograph by Vince Bagli

had the most profitable team in the NFL for ten years. Was that a wrong business decision?

We didn't act to keep him here. The problem with Baltimore and the state was that we always reacted instead of acted. But things are changing. I wanted an NFL team here, and we worked for it. We presented the best package of all for an expansion team. But the people of Baltimore have to wake up and realize that the NFL doesn't want this market in the league.

I'm involved with the CFL team here now. We lost money the first year; we needed help with the field and the stadium. The city realizes the economic impact of sports in this town. Now the state has got to understand that. They've got to recognize that we were a success the first year, and come and ask us what they can do to make us more successful, because it's going to bring nothing but money to the city.

Besides that, I had the greatest time of my life playing in this town, and I want to give some other kids the chance.

I also have a company called Tom Matte Sports Speakers. When corporations need speakers for sports banquets, I provide them. The kids today are making so much money, they don't want to go out and speak. And so many executives are about my age—fifty-five—they want the stars they remember, like Bart Starr, Roman Gabriel, Paul Hornung, Franco Harris, Steve Grogan, Chris Bahr. Rocky Bleier is in great demand—another garbage can back like I was, a Vietnam veteran, does a great job as a motivational speaker.

They can make $5,000 or more for one day or overnight. They're doing well, making some money, and I enjoy keeping in touch with the old ballplayers.

Let me tell you something about the Baltimore Colts. This team was a team that ate together, lived together; their families were friends. We were always concerned about each other, and about the people of Baltimore. And many of us stayed here and made our homes here.

DON SHULA

Born: 1-4-30
Painesville, Ohio
John Carroll
Defensive Back

6′ 0″, 190 lbs.
Drafted: #9, 1951
Cleveland
Colts: 1953–1956
Coach: 1963–1969

"You can't worry about friendship, or whether you're liked or disliked. You can be the most popular guy in the world and never win on Sunday."

I played at John Carroll, a small football program in Paul Brown's backyard in Ohio. One year we played Syracuse, and when the game was scheduled, the headline in the Syracuse paper read, "Syracuse Schedules John Carroll; Who is John Carroll?"

That became our coach's fight talk as we got ready to play the game. We were used to playing our games on a high school field, and 3,000 to 5,000 people was a big crowd for us. And here we were playing that strong team in Cleveland Municipal Stadium before maybe 20,000 people.

Paul Brown and his entire coaching staff were there, probably to scout Syracuse. And we beat them. I played both ways, and I think I had 125 yards rushing and played all over on defense. Carl Taseff also had a big day for us on offense. Because of that game, Cleveland drafted me number nine and Carl a little lower.

I was fortunate in having a good grade school coach, and Herb Eisely in high school. Our coaches went to all the Browns' clinics, and we put in the Browns' offensive and defensive terminology. So when I got to the Browns as a rookie, their system was not new to me.

That first year, 1951, I made the team and played in the championship game. Carl was on the taxi squad when the season started. Incidentally, that's where the taxi squad got its name. Art McBride, who owned the Cleveland team, owned a taxicab company.

During the year somebody got hurt and Carl was activated. Tommy James, the starting right corner, got hurt early in the season, and I played the rest of the year. James got healthy in time for the championship game, so I didn't start that one.

That's where I first met John Sandusky. Carl Taseff and I were together four years at John Carroll, got drafted together, got traded to Baltimore together, and went into the army together.

Paul Brown had the greatest influence on my coaching career. One of his assistants, Blanton Collier, was a teacher. He was the first to write

Sideline intensity with Don Shula and Lenny Moore.
Photograph © 1995 TADDER/Baltimore

things down in a notebook. With him, it was more of a teacher-pupil relationship than coach-player. I always said Paul Brown brought the classroom into pro football. The Chicago Bears were going around with a rough-and-tough image; the Browns' image was the classroom. I learned more from them than from anybody else—Paul from an organizational standpoint, and Blanton from the technical. Later I coached one year under Collier at Kentucky.

In Baltimore, Weeb Ewbank was like an extension of Paul Brown, using Brown's play book.

I played one year with the Redskins after I left Baltimore, then went into coaching. I spent three years with George Wilson at Detroit, and later replaced him with the Dolphins. George was a product of the Bears' hard-nosed, tough system, but he had a tremendous relationship with his players. He really knew how to get along with people; you couldn't help but love him.

Coming into Baltimore as the head coach in 1963 was tough, because I had been an average player here, and now all of a sudden I'm back, coaching guys who were great players, like Unitas and Moore and Parker and Berry—people who had won the championship for Weeb. They knew me as a defensive back who had ended up with the Redskins and coached three years at Detroit.

I knew I had the proving to do all over again. It was just a question of them realizing that I knew what I wanted to do, and I was dedicated. Then they joined in and helped me. The guys who helped the most were Gino and Pellington. They were player-coaches for me that first year. Gino was the team captain, and everybody looked up to him.

We started out that year 3 and 5, and then we turned it around. The next year was a great year, although we lost the championship game in Cleveland. But 1965 had to be the most exciting. At the time, with Unitas being hurt, then his backup, Gary Cuozzo, going down, you wondered what else can happen. That's when I called Woody Hayes at Ohio State and asked him if he thought Tom Matte could do the job. He assured me that Tom could, then said, "He only had one problem when he played for me."

"What was that, Woody?"

"Taking the snap from center."

I said, "Well, I guess we got to start with that. He's going to be my replacement quarterback."

And what a great job Matte did.

John Unitas was a guy who stood in there and waited and waited, trying to give the receivers a chance to take that last extra step to get open, and then he would put it in there and take the punishment. I remember John coming off the field bloody and battered, then go out and do the same on the next play.

You don't have to worry about whether a quarterback likes you or not. You hope you have mutual respect. With a John Unitas, you think:

"I've got a job to do; I'm asking him to do it," and you try to give him all the tools to do the job to the best of his ability.

I try to have mutual respect with all my players. You can't worry about friendship, or whether you're liked or disliked. You can be the most popular guy in the world and never win on Sunday, and you don't last long in the coaching profession. You don't really socialize with the players while they are playing. You get to know them better after they retire.

The loss to the Jets in the Super Bowl was the most devastating loss of my coaching career, because it made a good relationship come apart. That was really what came between Carroll Rosenbloom and me. After we beat Cleveland, 34–0, in the NFL championship game, he put his arm around me and said, "This is the last guy I'm ever going to hire as a head coach." After the Jets beat us, he was never the same. That next year you could just feel it coming apart. It was very unpleasant for a long time, although we did end up speaking to each other.

That's why, when Miami showed interest in me, I made the decision to follow up on it. I was fortunate to spend eleven years of my early adult life in Baltimore, four as a player, and seven as a head coach. I remember we had fifty-six consecutive sellouts. Those fans worked hard all week long for their entertainment dollar, and they spent it on watching the Colts. That was their entertainment. You felt that loyalty and sincerity and friendship. I don't think there's ever been a place like it.

I was forty when I went to Miami. I'm sure there was talk about my age to begin with, but after the first few weeks they didn't ask me how old I was. They were waiting to see how I taught and handled myself on the field. Once you establish yourself as their coach, then it becomes a question of: Can this guy teach me anything?

My second year in Miami, Dallas really dominated us in the Super Bowl, 24–3, and that really set us up for the next two years. We realized that it's not worth anything to be there unless you walk away the winner. And we did win the next two Super Bowls.

Going 17-0 in 1972 was the biggest accomplishment of my life. That Miami team never really got the credit they deserved. It wasn't a very glamorous team. We played great defense and held onto the ball on offense, and we didn't make mistakes. We just ground it out very efficiently.

Bob Griese was the thinking man's quarterback. Everything had to be in place and orderly. He didn't care if he threw the ball or not. He would just as soon hand it off to Larry Csonka.

Earl Morrall was a very unselfish guy. Watching him in practice, you'd never think he would be the guy he turned out to be on Sunday. He would win for you.

Paul Warfield was graceful and artistic, a very intelligent football player.

Larry Csonka's toughness gave us the identity that led to those two Super Bowls. Everybody relied on him to get that short yardage when we needed it.

Jim Kiick and Mercury Morris alternated as the first of the special situation guys. Whichever one didn't play was always in my office Monday morning complaining, "I want to play more." I told them to look at the score; we must be doing something right. But it was very competitive between those two guys.

Bob Matheson could rush or drop back into coverage, a great athlete. He was the first of the "53 defense" linebackers; we called it that because he wore the number 53.

Nick Buonoconti was bright, very competitive, probably weighed 215 and never lifted a weight in his life.

Garo Yepremian was a great kicker. Thank God he didn't cost us the game that time when he tried to pass.

I've had a lot of quarterbacks of not only different personalities, but different styles. And my backup quarterbacks have always come through for me when the number one has gone down: Morrall and Don Strock and Gary Cuozzo, and two years ago Scott Mitchell when Dan Marino went down. Then he got hurt and we picked up Steve DeBerg.

Of all of them, nobody's every thrown the ball like Dan Marino—quick decisions, quick release. It's an explosion. Everything happens and the ball goes out.

I've only been with two organizations, and in both cases, I always had control and made all the football decisions. Nobody ever told me who to draft and who not to draft, who to trade or not to trade. I've been very fortunate; a lot of coaches never have that. And I try to surround myself with good people.

I've enjoyed competing against so many great coaches, who were smart enough to chart themselves to make sure you couldn't get patterns on them. They had their own styles, but within that style they did things to keep you honest. I competed against George Halas, and it meant a lot to me to break his record for wins, a record that nobody thought would ever be broken.

One thing I've tried to do is not to get consumed by anything negative. I'm not an emotional extremist. I take losing probably as tough as anybody, but I know I can't change the score. So I try to learn something from it to use the next time. And if I'm successful, I don't get overwhelmed with success and stop learning. As for tension—I let it go. I'm not a guy who gets ulcers; I give them.

My son, David, started out to go to law school at the University of Baltimore. One year I lost an assistant coach and I called David to join me. We went to the Super Bowl that year. When I offered him a full-time job, he decided to go into coaching instead of continuing law school. Now, coaching against him, I have a sense of pride knowing that's my son on the other side. But once the game starts, you want to win.

Players have changed over the years. But I helped raise five kids, and at one time we had five teenagers in the family. That helped me understand young players better, because my kids were sometimes confronted with the same kind of problems. What's happened in football is the agents have gotten between the players and coaches, and between the players and ownership, and it becomes nothing but a business deal. If a young kid gets good representation, it can help him. But if he gets bad representation, it can work the other way.

The rule changes we're looking into include standardizing the face masks, and protecting the quarterbacks better from hits with the helmet. We're trying to make it as safe as we can without drastically changing the nature of the game. We don't want guys getting knocked out of their careers.

Prayer has been very important to me, and the belief in a Supreme Being. I feel that I have been very fortunate in my career, and I try to give something back.

Winners of eleven in a row, but no title in 1964.
Photograph © 1995 TADDER/Baltimore

JIMMY ORR

Born: 10-4-35
Seneca, South Carolina
Georgia
End

5′ 11″, 185 lbs.
Drafted: #22, 1958
L.A. Rams
Colts: 1961–1970

"I got a few cinders in my elbows down in that corner of Memorial Stadium near the dugout that they called Orrsville."

When I was young I always liked to catch things like footballs and baseballs. I was a walk-on halfback at Georgia. There was no such thing as wide receivers in college. The pros brought that in.

My time in Georgia was probably the worst three years in their history. We won ten games altogether. I led the SEC twice in receptions; never dropped a pass. Each year we had a different quarterback. We played both ways in those days.

Wally Butts was the coach, but the backfield coach, Sterling Dupree, was like a father to me there. He was a scout for the Rams, the first team to employ scouts. They paid him $500 for his opinion of the best players in the SEC. Because of him, the Rams took me in the 22nd round as a defensive back. But I never played for them. They traded me to Pittsburgh.

I played three years for the Steelers, 1958–1960. Bobby Layne was the quarterback. Bobby was a brilliant guy, more of a leader and play caller than a passer. The coach, Buddy Parker, could give Layne the game plan and he would remember it and call the whole game just like Parker wanted it. Parker had some brilliant game plans. He would study the films and cut out certain plays because of what he saw. For example, Andy Robustelli of the Giants took an outside release upfield, so Parker wouldn't include any play to go outside him.

As a passer, Layne was easy to catch, but he didn't throw that tight spiral that makes it easy to catch the ball and keep going. He threw a lot of ducks, but he got it there and his timing was good. He couldn't throw the quick out that Unitas threw so well, couldn't get it out there quick enough.

After 1960, there were some problems in Pittsburgh, and I decided I wasn't going back there. I tried to get them to trade me, but they wouldn't, so I was going to quit. Then, when I didn't show up for practice in July, they traded me to Baltimore.

Jimmy Orr. Photograph © 1995 TADDER/Baltimore

Lamar McHan was the backup quarterback to Unitas. He threw a heavy ball that felt like a 5-pound sack of sugar. You had to brace yourself to catch it. John threw a quick, soft pass that didn't break your stride when you caught it. You could just reach up there and pluck it without slowing down.

If we had had the bump and run rules then that they have now, it would have been a whole lot easier to catch more passes. But the reason I didn't catch more balls with the Colts was Raymond Berry. He caught the short ones and I had to clear out and go deep. By the time I'd get back to the huddle, he'd already have another play called for himself. I couldn't get back in time to get me one.

In that Super Bowl III against the Jets where I was wide open and Earl Morrall couldn't find me, it was the same play we had used to beat Atlanta in the second week of the season. It was a flea-flicker, and I was 20 yards out in the clear on that one.

In the Jets game, the defense was supposed to be rotating my way; that's the reason I was so wide open. The cornerback came up and the safety was supposed to have the deep outside. But the safety went with the run and the cornerback came up, so I went down the sideline. I was waving my arms in the end zone, 37 yards away from the closest guy. Whether the pass back to Earl was low and he didn't feel like he had time—I don't know. I never pressed the point, because I don't think he can give you a good answer. We never talked about that play after the game; in fact, we never mentioned it until we got together twenty-five years later.

I got a few cinders in my elbows down in that corner of Memorial Stadium near the third base dugout that they called Orrsville. One of the reasons that corner seemed to be the place I caught most of my touchdown passes was that every Thursday we'd go down there and work with Unitas on timing patterns without the defense. He'd stand at the 40 or 50 yard line and I'd go into that corner of the end zone, which sloped down and was 3 or 4 feet lower than midfield. I think it helped for me to know the terrain, because you were crowded into that corner and I was comfortable there, whereas the guy on the road playing there maybe once a year was not.

Wrigley Field had its peculiarities, too. Once I was going for a long pass and J.C. Caroline was covering me. As we got closer to that brick wall in left field, I'm trying to gear down a little bit and he runs into me and trips me, and the back of my head hit the bricks. I didn't remember much after that. My eyes were out of focus for a while, but it wasn't anything more than a slight concussion.

The other end of that field was Raymond's corner. You didn't have a full end zone; it was only 8½ yards. If you went down in the dugout and looked at the chalk line, you'd see it had a zigzag in it at the corner of the dugout.

Winning Super Bowl V over Dallas in the last game of my career has to be the highlight even though I didn't play. My legs were basically gone, and I was a backup that year. Gino didn't play that day either; he was in street clothes. It was a lousy football game—eight turnovers. But we won, 16–13.

Night Train Lane was the toughest I ever played against. He was bigger, faster, stronger, and tougher than I was. Herb Adderley and Jimmy Johnson, too. In one stretch of six games, I had to play against those three guys. I did better against Johnson, although I had some good games against Lane.

I coached receivers for three years for Atlanta. We didn't do a very good job; got beat, then got fired, then got in my car and drove out to Las Vegas and made my career change.

Colts buttons 1950s to 1970s. Photograph by Bob Miller

FRED MILLER

Born: 8-8-40
Homer, Louisiana
LSU
Defensive Tackle

6′ 3″, 250 lbs.
Drafted: #7, 1962
Colts: 1963–1972

"When I was growing up, I had two idols—Gino Marchetti and John Unitas. Then to get to play with them was almost unbelievable."

I grew up in Homer, Louisiana. We had such a small high school, we only had enough football players to field a team with maybe six or seven replacements, so we played the whole game. In practice, we had to run half the line against the other half, just to be able to practice running plays. Still, we went to the state playoffs, but we lost.

I signed up to go to Tulane and play for Andy Pilney, the old Notre Dame star. But that summer they discovered that I lacked one English credit, even though I had graduated from high school. They called me and said they could not admit me. My friend, Roy Wilkins, had signed to go out west to play for Texas A & M. So I decided I would go out there with him. But my mother said, "You're not going to do any such thing. It's too far from home."

When I went down to New Orleans to play in a high school All-Star game, LSU coach Paul Dietzel brought my whole family and my girlfriend down to the game, and by the time the week was up, my mother was sold that Dietzel was the greatest guy in the world. So I went to LSU. My friend left A & M and joined me there in our sophomore year.

That was 1958; freshmen didn't play varsity ball in those days. LSU had a national championship team that year, and the next year they lost only three guys out of thirty-three. One of the freshmen who moved up was Wendell Harris, who played in Baltimore. Another was Woody Winston, who played thirteen years for the Packers. I was redshirted, and played in 1960, 1961, and 1962 on Dietzel's Chinese Bandits.

Dietzel got the idea for the Chinese Bandits out of a storybook. They were the meanest, nastiest people in the story, and he instilled that attitude in his players. Everybody got to play. He had what he called the White team: they played both ways. The Gold team was a special offensive team. The Chinese Bandits were the defensive team. They would go in for three plays and stop the other team, and the Gold team

Fred Miller (76) sees the trap, eyes the quarterback.
Photograph © 1995 TADDER/Baltimore

would come in and return the punt and go on the offense. Then the White team would come in. Every time a guy looked up, there was a new face coming at him, pawing the ground to get at him. We played in 90-degree heat and high humidity down there, and went like crazy, sending in fresh players all the time to wear down the other guys.

I was drafted by Weeb Ewbank for the Colts, although I never got to play for him. I was drafted as a future in 1962; I was just a junior, so I had one more year to play and they had to wait until I graduated to sign me. I weighed about 230 then. I gained a little later on.

It wasn't easy to follow the NFL when I was young. We didn't have any television, and I didn't know who all was in the league or even who the teams were. But I had these two idols—Gino Marchetti and John Unitas. Then to get to play with them was almost unbelievable.

I arrived in 1963, Don Shula's first year as the Colts' coach. Shula had the toughest job in the NFL. He came behind a real successful coach who had had a couple lean years. You had on the squad four certain future Hall of Famers; you knew Gino, Jim Parker, Lenny Moore, and John Unitas were going. That was a given. You had John Mackey, who was also a rookie that year. You had Raymond Berry, who was set in his ways and wasn't going to change. You had Unitas, who was not going to learn a new system. You had Lenny Moore, who you were going to have to coax into working for you. You had a fairly old defense you were going to have to rebuild, with Gino and Bill Pellington at the heart of it.

So Shula came into all that, and he couldn't change anything. He took on the same game plan, the same system, and made the best of it.

It was easy for me. The play-numbering system was the same one I grew up with, through high school and college. Even was always to the right and odd was always to the left. With a lot of guys, every time they went to a new system, it was all different.

I learned more from Gino than anybody. He was a player-coach my first two years with the Colts. We lined up like ducks behind him; whatever he did, the rest of us did. I wasn't big enough, and I had to learn a lot just to make the team. I had to come up with some way to get around those 260-pound guys or take them out.

I tried to emulate Gino, do some of the things he would do. But he was so quick off the ball, he would be almost across the line before my hands started coming up. And that was my quickest move. I've seen him get behind offensive tackles before they could get up. That's why you wanted him on the outside of the line, not having to step over people. I was better in the middle of the line, stepping over feet and bodies.

We played team defense in Baltimore, not a lot of big stars. We used some defensive stunts, maybe in a pass situation, or where a team favored a particular type of play. But not the way they use them today.

After Gino left, Bubba Smith was the biggest star on the line. If Bubba had come along now, having grown up and matured, he'd rank just behind Gino. But at that time he hadn't fully left his college days behind him. He was still hearing, "Kill, Bubba, kill!" from the Michigan State crowd.

We had to pump him up to get him ready to play. When Bubba was coming at them, there were few players who could handle him. Rocky Freitas from Detroit was one of the better tackles, and he had his hands full with Bubba. Bubba would have his best days against the best opponents. But we would have to pump him up all week long.

I ran against one of the toughest blockers I ever saw in the very first game I started as a rookie. It was the second game of the year, in San Francisco. I'll never forget that game as long as I live. I started against John Thomas. San Francisco always had big linemen, and he was one of their best. All day long I didn't do anything that John Thomas didn't want me to do.

I can remember being so down and dejected on that plane coming home, I just knew no way was Shula going to let me play defensive tackle after seeing the game films. I was sitting next to Butch Wilson. I said to him, "If Shula doesn't send me home, no way is he going to start me next week after the game I played." But the next week, I was back in there and I had a little better game.

In 1963 we were 8 and 6, and we built from there. We had some winning teams and went to two Super Bowls and won one, but the only one you ever hear about is the one we lost to the Jets. Of course, the only football game ever played as far as Baltimore fans were concerned was the '58 championship game against the Giants. Even the championship game of '59 never gets mentioned. But I understand that. The 1958 title was the first one, and that makes a difference.

When we lost to the Jets in Super Bowl III, we just weren't ready. That year I learned something, and I think Don Shula did, too. We had a super team; the one game we lost, we didn't even look at the game film afterwards. We just said, "Let's go out on the field and work out." But after every game we won that year, Shula would beat us to death pointing out all our mistakes: "You should have taken a step here. . . you made the play, but you didn't do it quite the way you should have. . . ." Stuff like that.

When we got down to Miami, we all just got awed by the situation and we didn't get ourselves prepared. Shula tried to take the pressure off. He just said, "Let's work out, go through the formalities, and go out and play Sunday." That's all he said, instead of keeping us and driving us.

Mentally, we just did not put it all together to go out there knowing we had to play one of our best games of the year. We believed our press clippings and went out thinking we'd spend sixty minutes on the field and walk off as the champions.

The Jets were noted for trying to hold people, and they got by with it a lot. But they were only doing what Dan Sullivan used to tell us: "If a guy beats you, don't let him kill your quarterback. Tackle him or hold him or something. The least you can do is holler, 'Look out,' to Unitas, and give the guy a 'look-out' block." The Jets were probably doing that to protect Joe Namath, who was the savior of the whole group.

On the line, I remember Johnny Sample doing a lot of jawing for the Jets, but I don't remember Namath saying anything during the game.

Along about the beginning of the fourth quarter of that game, a feeling of frustration began to come on us. We knew we had to get this thing turned around. But we didn't do it.

I think we all learned a tremendous lesson.

The only black and blue spot I ever had on me after a game came that day. On one play, Ordell Braase threw their tackle, Winston Hill, inside when I was pushing off my right foot, and Hill fell right on my ankle. It swelled up and my whole foot turned black. After the game, I went to Jackson Memorial Hospital to have it x-rayed, but there wasn't anything broken. Then I had to leave at five the next morning to go to the Pro Bowl. I kept the foot in a whirlpool for a few days and played.

We fought hard to beat Dallas in Super Bowl V, 16–13, in Miami. A defensive tackle has to battle the center and the guard. Prior to 1971, Dallas used a lot of technique blocking, and you had to prepare differently for them. We didn't use all those techniques and stuff. Our approach was just to go in there and deliver a shot and get it over with, and it worked for us. About the time of that Super Bowl, Dallas had gone back to playing good old hard-nosed football. Craig Morton was their quarterback, and I believe if they had brought Roger Staubach in, they would have won it. It was hot down there, and we had given it everything we had. If we had had to chase Staubach around in those last seven or eight minutes, he'd have killed us.

Duane Thomas's fumble on the goal line in the third quarter also saved us. That's still a controversial play. Billy Ray Smith came up with the ball out of the pileup, and he never would talk about it much—whether it was an actual fumble or he took the ball away from Thomas in the pile. However he did it, it certainly made a difference in that game.

Despite my experience on the LSU Chinese Bandits, I was not one of the nasties on the line. Only once did I ever get worked up. Chicago had a big offensive guard, George Seals. We were playing the Bears in an exhibition game in Birmingham, Alabama, and he hit me in the head with a forearm and knocked me goofy for about half the game. Seals was good enough at throwing it so the official didn't call it, but he was doing it all through the game.

The next time we met, I got smarter and managed to dodge that forearm pretty good. About the fourth quarter they ran a rollout where the quarterback comes out backwards and the offensive guard comes out backwards and they set up, and if you don't see him he'll kill you. I'm in a chase pattern, and I just barely catch a glimpse of Seals out of one eye and I see him crouched, ready to tear me in half. I came from as far back as I could get and hit him in the head. He just crumpled and sat there.

An official came over and said, "All right, you two are even now."

Ordell Braase was asking me, "What's he talking about? What's going on here?" But as far as I was concerned, it was settled. I said, "It's okay, Braase." By that time my hand had started hurting. For the next three days I had to carry it high up to keep it from hurting so much.

The next year I'm playing opposite Seals again, and he's still throwing that forearm and I'm ducking. He's trying to clamp me and he got called for holding three plays in a row. After that the Bears took him off offense and put him on defense.

My best games were against the better players. Mentally, you know you're going to get your butt kicked if you're not ready. When New Orleans first came into the league and we didn't take them seriously, the first few times we played them, we weren't up enough and just squeaked by.

If you didn't do well against a guy the last time you played against him, you'd sit and watch the game films and try to pick up something from those three or four players on the line, or maybe from somebody in the backfield, trying to pick up some tips on what might happen. Then it was a matter of getting out there and working hard.

Offensive linemen I had a lot of respect for included Howard Mudd of the Bears and 49ers, Tom Mack of the Rams, John Gordy from Detroit, and Fuzzy Thurston of the Packers. Thurston would try anything to keep you out of there. If he lost you one way, he'd try another way.

The ball carrier who gave me the hardest blow in tackling him—and I still remember it vividly—was Jim Brown in the 1964 championship game in Cleveland that we lost, 27–0. They ran a sweep around to their right side, and I'm playing right tackle, so I'm coming across in pursuit. Brown ran over Jerry Logan or got by him somehow, then got by the linebacker, and it was just him and me.

I had a perfect angle on him near the sideline, and I'm coming full tilt and I'm thinking, "I'm going to kill you. . . I'm going to hit you so hard you're not going to get up." Coming with a full head of steam, I hit him with my best lick and knocked him out of bounds. I'm sitting there, and my bell's rung. I could hardly sit up, much less stand up. And Brown gets off the ground in his usual slow way and ambles back to the huddle like I haven't even touched him. I'm still sitting on the ground, trying to gather up enough strength so that when I do manage to get up, I won't start stumbling and staggering and fall back down. Brown was 4 or 5 yards away before I could get my resources together and stand up. I said to myself, "That is one hell of a man. I gave him my best shot and it didn't appear to affect him in the least."

I guess the other toughest guy I ever hit would be Larry Csonka of the Dolphins.

Some defensive linemen had a tough time stopping Jim Taylor, but I never had any problem with him. Taylor had been an All-American running back at LSU just before I got there. We were playing at Green

Bay in my rookie year and we got into a pileup, and Taylor was mumbling and groaning and kicking and squirming in the pile. I cursed at him and said, "Taylor, be still. Be quiet."

He looked at me, and when he saw who it was talking to him that way, he just got quiet and got up. We were longtime friends. He was a tough-looking guy, and still is. Still in super shape, too.

I played in three Pro Bowls. The first time Merlin Olsen, Roger Brown, and I were the three tackles. The second year it was Olsen and me, and Alan Page from Minnesota was the backup. The third time Olsen and Carl Eller were there, and I was the backup. That was fun. You get a lot of respect for the guys you play against all year, and when you get to know them, you kind of hold them in awe. Merlin Olsen is a gem of a guy; he could politic all day long and not make anybody mad. And he was a super smart football player.

I'm proud of all my years in Baltimore except the last one. By 1972 a lot of us were winding down, getting old. I had some knee injuries and could run a 100-yard dash in maybe a week. When Bob Irsay and Joe Thomas came along, it was evident that they were going to make a lot of changes.

I went in to talk to Thomas. "I've learned a lot over the years," I told him. "I think I can help the younger players. I would be perfectly happy to play a backup role for one more year, and I can contribute."

We had Billy Newsome and Jim Bailey coming in at tackle, and they were just out there running around and hitting on people. They hadn't paid much attention to learning good football and how to use their abilities. Joe Ehrmann and Mike Barnes were coming along, and I wanted to work with them for a year. Barnes had the talent. I think I could have made him an all-pro the first year. Ehrmann was a dependable, hard-nosed football player. Put those two guys together, turn Barnes loose and let Joe mind the gate, and I think it would have been phenomenal.

Joe Ehrmann is such a fine individual and a great ball player. He has all the respect and support that I can give him now as a minister. He's one of my favorite people. I just wish I had the courage to do some of the things he's done. A gutsy guy.

So that's what I proposed to Joe Thomas, but he turned me down. Then I said, "Well, if you're going to get something for me, send me to Washington or Philadelphia. I'm not going anywhere else."

He traded me to Washington, where George Allen was the coach. I have never in my life seen anything like that George Allen training camp, or anybody like Allen.

Allen would call Baltimore coach Bobby Boyd at three, four o'clock in the morning and ask him something about the nickel defense or whatever, and when Bobby mumbled or grumbled, George would say, "You mean you guys are not working? I'm working." But he had set his clock to wake him up so he could make calls like that.

George's wife used to come out to the camp after practice a couple times a week and they would go out to dinner, and all the other coaches had to stick around and wait until George got back to have a meeting that night.

I still have a little book I kept of all Allen's audible calls that pertained to the defensive line that I needed to know. I translated them into what we called them in Baltimore. He had fifty-three different audibles just for the defensive tackle and end. Then they had another thirty-five or forty for the linebackers. The linebackers had to know all of our calls plus their own plus the safety's. It was unbelievable.

In a meeting before an exhibition game, he'd tell Ted Marchibroda, one of his assistant coaches, "Don't let your offense get my defense in trouble." That was his philosophy. He'd say, "You remember those audibles we used to call just before the ball's snapped? We did that a couple times two years ago and got them to jump offside." He'd look at the quarterback. "You remember that?"

The quarterback would say, "Yeah, George, I remember." He no more remembered than I did. It was not even the same quarterback, not the same coach, not the same opponent, but George was still on that same crap about what they had done two years ago.

Or he'd say, "You remember that tackle used to twitch his little finger?"

I'm making light of it, but that's the kind of stuff George would go over. He'd go over the signal count and the cadence; didn't make any difference if it was another quarterback. It was whatever he had done a year or two before. That was George.

They had Manny Sistrunk at tackle, been there a few years. Sistrunk concentrated on beating the guard, slamming him, and letting the ball carrier run outside. He was never going to change. But Allen kept playing him in exhibition games. Finally I said to George, "There's no use me hanging around if you're not going to play me."

Allen said, "I know what you can do, playing against you all these years. Don't worry about it."

"But if I don't get into some exhibition games, and get some playing time, I'm not going to be worth a damn."

I got in a little action after that, but one day in camp I hit the blocking stand and pulled something in my back. It didn't respond to treatment, and I told him, "This thing isn't coming around. There's no use my being here. I'm going to call it quits and go home."

He told me to go home, but stay in shape and see what happens. I spent two months around the house, the most miserable time of my life. I had just moved out to the old farm and there were all kinds of things I wanted to do, but I couldn't do anything. If I drove somewhere, I couldn't get out of the car after sitting a while.

I never played again.

After talking about George Allen, I want to say something about Don Shula. When he went to Miami, he had figured out his own system and how he wanted to coach. I admire him for this: he took the players that he had and built the system around the players. He had a 3 and 10 season, and went out and got one guy, Paul Warfield, and they turned it around with a 10 and 3 season.

Shula took a look at what he had: a big old bruising back with decent speed in Larry Csonka. Shula said, "To give him one step to get up some speed, let's get the defensive line to take one step the wrong way."

Fred Miller.
Photograph by Vince Bagli

He had Jim Kiick, who could run a little, throw the ball, block a little, do a little of everything. He said, "Let's make these two guys complement each other."

He didn't have much of an offensive line, so he set up the influence stuff—influence the defensive line just enough to get them going the wrong way, then take them that way.

The difference between two great coaches is a guy like Tom Landry, who had a system and went out and got people to fit his system, and Shula, who takes the players he has, looks them over, and figures out how best to use them.

We had a lot of fun playing in Baltimore. I wonder if the guys today have as much fun. We did a lot of things as a team. Guys cared about each other. You had a lot of friends on the team, and did a lot of things together.

When I went to the Pro Bowl and over to the Redskins, other players would say to me, "What have you guys in Baltimore got?" I didn't know what they meant. I thought all teams worked together like we did and had as good times as we did. I didn't understand how much difference there was until the year I went over to Washington, and I saw all these little groups. They acted like they were a team because that's the way George Allen wanted them to be, but as soon as they could, they would split in all different directions in groups of two or three. They didn't think anything of cutting another guy's throat. I don't think Allen was aware of it, he was so busy trying to carry a pretense of his own, or he overlooked it. He had one guy on the roster who was under orders to make noise during practice, yelling and clapping and all that stuff, to give the appearance of team spirit. Had it in his contract that he had to do that.

I have a video of highlight films put together, and every once in a while I show it to my kids, or to visitors, and I'll say things like, "You see Lenny Moore making a 40-yard run into the end zone and pitching the ball to the official and jogging right on over to the sideline to get him a little air to get ready to go back in? . . . Do you see Jerry Hill scoring? . . . Did you see Raymond Berry catching that pass, and flipping the ball to the official and going over to the sideline?"

What I'm pointing out to them is that there was no showboating. I don't appreciate what they do today. Don't like it at all. It aggravates me that coaches allow it, and the media seems to want more of it. If a guy's putting on a show out there, they are on him with the cameras. I don't think it's very professional. If they want to be in a dance team, go join the Rockettes or a dance team in Las Vegas.

While I was playing, I had operations on both knees, the right elbow, and the right eye for a detached retina. Since I finished playing, I've had two discs removed from my back, and a spinal fusion. I've had a rotator cuff pinned in my left shoulder. I finally told the doctor, "This is it. Keep your knives in your pocket. I'm not coming back. If something else happens, I'm going to find a way to live with it."

I started drawing a pension when I turned 55 in August 1995. I have eleven years' credit, so I'll draw about $1,100 a month. Our pension is the worst in all professional sports. But I hope to get back into manufacturing management.

I still fish and hunt, but my injuries have slowed me down. As a result of my back problems, my right foot is numb and the calf of my right leg has atrophied quite a bit. I don't have much control of the right foot. If I sit it up there and tell my toes to do something, they sit there and say, "What do you want me to do, turkey? You don't have control anymore."

In the last few years, there are a lot of things that I have had to adjust to. It was frustrating at first, because I always wanted to do things the same way—fast and furious. I've come to the point that I'm not going to quit doing anything I enjoy or want to do. I'm just going to do a little less of it, and not quite at the same pace I used to go at. But I'm still going to hunt, fish, cut wood, until they roll me over and put a little dirt on top of me.

Willie Richardson

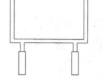

Born: 11-17-39
Clarksdale, Mississippi
Jackson State
Wide Receiver

6′ 2″, 198 lbs.
Drafted: #7, 1963
Colts: 1963–1969, 1971

"Don Shula had that burning desire to win more than anybody I've ever been around."

Growing up in Mississippi, the only team we saw on television was the Baltimore Colts. I went to Jackson State, and played right cornerback and wide receiver on the right side. The biggest thrill I ever had was just being drafted by the Colts in 1963, and having a chance to be on the same team with all those great players I had watched on TV.

Weeb Ewbank was still the coach when the draft took place; he drafted me to be the right cornerback. Then Weeb was let go and Don Shula took over. When I got to training camp, he tried me both ways and decided I couldn't play defensive back, so I went to wide receiver.

I had two advantages: we had used a pro set in college, and I had played wide receiver there, so the only changes for me were in the terminology and the routes you had to run.

I was lucky to play on a real good club. I felt like it was family. The only problem I had when I arrived was the presence of Raymond Berry and Jimmy Orr. But Jimmy got hurt early in the season, and I got to start four games and caught 17 passes.

The next two years I didn't play much; caught only one pass in 1965, but it was a 14-yard touchdown pass. I practiced a lot, and although I wasn't playing much, I felt that I was going to be a part of the team, and that made a difference. I didn't worry too much about the new players coming in, or about being traded. Over the years, the good teams didn't move guys around a lot. They kept the teams together.

Then Jimmy Orr got hurt in the first game of the 1967 season against Atlanta. I finished that game, then we went to Philadelphia, where I caught 11 balls and scored 2 touchdowns. I was ready. I went on to have a real outstanding year. [Richardson led the team with 63 receptions and 8 touchdowns.] I made the Pro Bowl.

One of my football thrills was the catch I made against the Packers at home that year to beat them, when we hadn't beaten them since 1964.

Willie Richardson. Photograph © 1995 TADDER/Baltimore

Willie Richardson.
Photograph © 1995 TADDER/Baltimore

More than anybody I've ever been around, Don Shula had that burning desire to win. His first year was my first year, and I think there was some pressure on him from the start. He was uptight. He worked hard to prepare us, and didn't like mistakes or dropped passes, even in practice. He'd get on you for little things. But that made the difference. The way we had to be so rigid in practice, catching everything and running the correct routes, paid off. It all carried over into the game. The games were really a lot easier than the practices.

In the Super Bowl against the Jets, the preparation wasn't there during the week before the game. We watched the films and commented that the Jets didn't look like a professional team. A real case of over-confidence. And we were a little off that day. Tom Mitchell had a pass knock off his shoulder for an interception. Once I was open in the end zone and Earl Morrall threw behind me for an interception. And the time Jimmy Orr was open. You're looking at three scores.

I played the tight end on the stronger side of the field, opposite the left cornerback, who is supposed to be your best. The toughest I ran into was Night Train Lane. Jimmy Johnson was outstanding. So were Herb Adderley, Ken Reeves, Abe Woodson.

Today I'm one of the five members of the appeals board of the Mississippi Department of Transportation. We hear appeals for truck violations. I also play a lot of golf, average in the 69–72 range. I've been trying to get on the professional athletes' tour that's really getting popular.

John Mackey. Photograph © 1995 TADDER/Baltimore

JOHN MACKEY

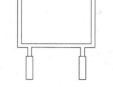

Born: 9-24-41
Queens, New York
Syracuse
Tight End

6′ 2″, 225 lbs.
Drafted: #2, 1963
Colts: 1963–1971
Hall of Fame: 1992

"[Freddie Schubach] said to me, 'Welcome to the world champion Baltimore Colts. I shine your shoes every day. I polish and clean your helmet every day. I press your practice uniform. And I demand that you play the way I make you look.' "

I was a tight end in high school, but when I went to Syracuse, they wanted to make me a running back. The coach, Ben Schwartzwalder, said to me, "John, I will give you number 44 when Ernie Davis graduates."

Number 44 was an honor at Syracuse; Jim Brown had worn it, then Ernie. Later Floyd Little had it. But Ernie, who was my roommate, was only one year ahead of me. So I said, "That means I'm going to have to sit on the bench."

After my first year, I told the coach I didn't want to play running back because I didn't want to sit on the bench while Ernie played.

He said, "Then you're going to have to be a tight end."

I said, "Will you give me number 88?"

And that's how I got number 88. Every day we'd go back to the room and I'd say to Ernie, "You know why they gave me number 88? I'm twice as good as 44."

When I was a senior, Floyd Little and Larry Csonka were frosh, and Jim Nance was a sophomore. Can you believe that? That's why I knew how to block. Everybody talks about my running, but I was a total blocker.

In 1963 I was drafted by the New York Titans in the American Football League, and the Colts. I never heard from the Titans. But Buddy Young came to see me, and the Colts general manager, Don Kellett, invited me to come down and see a game. Carroll Rosenbloom sent his private plane for me. The Syracuse team flew all the time, but that was the first time I had ever been in a private plane, and it's the only time I can honestly say I was afraid. I took my agent and his wife, and Sylvia, my girlfriend at the time who became my wife, and we flew in this little plane, and all I could think about was, "I know they always say if it's your time to go, you'll go, but I don't want to go just because it's the pilot's time." We only had one pilot.

That summer I was on the College All-Star team that beat the Green Bay Packers. We were the last all-stars to beat the pros. We had never had a losing season at Syracuse and we had a real good program, but we didn't throw the ball. I didn't know how to run pass patterns. I never will forget that at the All-Star game, Otto Graham and Dante Lavelli told me, "Don't feel bad if you don't make it to the NFL." They said I was too small to play tight end, I didn't know how to run pass patterns, and I was going to a throwing team in Baltimore.

That probably helped me, because I always had people telling me what I can't do, and I've always tried to prove that I can do it. I left that night right after the game and went to Baltimore to prove that I could do it. And I never will forget, man, the only time I got fined was in an exhibition game against the Washington Redskins. Otto Graham was coaching there. I was going for a touchdown but I ran out of bounds in front of their bench so I could say to Otto, "Do you think I can make it in the NFL?"

After that it became a joke between us. When I went into the Hall of Fame, Sylvia said to him, "Do you think John can make it in the NFL?"

And every time Graham sees me, he says, "All right, I was wrong. I was wrong."

But when I first got to Baltimore, I was worried about my chances to start, 'cause I always wanted to start, not just make the team. And Sylvia had been sending me clippings from the Baltimore papers saying, "The tight ends look good on the team."

When I landed and she met me, she said, "Don't worry, John, just try to make the team."

"Forget making the team," I said. "I want to start."

The first guy I met at the Colts' training camp was the equipment man, Freddie Schubach. I never will forget this, because he set the stage. He said to me, "Welcome to the world champion Baltimore Colts. I shine your shoes every day. I polish and clean your helmet every day. I press your practice uniform. And I demand that you play the way I make you look."

I had never heard anything like that in my entire life. I was so impressed. Then I went in to see Don Shula, who was in his rookie year as a coach. Shula says to me, "What are your goals?"

I said, "I want to be your starting tight end."

He says, "All you got to do is beat out the guys in front of you. Your problem is, they've been here and they know the system. But I'll tell you what I'll do. If you're willing to give up your afternoons instead of sleeping, I will bring in Jim Mutscheller to tutor you in the afternoons."

And he did. The most important thing Jim taught me, which helped me all through my career—and I tell him every day—is when he said to me, "John, if you don't remember anything else, always get off on the count. If you get off on the count, you can block a 300-pounder, because you'll hit him before he moves."

And you know what? I practiced that with Unitas through the off-season, during the season, and there were times when it looked like I was offsides, because I got off exactly on the count.

Another Colt I worked with was Raymond Berry. Raymond was outstanding and a great teacher. There's a little pattern where you release along the linebacker and you go 10 yards and then you go across. If it was on the right side, we called it an R, and if it was on the left side, we called it an L. Every time I tried to catch it from the right side, I caught the ball wrong.

Dick Bielski, an assistant coach, kept saying to me, "John, you're going to drop the ball more than you catch it, because you can't see it the way you're catching it."

But I couldn't catch it the way he and Shula wanted me to catch it. So I went over to Raymond Berry's house and I asked him, "What should I do?"

And Raymond asked me a very simple question. "What would make you happy, and what would make the coach happy?"

"If I catch the ball."

He said, "I don't care how you catch it; just catch it."

And you know what? I always caught it the wrong way. I didn't see it, but I would catch it in my arms because I had my arms a certain way so I could tuck it, punch the guy, and run. But I always caught it.

That first year, when I'd get in the huddle, it took me time to adjust, because I didn't really hear the play. I was just so happy to be there. I'm looking around in this huddle and there's John Unitas, Raymond Berry, Lenny Moore, Gino—and I'm thinking, "Man, I heard about him and I heard about him. . . ." I had heard about these guys when I was in high school.

Everyone says I was the first tight end to go deep. You know why I went deep? 'Cause when I got to Baltimore, I didn't know how to run pass patterns. I saw Raymond Berry go deep. So I figured, why couldn't I go deep?

Then Raymond took me aside and said, "John, there's one thing you gotta always do. Whenever Unitas looks at you, give him something that you know you can do."

There was only one play that I knew—tight end out and tight end option.

Well, it's impossible to catch a pass on the full out or the option against a zone defense. But I caught five touchdown passes over 50 yards each against zone defenses my first year. I ran the pattern and Unitas threw it. And the veterans are standing there laughing, and the defense is saying, "He can't run that against this (defense)." But I did it.

And I never will forget, we're in a Monday meeting and Shula stops the film and he says, "I know why Mackey ran that play. He had no idea what he was doing. But Unitas, why in the hell did you throw it?"

And Unitas said, "Because Mackey didn't know he couldn't do it."

It's funny; after my first year I never ever caught another pass like that, because I became an intelligent tight end. Whenever you released and could read the defense, and you see them go to zone, and you're supposed to run a full out, you hook in the open spot. That's the right way.

That year Bob Vogel, Jerry Logan, Willie Richardson, and me were all rookies. We all came in and played. And for the next ten years, we never had a losing season.

The only player I really had a big problem with was Dave Wilcox, a linebacker for the 49ers. The first time I played him was in 1964. Because he was a rookie, I went offsides deliberately to nail him, and I stuck him. It was a 5-yard penalty, but I got the first shot in.

Shula's going crazy on the sidelines. Then we go back to the huddle and Unitas says, "If he's soft enough, let's go get him." He calls a 36 trap, where I'm supposed to crack back on the defensive end, unless I know I can hook the linebacker, and we'll go outside instead. And if I say, "Solid!" that means I'm hooking the linebacker and we're going outside, right? So we come up to the line and I say, "Solid!" I came off the line to stick him, and he picked me up and threw me, then knocked Lenny Moore down for another 5-yard loss.

Man, I went back to the huddle and said, "Call it again! Call it again!" And Unitas told me, "Shut up." He didn't call it again.

From then on I had big problems with Wilcox. Finally I went to Raymond Berry. He told me, "Get the film of the first time you played him, and the last time you played him, and let me take them home, and then you come over and Sally will fix dinner for us."

I went over there and he said, "You're intimidated."

Man, I prided myself on never being intimidated on the football field by anybody. I said, "I'm not intimidated."

So we looked at the films, and I saw that, after that first game, every time we played San Francisco, I played closer and closer to Jim Parker. I didn't have the natural split. And Raymond picked it up. He said, "You're intimidated. You think by getting close to Jim, he's going to help you. But we can't run inside because your body's in the way. We can't run outside because (Wilcox) is out there. Now they're forcing our offense and they know what they're doing."

I said, "But we beat them."

He said, "We beat them just because we're better than they are. That's dumb football."

"What must I do?"

He said, "Move out 5 yards."

And you know what? He was so right. I moved out 5 yards. When Wilcox came out with me, we were battling, man, but Lenny Moore went 35 yards inside him. Then the San Francisco coach said, "Get rid of Mackey."

Wilcox came down to the inside, John checked off, and I cracked back on him and we went outside. And I said to myself, "I should have never had a problem with him."

In the 1964 championship game in Cleveland where we got beat, 27–0, we found out later that they realized we ran our primary receiver at 10 yards. They knew he was open at 10, our secondary at 15, and the outlet at 18, and they challenged all of them at 7 to 9 yards, and threw off our passing game.

At the start of the 1968 season, Carroll Rosenbloom basically told Shula in front of the team that if he didn't win, he was history. Carroll always talked to us at the beginning of the season. This time he said, "I had a coach who brought me two championships, and he couldn't bring me the third one. We're always a bridesmaid, and never the bride. This year we better be the bride."

That year was the best coaching job that Shula did here. We lost to Cleveland at home, then we blew them out for the conference title. After that game, Rosenbloom came to the team and said, "You did what I asked you to do. Now, to show you what kind of guy I am, I'm taking everybody to Miami for the Super Bowl—the wives, kids, everybody."

Everyone went to Miami. We're down there, and we'd never had our families with us on an away game. The only time ever playing pro ball that Sylvia was in the same room with me the night before a game was the night before we lost to the Jets. It was little things; like she would say to me, "How am I going to get to the game tomorrow?" She didn't mean any harm; it's just the time. And you really want to say, "I don't care if you go," but you can't say that, 'cause you'll fight all night.

Ordinarily at an away game, you'd come in after practice and sit down and talk about things you're going to do in the game. Now, my little boy would run up to me: "Hi, Daddy," you know, and you never talked about the game.

It was a clear case of overconfidence. The day before the game, we announced a victory party. "Carroll Rosenbloom is having the party at his house, and don't invite too many, because he can only accommodate three hundred." That's what we said. The night before the game, he takes everybody out to dinner, trying to show the wives a nice time.

I don't know if Shula was upset over all this. If he was, he never showed it.

In the Super Bowl win over Dallas two years later, I had just come off a knee operation. I wasn't supposed to play until I rehabilitated my knee, but the tight ends got hurt and I played. I caught a pass that was tipped twice. Mel Renfroe hit it, and then Eddie Hinton, and then I got it. The play went 75 yards for a touchdown.

I got involved in the players' association through Ordell Braase. He was active in it, and his locker was next to mine. I became the president, but I resigned when I retired because I thought an active player should be in that position.

I got a call one day recently from NFL Films. They said to me, "John, there have been 44,000 touchdowns up to this point, and out of the top 100 in the NFL, you're in the top ten of the greatest runs ever made. One of yours is number eight."

You know what I said? " 'Cause I'm a Colt, man; I never played to be number eight. I wanted to be number one." I said, "Why am I not number one?"

He said, "It's the criteria. The only reason is that your run didn't change the outcome of the game."

He said the number one was the Immaculate Reception with Franco Harris, where the Steelers threw up the pass and went from defeat to winning against Oakland.

"We're coming out with this film of the top one hundred based on individual effort," he told me. "And you got ten plays in the one hundred."

The run he said was number eight was a short pass and a 65-yard run against the Lions. But I don't remember the game or even the year where I made the run. All I remember is that I knocked Lenny Moore down. I didn't see it at the time, but in the film he was coming over to make a block and I knocked him down.

You know why I don't remember the game? Because as a Colt, I never thought about scores or anything like that. All we ever thought about was how much we were going to win by. We were confident; you know what I mean? But we didn't always win. And I'll tell you, I didn't learn to appreciate that until they sent me to San Diego in 1972. When I got there, I'd never seen anything like it.

When I reported to their equipment man, I thought I'd beat him to the punch. I said, "I'm John Mackey, reporting from the world champion Baltimore Colts. I'd like my shoes shined and polished every day. I like my helmet cleaned and polished every day, and I want my practice uniform pressed. I play the way I look."

He handed me the shoe polish and said, "This is for your shoes. There's a spray for your helmet. I put the jocks, T-shirts, and socks in the middle of the floor. If you get here early, you'll get your size."

That's how they played.

But, hey, I went to the Super Bowl last year in Miami. San Diego's in it, and I walk into their locker room at Joe Robbie Stadium and guess what—they're in there polishing helmets. I laughed and said, "Now, that's why they got here."

When I played tight end, we did it all. Now everyone's a specialist, they take them out in certain situations. I don't rate players today. I'll tell you why. When Raymond Chester was at Oakland, he made all-pro. Then he came to Baltimore and he didn't make it. He went back to Oakland and he made all-pro again. That's an example of it's not how good you are, it's what the team asks you to do and how they use you.

Pettis Norman played with me at San Diego. I didn't know he could catch the ball until I got there. He came over from Dallas. He was a pretty good tight end, but they never threw the ball to him in Dallas. And he never played with a Unitas.

People ask me if I could still play, and I tell them I have the George Foreman look, but I'm not George Foreman. I was up in New York on business, and there was another player, who had been coached by Raymond Berry at New England. I was old enough to be his daddy. He came in hobbling, and the receptionist looked at both of us and said to him, "You both played football, and you're so much younger, and there's nothing wrong with Mr. Mackey. Why is that?"

I said, "I played on a winner. It doesn't hurt as much."

I've been involved in an investment firm with the same partner for thirty years. I met my partner, Leon White, at the College All-Star game. He was the first black kid from Atlanta to go to a major white university. He played football at Northwestern.

At the All-Star camp we made a deal. If I made it to the pros, I would skip law school, and he would skip pro ball and go for his MBA. He was drafted to play baseball, but he didn't play. I would save my money and go into the business, and he would make sure that when we invested it, we wouldn't lose. Today we own Blockbuster Videos and Denny's, and hair care and skin care products. It's been pretty good.

Going into the Hall of Fame in 1992 was a great honor for me. It was a sore point for them, because they had voted me the best tight end in the first fifty years of the game, and I was on the all-time all-pro first team. Mike Ditka was on the second team, and Mike went into the Hall of Fame ahead of me. When he went in, he said, "How did I get here before John?"

You know when you're going into the Hall of Fame? They announce it and they introduce you at the Pro Bowl game in Hawaii. I'm out there and the place is packed, and they call "Lem Barney," and he comes out and all Detroit Lions who are on the Pro Bowl team run out and hug him.

They call, "Al Davis," and all of the Raiders on the team run out in the middle of the field and hug him.

Then "John Riggins," and all of the Redskins run out and hug him.

Then they call, "John Mackey," and there are no Baltimore Colts there, and no Indianapolis Colts on the Pro Bowl team. And I'm walking, and I'm walking, and Reggie White ran out and he gave me a hug, and he turned to the other guys and said, "He doesn't sue 'em—we don't get paid" (referring to my union activities). And they all came out.

I said, "I'm going to Baltimore. I'm going where my family is."

I think Baltimore deserves an NFL team. The key is not to give up. I'm a Baltimore Colt and I'm part of that legacy. I have no connection with Indianapolis. If we're going to give our kids and grandkids a true history, Baltimore did exist. I've never seen my display at the Hall of Fame. If it shows me with an Indianapolis backdrop, I'm going out there and I'll change it.

Mike Curtis. Photograph © 1995 TADDER/Baltimore

Mike Curtis

Born: 3–27–43
Rockville, Maryland
Duke
Linebacker

6′ 2″, 232 lbs.
Drafted #1, 1965
Colts: 1965–1975

"You want to get a cheap shot on one of my receivers? Listen, buddy, we're going to run some plays over you until you are a dead man."

I played both ways at Duke, linebacker and fullback. When I got to Baltimore, I played wherever they wanted me. First they decided they wanted a third fullback behind Tony Lorick and Jerry Hill. Since I'd made All-American as a running back, it was okay with me. But I started as an outside linebacker; then Shula switched me to the middle. I figured I'll just play as hard as I can wherever they put me. I work for the company and they pay me.

In 1967 I was on the outside, and on a play against San Francisco they cut back and I hurt my knee and had to get cut on it. But it never bothered me again. I went up against Leroy Kelly in a game and got a compound fracture of the thumb. I would have stayed in the game, but it kept popping out. They stuck a pin in it and a big cast on it, and I think I played the next week. A lot of guys played every week; that was your job.

We had a better team in '68 than when we beat Dallas in the Super Bowl. Everybody clicked. The team working together makes a lot of guys look good. Earl Morrall was doing a good job hitting the receivers, who were making the right turns. The offensive line was all working together. Everybody liked Earl; they played harder for him. Earl doesn't have an ego problem, no bone to pick. He gets along with everybody, and he made a lot out of his ability. We kidded him about how slow he was. His arm wasn't any rifle, but he worked hard, got the job done, and had a great year.

I think you can use the word "humiliating" to describe the loss to the Jets in the Super Bowl. It's been twenty-six years, and that is one of the most painful things in my sports career. Of all the good things that happened, that one negative thing weighs disproportionately.

Intercepting a pass and winning the Super Bowl two years later did not make up for it, didn't even put a dent in it. That was another game. We had a good team, a lot of camaraderie, worked hard, lost one game all season. We should have killed the Jets, like we did on a regular basis in those years. It was like nowadays, the way the press makes such a big deal out of everything. Joe Namath said they were going to win, and after they did, the New York press jumps on it like they were the greatest thing since sliced bread.

The loss was a combination of things. Bringing the wives and kids was not good. Too much distraction. Shinnick was a smart player, but slow and weak. Ordell Braase had to cover a lot of ground on the right side of the line. Then we had passes bounce off pads and guys open not seen, and that's all part of not being mentally up.

Joe Namath was the beginning of the Hollywoodization of the game. The Jets paid him $400,000 when they drafted him. I didn't know what that amount of money was—the national debt or what? It had no relevancy to me. I was making about $30,000, and that was probably three times what my dad was making. What am I going to do with that kind of money? I was not used to having it. It was unbelievable to me.

I just wanted to be left alone and let me play. I didn't want to be distracted. I don't know how I'd do today with all the show biz in the business. Maybe I was naive.

Like breaking the picket line in training camp in 1970. The team asked me to go to work, I go to work. I didn't figure it was that big a deal. I was never involved in a union. I was naive about a lot of that stuff. If I had known the significance of all that, I probably would have done a little more soul-searching. I just drove in to go to work. Everybody else made a big deal out of it.

Bill Curry was my roommate. He was a leader in the union; John Mackey was also involved in it. Curry called me at the time and tried to convince me not to go in. I told him the uncomfortable part of it was that I would share in whatever they sacrificed to get in the way of a better retirement. My primary responsibility was to the people who pay me.

That made me look doubly worse, because I would enjoy the benefits, and the owners would love me, too. But I told him, "I don't need anybody else to take care of my retirement. It's my responsibility to invest any money I have so I'll have something when I retire. It's not their job to take care of me, and that goes to the very essence of our argument. You guys have the right to do that, but I'll take care of myself."

I felt lucky to play NFL football. Not many guys get that opportunity. So I wasn't going to walk out the door. I still had another thirty or forty years to work in a real job.

I got along real well with my teammates, although I had to smack one of them once because he wouldn't turn off the radio while I was trying to rest at training camp. It was the guys who had an agenda other than football who I didn't get along with. The guys who decided that how they performed was more important than how the team performed. That's where I would get in trouble with somebody. If they were going to affect the team's ability to win, that's when they'd get their ass kicked, and they didn't like it. I had enough hammer to make my point. Except maybe with a Billy Ray Smith. Then it was the team that had to get after him.

Even though we remained roommates, there was a bone of contention between Bill Curry and me. I don't believe in his general political philosophies. Like the time I popped the fan.

We were playing Miami at home in 1971, a game we had to win to be in the playoffs. Miami had the ball down in the open end of the field. So we're playing, and this guy comes running out on the field. I see him out of the corner of my eye, and he's smashed. I was afraid the game would stop and we would lose our momentum and maybe lose the game. If he's running around and the cops are chasing him all over the field, you take off ten or fifteen minutes and everybody's resting and gets cooled down.

A few years earlier, we had been watching a Chicago Bears film when this same guy ran out on the field and came up outside their huddle. Mike Ditka put an elbow right on the guy's nose, and the blood that came out of that boy's head—I didn't think we'd see him anymore. So when the guy ran up to us, I gave him a "flipper" with my padded forearm—my weak arm, the left—not to hurt him or kill him. Ditka had tried to kill him; all I wanted to do was get him off the field. Down he went. They helped him off the field.

Some guys wanted me to put the guy's lights out permanently. But Bill Curry, being a Clinton type of person, thought what I had done was the worst thing in the world. He kept saying, "Why'd you do that?"

I said, "Why'd you think I did it? I just wanted to get rid of the nuisance."

The guy wasn't hurt, no blood or anything. But he tried to sue us. They took depositions, and the guy kept moving and his lawyer had to keep finding him. He even flew up to Baltimore from Florida to take depositions. After about a year of that, and the lawyers dickering back and forth about an amount of money, it finally came down to where they would settle for an autographed football. I told them to forget it. It cost the club to defend us, but the guy wound up with nothing. Not even a signed football.

That wasn't the end of it, though. This was during the time when all those anti-Vietnam protests were going on. So I had people writing me letters. Some people wrote that I should have killed the guy, and others called me a war-monger. I got some from older guys who called me a bully and said, "Your father must be a bully, too, so I'm ready to fight your father."

I showed these letters to my dad and he said, "What's the guy's address? I'll go look him up and see how tough he is."

When Joe Thomas came in and started making changes, he broke the back of our morale. Then he went 2 and 12 in 1974. The family that was started and built up beginning in the 1950s, then continued as new guys came along and became part of the family as the older ones left—it got cut off. You got divorced. It broke the continuity and the tightness of the team and the town. Guys like Sully, Raymond Berry, Unitas, Fred Miller, who could still contribute more than just the physical side of it, were gone. Bert Jones and that group came along, but it was never really the same.

I got into the family and grew up in it for eleven years. Joe sent me to Seattle, then I finished up with two years in Washington. My whole life was the team, but just as I had done when I left Duke, I moved to the next step, and it's almost like the shades went down behind me and I put the blinders on.

Photograph by Bob Miller

After being with the Colts all those years, I didn't like the Redskins. And the coach, George Allen, was a flake. I was at the Pro Bowl one year when he was the coach. There was a guy on the other team, a receiver, who couldn't see very well out of his left eye. Allen is talking to his defense, and he says, "You don't have to worry about this guy when he lines up on your left, because he can't see out of his left eye."

The guy caught about ten passes on the left side that day.

So even before I went to Washington, I knew this guy was a nut.

So I'm sitting in the back of the locker room with some of the older players before a game against Dallas, and everybody's wondering where Allen is. Then suddenly he comes in screaming and dives on a guy up front and starts beating him up.

He gets up and says, "This is how I want you guys to beat Dallas."

It's the first time there for me, but the other guys are rolling their eyes.

Another time he brings in a karate guy. He wants to show the team how he wants them to win. They bring out a board and Allen's going to hammer this board and splinter it with his hand. He lets out a scream and hits the board and it doesn't break. His arm hangs limp at his side and he goes down, and the trainer had to get down on his hands and knees and administer first aid to this stupid flake.

There was more violence in football when we played. Guys could do more things than they can do now. Our attitude was, "You want to get a cheap shot on one of my receivers? Listen, buddy, we're going to run some plays over you until you are a dead man." That's what happened.

Today you see defensive backs acting tough, but they act that way when there's somebody skinnier in front of them. But if somebody else is carrying some guns with them, you don't see so much toughness. It's a showboat toughness. It's almost like they pick on guys; they're not gentlemen about it. There's always somebody bigger and tougher. If they were playing with some of the guys I played with, they'd have their asses whipped right on the field to where they wouldn't be playing anymore.

If I played with guys who hot dogged so much, I would wait for them to come off the field and get dressed, and I'd follow them. Then I'd pull them out of the car and say, "Now is when you're really going to find out how tough you are, 'cause you're talking to somebody who's dangerous, and I'm going to kick your ass."

I've got three children. One's a senior, has a lacrosse scholarship at Duke. Another boy is a senior at Landon in Bethesda. He made first string all-metropolitan in lacrosse. Both played football at Landon. I have a daughter who plays soccer. Whatever sports they play, I just tell them I expect them to play as hard as they can, and do the best they can. I don't care what it is.

I never had any interest in coaching, never got into the finery of play calling and psychology and working with players. When the curtain went down on my playing days, the curtain went down. I'd invested in various types of real estate and had gotten my license. I used to have a Pappy's Restaurant.

I had a 3,000-acre ranch in Wyoming. That's one thing I miss. I wish I could have kept it.

The continuing loyalty and family attitude among the old Baltimore Colts is attributable to a lot of things. First, the management of the Colts brought together a lot of good guys, with good character. We liked each other and that helped us win.

Then you had a town that had pretty good character.

That's one of the tough things about getting out of football; you never find that camaraderie again in any other job. We were all concerned about each other and our kids, and we still are. That was a great part of the game.

Rick Volk. Photograph © 1995 TADDER/Baltimore

Rick Volk

Born: 3-15-45
Toledo, Ohio
Michigan
Defensive Back

6′ 3″, 195 lbs.
Drafted: #3, 1967
Colts: 1967–1975

"Here I am . . . playing with John Unitas, Lenny Moore, Raymond Berry, Jim Parker . . . all these guys, and they're counting on me? *It makes you want to play harder."*

I came from Toledo, but I didn't want to go to Ohio State. I was a quarterback in high school, and I knew that Woody Hayes called all the plays. I wanted to call my own. Besides, I really wanted to play for Michigan. My uncle, Bob Chappius, had been an All-American there, runner-up to Johnny Lujack for the Heisman Trophy in 1947. I just wanted to go there and wear those colors.

Bump Elliott was the coach, and he had played with my uncle, so when he offered me a scholarship, I took it. Today the recruiting of high school players is so intense all over the country, the will to play for a certain university is not there like it used to be. They're all thinking of it as a stopping point to get to the NFL.

I became a defensive back in 1963, covering wide receivers. At that time there was no free substitution, and we played both ways. Free subbing came in the next year. Since we only had three defensive backs, I had a better chance of playing in that position.

We won the Big 10 championship in 1964 and beat Oregon State in the Rose Bowl, 34–7.

I was drafted by the Colts in the second round in 1967. They had traded with New Orleans and gotten their number one pick, so I was actually their third choice, behind Bubba Smith and Jim Detwiler, a back from Michigan.

Bubba was 6-foot-7, 300 pounds. At that time that was huge. When he got down to 275, he outran anybody on our team for 10 or 15 yards. He had that kind of quickness.

After playing Big 10 football in a big school, I knew I could play in the NFL. I missed the first three weeks of training camp because of the College All-Star game, but Chuck Noll took me aside and went over everything with me. When you're breaking in, you've got a lot to learn.

Joining a team with all these guys you'd heard about all your life—I was ten years old when John Unitas had started, and now all of a sudden they're counting on you to help them win, that's a big thing. It makes you want to play harder. You're all excited, all that enthusiasm and adrenaline flowing. But when you're young, you don't even think about it.

When I arrived in Baltimore, they had a pretty set team. They were looking to fill a few openings, and when Alvin Haymond dislocated a shoulder in training, I plugged in at the right safety position, the same as I had played my senior year. I had a lot of good people around me—Jerry Logan and Lenny Lyles and Bobby Boyd—and they made me look better. When I needed help, Lyles was there. If I got beat by a receiver, Bubba or Fred Miller was sacking the quarterback. I was lucky to come in when I did.

Jerry Logan was a great hitter and very intelligent person who knew how to play the game. He solidified the whole secondary. Jerry always used to say, "Keep it simple, stupid. The simpler the better." Whenever the coaches tried to get too detailed, he'd tell them to keep it all on the same page; don't get too complicated. He and Bobby Boyd worked together, using hand signals to change defense.

Jerry played with knee and shoulder problems a lot of times. Boyd said Jerry had the highest pain threshold of anybody he knew. But in those days everybody played hurt. If you didn't play every week, they considered you a softy. Unitas, Fred Miller, Billy Ray Smith—all those guys played hurt. Nobody wanted to sit out. I remember Tom Mitchell going out and playing a whole game with two sprained ankles and not even looking like he was hurt, then sticking his legs in buckets of ice after the game. Maybe we were scared that somebody else would go in and take our job if we sat out a game.

Mike Curtis was the most intense guy I ever played with. An awesome individual. He had the physical abilities and the smarts. In professional sports, you can get yourself ready, play the game, and not have to associate with anyone else. In order to play, Curtis had to be focused solely on his own responsibilities. They wanted him as a middle linebacker to call the defensive signals—look over to the sidelines, read the hand signals, call the defenses, and make changes at the line of scrimmage. Mike could do it, but if he did, he was not able to play his game. So Stan White took over that responsibility. Stan loved it. He had the game plan in his head, and he could think on the field and anticipate the other team's tendencies.

The atmosphere going to Miami for the Super Bowl game against the Jets was that this is a fun game; bring the wife down for a week in Miami. We had been there the two previous years in the runner-up bowl, and the first two Super Bowls hadn't even sold out. We were all relaxed, including the coaches. It was only after we got beat that we realized what an opportunity we blew. We got humiliated, what with Joe Namath sounding off and all. But that was Joe's time, and the game needs characters like him to keep it going.

In that game, I got knocked out on the third or fourth play. Matt Snell came up the middle and I met him and ducked my head and took a hit. I came out dazed. On the sidelines they asked me questions: "Where are you. . . what's the score. . . who are you playing against. . ." You could answer those, but five seconds later you couldn't remember what you said. They asked me if I was okay, and I said I was, so I went back in.

I knew what I had to do instantly, like when they called a 4–3 defense. I knew what to do, but I was not reacting as quickly as I had before then. And after a play was over, I'd forget what happened.

Later I watched the game film, and there were a lot of times where I was waiting. I would figure that they were going to run a sweep off to my side and I'm waiting, you know, like where am I? They kept running away from Bubba to our right side, at Ordell Braase and Don Shinnick, and we weren't stopping them. I should have been coming up and supporting the defense.

Normally I would have been up there a lot quicker supporting the weak side, because we had responsibilities to stop the run on that side. I was just late coming up. I'm watching the films and I'm not even in the frame until the running back is maybe 5 yards down the field, then here I come. That was not normal for me.

Usually, watching the films, you know what's going to happen next. But this time I didn't know what to expect. You know at the instant of the play who you are and what you're doing, but you don't have any recall when you've been dinged the way I was.

But my troubles in that game were not over. On the on-side kick that Tom Mitchell recovered for us with under two minutes to play, I got kicked in the head and was really out for the count. They threw me on the sidelines so as not to take a time out. (The next year they changed the rule so if anybody got hurt in the last two minutes, the team would not lose a time out.)

There were other things that we self-destructed on, but that was the best defensive team I ever played on. When you have a guy who is not playing to his capability, you lose that little edge you had. I think that was a big factor in our loss.

When Unitas came in late in the game he got us a touchdown. Had he come in the game earlier, it might have made a difference. Might have.

By the time I came to after being kicked in the head, I was in the locker room with a real bad headache. We got on the bus to go back to Ft. Lauderdale, and I was getting sick. When I got back to the hotel, Dr. Norman Freeman told my wife, Charlene, to keep me awake. When you have a concussion, the worst thing is to fall asleep. I was really tired, but she kept me awake. Then I got sick to my stomach and went into convulsions, and Charlene ran out into the hall screaming.

I was in the hospital for several days. Charlene says when Don Shula came in to see me, the first thing I said was, "Coach, are we still going to get our rings?"

That was the last game of the year, so I had six months to get back to normal. I got knocked out a few more times after that.

As far as I'm concerned, Don Shula was the best. Sometimes he said things to me and other guys that I didn't like. He'd start off with a couple bad words, then he'd start cutting you down. You know you're out there doing your best, and he's on your butt because you didn't do something right. But he didn't do that to me until after I'd been there a few years, and he didn't do it to everybody. He would yell at those he knew would be motivated by it. I felt that if he said it to me, at least he was concerned about me. It's when they stop talking to you that you have to worry. He also knew I was professional enough so that I wasn't going to bad-mouth him and sulk on the sidelines. When I went back in, I was going to prove to him that he was wrong.

When Shula was gone, and Don McCafferty was the coach, it was different when we went down to the Super Bowl the next time. No wives, meals at certain times. We beat Dallas, but it was not a well-played game.

Fullback Tom Nowatzke had come over from Detroit in 1970. He had been a number one draft pick for them, and to be traded to the Colts was devastating to him. He felt a little like an outsider when he got here. He made a big contribution all year, and in the Super Bowl he punched it out on that "19 straight" play all day on the weak side against Bob Lilly. He was proud to return to Detroit wearing a Super Bowl ring.

Tom Nowatzke.
Photograph by Vince Bagli

It was late in the fourth quarter of that game when I made my big interception, but it wasn't an outstanding play, just an overthrown pass. Craig Morton was trying to throw to a back in front of me, and Roy Hilton made a good pass rush on Morton, forcing him to throw it a little higher than he wanted to. It sailed over the receiver and I was able to scoop it up and run with it. Dallas wide receiver Reggie Rucker was chasing me, and I knew he was behind me. I saw Ted Hendricks ahead of me. He got down and I hurdled him, but about the 8 yard line Rucker started grabbing my back. I made it to the 3 before he got me.

If I had gone all the way in, I might have been named MVP of that game. Chuck Fowley won it, the only time a player on the losing team got it. But Tom Nowatzke punched it behind Glen Ressler and Sam Ball for the tying touchdown.

Rick Volk. Photograph by Vince Bagli

With about eight seconds to go, Mike Curtis intercepted a pass and Jim O'Brien kicked a field goal to give us the lead, 16–13. Now we had to kick off again. They had Bob Hayes on the far side, but we didn't kick it to him. They had time for one play, and tried a Hail Mary pass, but Jerry Logan broke it up.

Soon after that, Carroll Rosenbloom sold the team to Robert Irsay, and Joe Thomas came in and started making changes, and it all began going downhill.

I used to wonder how a guy like Carroll Rosenbloom could ever tell any of us he was trading or cutting us. If we couldn't play anymore, I think he would bring us back into the organization to coach or teach the younger players.

Thomas got rid of a lot of players the fans loved—Tom Matte, John Mackey, Johnny U, Bill Curry—the heart of the team. He drafted young players and just threw them in there to play. When the fans lost all their heroes, the players everybody looked up to, and the people who replaced them on the field were guys they never heard of who couldn't play as well as the ones who were let go, the fans began to boo for the first time in the team's history. The product was not a good product and the fans could see that.

Some people say Thomas knew talent. I heard this story about him:

When he was the player personnel man for the Dolphins, he was at a pre-draft session, and somebody added a fictitious name to the list of players. So they were going through a mock draft, and Joe was talking about each name that came up. Then they got down to the made-up name, and Joe starts giving a big description of the guy. Everybody started laughing so much, they had to let him in on the joke.

They began to shuffle coaches. We had Howard Schnellenberger, who had a minus personality. He thought he could be the disciplinarian, a Marine kind of guy. Some players don't function for that kind of coach, but he wasn't able to see each player as an individual. A successful coach has to be able to motivate each individual to produce, and know what their hot button is. In practice, you may say something to cut a guy down, but you know that guy has enough guts to come back and show you.

My last year with the Colts was 1975. I went out on a bad note. I felt I could still play, but I was not a starter after Ted Marchibroda took over as head coach. I remember Ted always hitting his hand with the game plan and yelling at the coaches.

Unlike Shula, Ted could not stand up to people. After a few games, they sat me down. I went to Ted and said, "Ted, this doesn't seem to be like you. In the past you've always gone with your vets and not the rookies, and now you're playing Jackie Wallace in my position. It doesn't seem like your move, more like Joe Thomas telling you what to do."

He said, "No, it's my decision."

I accepted it, but I never felt that it was right. I believed that Thomas was telling him who to play. Years later Thomas said that it had been his decision, and my feelings proved to be true. Ted did not have the backbone to stand up for who he wanted to play. I never really respected him after that.

I blamed Ted for Bert Jones's problems here when everybody got on Bert for complaining to the refs all the time. If he didn't stand up for himself on the field, who would? Marchibroda didn't have the guts to get the refs to call the penalties.

Bert had the best arm I've ever seen. He had accuracy, strength—maybe too much at times. If Unitas had been here, he'd have taught Bert how to go from one receiver to another. But Marchibroda told him, "If your number one guy is not open, dump it to the backs."

That's why Lydell Mitchell led the league in receptions. Bert did not know how to go from his number one to two to three receivers. Maybe it was because it was a young team and the line couldn't give him enough time to do that. I don't know. But Marchibroda told him to dump it off.

I also blame Ted for the way Roger Carr played. When Carr was a primary receiver, he worked hard running a pattern. When he was not the primary receiver, he dogged it. I played against him; I saw it. When he was not the number one receiver and didn't bother to run out the pattern, that gave away a lot of stuff the Colts were trying to do.

Carr could run and had great hands, but he didn't have a big heart. He didn't want to come across the middle. He'd tear off down the sidelines, so if he had to break it off, you were ready for it. If I had to line up against him, I'd definitely get some yardage between me and him.

But the team started winning in 1975—nine in a row. They had the talent, and when they beat a couple teams, they began to realize they were good enough to win. As the year went on, that's what happened. We made it to the playoffs, and got beat by Pittsburgh.

Even with the Sack Pack and George Kunz at right tackle and the rest, I don't think the Colts would have gone any farther than they did in the 1970s, even if the Steelers had not been so dominant.

After a few weeks Irsay shuffled his coaches some more. Mike McCormack, then Frank Kush, whose reputation was an outlaw kind of coach, a snake in the grass kind of guy. I didn't play for him; that's just what I thought. Maybe he wasn't. Maybe he was good to his players. I don't know. I just didn't respect his character coming in.

I played in New York in 1976, then spent two years with the Miami Dolphins. We got to the playoffs in '78, but lost to Houston in the first game. Don Shula, George Young, John Sandusky, Carl Taseff, Tom Keane, Norm Bulaich, Don Nottingham were all there. It was a quality organization.

For me it was great being back among a lot of the old Baltimore Colts.

Captain Jack Fellowes

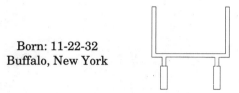

Born: 11-22-32
Buffalo, New York

U.S. Naval Academy, 1956
U.S. Navy (Retired), 1986

"This guy saved my life—trying to remember Earl Morrall's name kept me from going crazy."

The mind is really something. I was a POW in Vietnam from 1966 to 1973. I spent seven years in a lot of "Hanoi Hiltons." The name of the game was to try to think of things that would not put you where you were. So I would think of anything. I used to go through baseball lineups, like the Red Sox in the 1946 World Series. I had grown up in Arizona, where I would listen to USC and UCLA football games on the radio, and I would replay those football games in my mind.

One day there crossed my mind an old television program called "What's My Line?" Earl Morrall had just been traded or somehow had hooked up with the New York Giants, and they were talking about something on the panel, and I'm recalling Kitty Carlisle saying, "Well, the Giants are saved now, because they got a new quarterback, Earl Morrall." Except when I got to that part, I couldn't remember the name of the player she was talking about.

For the next two and a half years, I was going batty trying to remember who was that quarterback that she had mentioned on that program. I even remembered seeing him play once and being very impressed. But the name? It wouldn't come to me.

Then one day I was with some Air Force prisoners. We were singing songs and trying to remember lyrics. The song, "Lucky Old Sun," came up, and I was singing it mentally trying to remember the words, and suddenly it came to me—Earl Morrall—just like that. I jumped up and danced around the room, and this group of Air Force guys said, "What the hell's the matter with you?"

I said, "I'm not crazy. I remember his name."

Of course, to most people, that sort of thing is not very exciting, but it was exciting to me. It's fascinating, because here he was a football player, didn't know me from Adam, and I certainly don't know him, but his name was very important to me. After 1969, when it finally came to me in that song, I've never forgotten it, of course.

I was a captive for another four years after that. It was always awful. But we made some good days because we passed jokes to each other, but I don't think it was worth a darn. It just wasn't fun.

You sit there for so long and you think your mind's going to atrophy, but it doesn't. There's so much back there. It just made me feel good that I remembered Earl Morrall's name. It kept me going. I give Earl credit for keeping me going for the first three years because I forgot his name. He doesn't know that I forgot it. But the next four years, boy, I was solid. I knew I could remember these things. He was a kind of a turning point, to be perfectly honest with you.

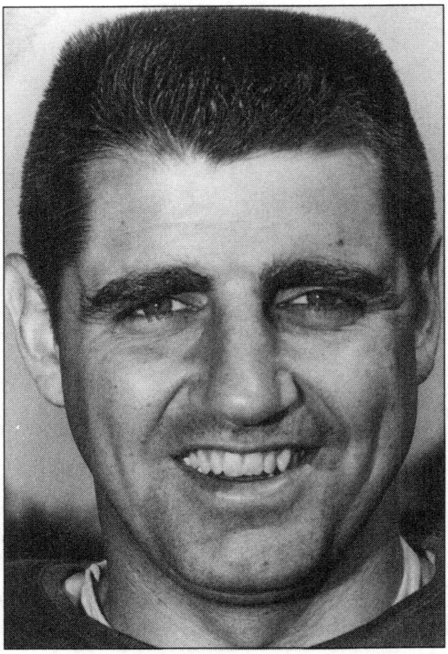

Earl Morrall.
Courtesy New York Giants

Commander Jack Fellowes reunited with his family following release from captivity. Courtesy Jack Fellowes

Earl Morrall

Born: 5-17-34
Muskegon, Michigan
Michigan State
Quarterback

6′ 2″, 208 lbs.
Drafted: #1, 1956
San Francisco
Colts: 1968–1971

"I played twenty-one years with six teams, and the Super Bowl loss to the Jets was the biggest downer."

I played two years at Michigan State under coach Biggie Munn, and two for Duffy Daugherty. We went to the Rose Bowl twice, in 1953 and 1955.

Detroit and San Francisco had tied for last place in the NFL, so they flipped a coin for the first draft pick. The 49ers won, and selected me. San Francisco had Y.A. Tittle, and the next year they drafted John Brodie number one, so they had three quarterbacks. Then they found out they needed a linebacker, so they traded me to Pittsburgh.

Buddy Parker was the coach there. He had been at Detroit when they wanted to draft me. He was okay, but moody. I don't know if I would have lasted there. My second year there, they traded me to Detroit for Bobby Layne. Then the Lions made Len Dawson their first draft pick, and they picked up Jack Kemp, so there were three quarterbacks again. But I was the veteran, with two years' experience, so I played the most.

Colts fans remember that game in Memorial Stadium in 1960 when we beat them in the last ten seconds. The scoring had gone more like a baseball game: 3–0, 3–3, 5–3, then 8–3. I came in in the fourth quarter and hit Hopalong Cassady on a post pattern. It was literally a post pattern, 'cause he caught it, took two steps into the end zone, and ran into the goal post. Put his head down and ran right into it. He thought he had hit a defender. When he came off the field, he was dazed. Didn't even notice me trying to congratulate him.

That made it 10–8. Then Jim Martin kicked a field goal for us and it was 13–8, with 2:53 to go.

Then Johnny Unitas did his patented move down the field—this and that—and hit Lenny Moore with the 35-yard touchdown pass over Night Train Lane. That gave the Colts the lead, 15–13, with fourteen seconds on the clock. The crowd went wild. They had to clear the field to get the final play in.

Baltimore kicked off and Bruce Maher ran it out to the 35. On the play, one of the Colts leveled Steve Junker in front of our bench. I helped

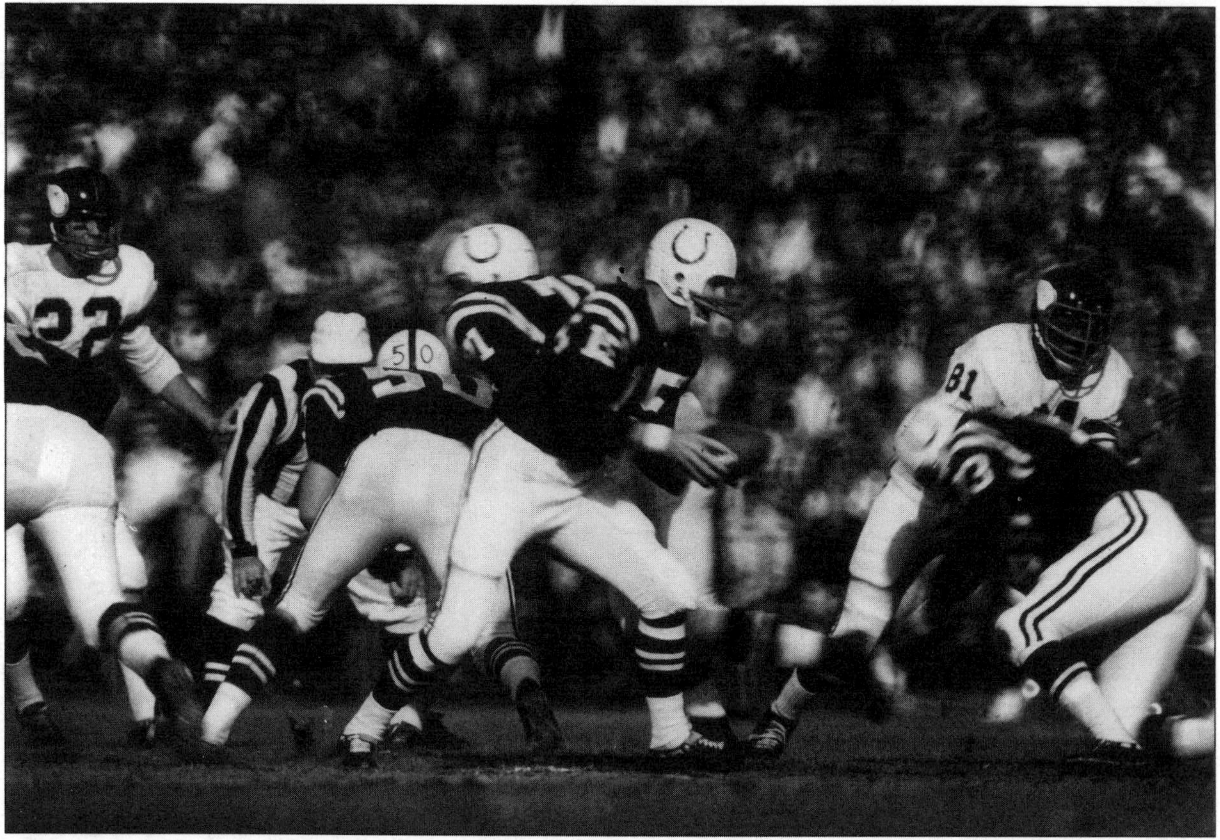

Earl Morrall, the "backup" quarterback who became 1968's MVP. Photograph © 1995 TADDER/Baltimore

the official pull the red flag out by hollering, "He can't do that!" He threw it down—15 yards. Meantime, Carl Brettschneider comes off our bench from 10 yards farther down and kicks the Colt player who is still on the ground. So there's an offsetting penalty, and we're still on the 35.

I ask coach George Wilson, "What do you want to call here?"

He said, "Call anything."

I went out there and see the official standing over the ball. I asked another official, "Is he going to start the clock whenever he wants to?"

"Yeah."

"But a penalty stops the clock."

"There's two offsetting penalties. He'll start it when he walks away."

So I called a time-out.

I stepped in the huddle and called a play for Jim Gibbons over the middle. I was trying to get 15 yards to midfield to go for a field goal. The goal posts were on the goal line then, and Martin could kick it that far. The record was 56 yards, set by Bert Rechichar. In practice, we always finished up by going for the record. We'd put it down at 57, and most times Jim would make it. He had a strong enough leg. I figured if we complete the pass, I'd call another time out, and if Martin makes it, we win, 16–15.

I hit Gibbons coming from the left side across the middle. The pass was up high in front of him; he had to reach up for it. Carl Taseff and Andy Nelson were chasing him. Nelson went up for the ball. Gibbons caught it and ducked, and Nelson slid off his back and collided with Taseff. Taseff might have tackled Gibbons if they hadn't collided. But Gibbons springs out and goes down the sidelines. Our fullback, who was in the flat, got down there and helped shoulder Bobby Boyd, and Gibbons scored with no time left on the clock.

I played twenty-one years with six teams, and the Super Bowl loss to the Jets was the biggest downer. I still have thoughts about it. You remember the big plays, like the one to Gibbons, but you still remember the plays that "could have been" in the Jets game. They could have changed my whole career.

There were a number of them. You look at all the different things that happened to the Colts that day. Four times we were down in scoring territory, and came away with nothing. Missed the first field goal. Then I didn't see Jimmy Orr in the end zone. Another time, we get down there, Willie Richardson runs a quick in; I was looking for a little bit slower, and I threw behind him. Sample makes the interception. On another one, I hit Tom Mitchell on the shoulder pad. The ball bounces 20 feet in the air. If I don't hit him there and he catches it, grand. Later a linebacker said he had gotten a fingertip on it. They stopped us there.

After the half, there was one to John Mackey on a little delay over the middle. There wasn't a defender within 20 yards of him. If he catches it at midfield, he goes down to their 20 most likely, running over somebody. But he dropped it.

Tom Matte had the longest run, got caught at the 10, and fumbled.

Another thing that people forget is that Joe Namath threw a quick slant out in the flat that hit Rick Volk in the belt buckle and he dropped it. If he catches it, he'd be gone the other way. Namath couldn't catch him.

When things are working for you, they work. When they don't, they don't.

I don't think it was overconfidence. People said we were out there kidding and prankstering in practice. We always did that. Teams don't change. If we had been out there serious and not making any noise, that would have been a change. But when you're winning, you don't change things.

I don't think the Jets ever beat us again after that.

One of my biggest kicks in football was holding the ball for Jim O'Brien's 32-yard field goal with nine seconds on the clock to beat Dallas in the Super Bowl two years later. O'Brien was worried about the wind. I told him, "Just kick the ball through the middle. Don't worry about anything. Kick it through the middle and it ain't going anywhere else."

Jim O'Brien. Photograph by Vince Bagli

That Super Bowl didn't wipe out the loss to the Jets. Nothing can do that, when you don't win and you know you should have.

I threw the ball more in Baltimore than I did when I went to Miami in 1972. The ground game was going so good down there, why change? Give it to Jim Kiick, or Larry Csonka, or Mercury Morris. And the line was blocking so good. I was the holder for Garo Yepremian. With sidewinders like him, you watch how they're kicking. I'd lean it in or out, depending on how he was kicking. If he was hooking a little bit, I'd lean it away from him and keep the ball straighter up and down. Things like that.

Playing in 1972 after Bob Griese got hurt, it was a great feeling to be part of a perfect season. You start out every fall trying to win every game, and we accomplished that. We weren't looking back, and the press didn't make a big deal of it at the time.

Don Shula kept us focused on what was coming up each week. He has been able to adapt to the players and talent he has had over the years, working with them and getting the most out of them. He has the right words, the right way with people. He looks for the small mistakes, and does not tolerate the mental mistakes. He knows how to stay in control of practice. There's humor, there's laughs and jokes. But there's times when it gets too free and nothing's getting accomplished, and he knows how to call the players back to attention, get them sharp and thinking again.

It took me twenty years to catch a knee injury. I cut off a toe with a lawn mower in 1962. Doug Atkins broke my collar bone in '64. I broke a wrist in '66, and tore a media collateral ligament in my knee December 1, 1975. I got operated on after the season.

It was possible that my son, Matt, and I might have played as the first father-son combination in the NFL. He was a center at Florida until he broke both bones in his right arm in '76, my last year.

Matt was a ballboy in spring camp and one time we were having skeleton passing drills, just me and Griese and the receivers—no line—just going against the defense. Shula was watching and he told Matt to go in and do a few snaps. So he was snapping a few back to us, and one time he snapped one to Griese. Either Griese pulled back too soon or Matt snapped a little late. The ball hit the ends of Griese's fingers. He grabbed them and said, "Goddamn, Matt, you'll do anything to get your dad to play, won't you?"

Shula said, "Matt, you just center your dad from now on."

But Matt and I never played in a game together.

Marty Domres (14) spins back to throw.
Photograph © 1995 TADDER/Baltimore

MARTY DOMRES

Born: 4-17-47
Ithaca, New York
Columbia
Quarterback

6′ 4″, 220 lbs.
Drafted: #1, 1969
San Diego
Colts: 1972–1975

"[In 1975] the swagger was on our side of the field, and that element of confidence in sports—individual or team—is so important."

I never had any grand ambitions of playing any professional sport. I was a 6-foot-4, 197-pound quarterback in high school in Syracuse. We tied for the championship two years in a row, but I was only second team all-area. I was recruited by Syracuse, Penn State, Boston College, and Rutgers, but I intended to go to an Ivy League School.

Hubie Schultz recruited me for Columbia, and I flew down to New York one weekend to look it over. There was about four inches of snow on the ground when I landed at LaGuardia Airport. One of the coaches, Al Paul, who was from Baltimore, had instructed me to take a cab, give the driver directions to take me to 116th Street, and not to pay more than $1.25 for the ride.

The city was safer than it is now, and I had a tremendous weekend. The campus was beautiful and the coach, Buff Donelli, made a very positive impression on me. I fell in love with the city and the people I met, and that's why I went to Columbia.

Columbia was the smallest school in the Ivy League. We had 3,400 undergraduates; other schools had three or four times as many. Sports were treated as an extracurricular activity. When I got there in 1965 we had just enough players to make up one side, either offense or defense. The three years I played there, we had the same record each year. In my sophomore year, we put most of the good players on defense; we won 2 and lost 7. The next year we put most of the good players on offense; we were 2 and 7. As a senior, we stacked the defense and figured we'd throw the ball and score a lot of points; we were 2 and 7.

But we weren't as bad as it sounds. We did score a lot of points, and I set all the Ivy League passing records and four national records. It just seemed that there was always something that happened in a game. For example, against Princeton, we're down by two with eight minutes left. We try a two-point conversion; I throw to Billy Carey on a slant and the ball bounces off him as he is hit by a defender.

We kick off, they run it back 70 yards. Next play they score. We get the ball and march down the field passing, and on fourth and four we go for it. I throw a square-out to the receiver, and as he squares out he catches the ball and tries to cut back, because the defender's on him, and the ball pops up in the air and the defender catches it and goes down the sideline and out of bounds on about the 20-yard line. They score on the next play. They score again, and we lose something like 41 to 15. But the reality was that we were right there with eight minutes left to go. And that's the sort of thing that happened constantly.

The San Diego Chargers of the American Football League made me their first draft pick in 1969. [The next year the league became part of the NFL as the American Conference.] Sid Gillman was the coach. Their quarterback, John Hadl, had had a poor season the year before, and everybody was calling for his head. But he came back and had three great years while I was there.

Each year I saw less action. I threw 112 passes the first year, 55 in 1970, only 12 in '71. Gillman was out one year because of illness; he came back in '71 and they fired him late in the season, and Harland Svare took over.

I signed three one-year contracts, and now they were up. I went to training camp in 1972 very unenthusiastic, and requested to be traded. The Colts were looking for a successor to John Unitas, and they wanted somebody with experience, so Joe Thomas traded a first-round draft pick for me.

As a New York Giants fan, I had grown up watching and rooting against Unitas. When I arrived at the Colts' training camp and walked up to him and said hello, that was a special event for me.

I thought John was great. He was very quiet, very matter-of-fact about playing football, like a stoic golfer who doesn't wear his emotions on his sleeve. John was just John, friendly but not effervescent. If I asked him any questions about the offense, he was cordial.

I don't think John was a tremendous natural athlete. While he was definitely not a cheerleader, he was a great leader. A fierce competitor, he could crack the whip and demand of his guys. But there was nothing divisive within the team. He played on a strong team most of his career and got a lot out of them. He reflected the same personality you knew on the field all the time.

Later, he and Bert Jones did not get along. They were just different personalities. To John, Bert was a wise guy. Bert would kid him, and if there is one thing you don't want to do, it's try to stick the needle to John.

I'm sure it was a culture shock for John when he went to San Diego. Having Harland Svare as a coach there was the equivalent of not having a coach.

Five games into the 1972 season, the Colts were 1 and 4, and they fired Don McCafferty. John Sandusky replaced him and told me I was going to start the next Sunday against the Jets in New York. Unitas always stood up in the huddle, and I had a habit of going down on one knee. Danny Sullivan knew that, so the first day of practice that week, he had the rest of the guys ready, and the first time in the huddle, when I dropped to one knee, they all did the same. We started laughing, and I felt completely comfortable about the situation.

We had the Jets beat late in the game. Then Joe Namath threw the ball up for grabs and our defensemen, Charlie Stukes and Jerry Logan, collided and tipped the ball up in the air, and a little guy, Eddie Bell, caught it on the dead run and went in to score, and they led 24–20.

We got the ball with about forty seconds left. On the last play of the game, I threw a pass from the 50 to John Mosier. He caught it on the one and got stopped there. That's the kind of would-be moments of satisfaction that I don't have from my pro football career.

Four weeks later, at Cincinnati, we went down the field in our two-minute drill and Jim O'Brien kicked a field goal in the rain. We had done everything we had to do to get ourselves into position to kick it, and we won it, 20–19.

My most memorable event in professional football was the last home game of the 1972 season against Buffalo. We won, 35–7. I had a good game, and was named player of the week. But the highlight came when a plane was circling overhead pulling a banner: "Unitas We Stand" as John went into the game with that unique canter—that waddle of his—and threw a touchdown pass. The place went wild. I got to see John in action, and the reaction of the crowd. It was his last home game as a Colt.

Coming along and replacing John that year, I think I had a reasonable year under the circumstances. We were 5 and 9. During the off-season, I worked at Citibank in New York. So on the day of the draft, I went down to watch it.

The Colts were in a transition time, and I thought it would work out. We'd have Don McCauley and Lydell Mitchell in the backfield. We had Jim O'Brien, Sam Havrilak, and Eddie Hinton, whom they traded. I thought the Colts would draft Isaac Curtis, a wide receiver from San Diego State. Instead they drafted another quarterback, Bert Jones, from LSU.

My first thought was, "This is the end of me." I was twenty-six. I was livid. I was also embarrassed. I left the meeting and immediately called Joe Thomas. "What's this?" I asked.

"You always take a quarterback when he's available," Joe said. "He's a good guy and you'll see, it'll be fine. Just come in and compete and you'll be here a long time."

Later, I wished I had been traded right then and there. I would have been better off to have stayed at San Diego or gone someplace else. I was told they had been thinking about taking Jones all year, no matter how well I might have played.

Howard Schnellenberger took over as the coach in 1973. We had an inexperienced team and went down to the bottom.

I started the 1974 opener at Pittsburgh, got hit by Dwight White and L.C. Greenwood, and went from the floor of the Astroturf to the hospital with three cracked ribs. Bert Jones finished that game.

The next week I tried to play against Green Bay and didn't play very well. So Irsay was hollering for Bert to start the third game, at Philadelphia, but I played the first half. They were ahead by something like 17-10 when I threw an interception to Joe "Birdman" Lavendar, who ran down the sideline for a touchdown. My receiver, Ollie Smith, had slipped and Lavendar picked it off.

When I came to the sidelines, Irsay was there hollering at Schnellenberger. Howard took off his headset, threw it on the ground, and said something to Irsay. Irsay stood there, flushed, holding one of those sideline cups, telling Howard he wanted Bert Jones in the game. Howard replied that I was going to stay in.

I went in for another series, we punted, the Eagles went down the field and scored, and the half ended.

After the game, Irsay told Joe Thomas to fire Schnellenberger. He was gone that day.

We were a transition team. Our continuity hadn't developed yet, and Howard was a victim of that. He knew the pieces were not ready to win. Joe Thomas coached the last eleven games of 1974, which was a waste. We finished 2 and 12; we were in the games we lost, but we would have been farther along on the curve if it hadn't been for Joe Thomas.

Then Ted Marchibroda took us from the worst record to the playoffs in '75. Marchibroda was a very savvy, knowledgeable guy, great at reading the psyche of a team and saying, "This is the chemistry I need to create for this team to be successful."

Later, I saw him do that at Buffalo, where he put the entire burden of play calling on the quarterback and allowed them to have free rein with their no-huddle offense.

In Baltimore he was always criticized for being too conservative, but maybe that was the right strategy to have, given Bert's temperament, and the fact that we had a solid defense that could hold the other team and give us back the ball. When we had the opportunity to make a big play and score, we could take it, rather than forcing the issue. A good strategist, Marchibroda knows people. I'm surprised he's coaching for Irsay in Indianapolis.

So it's 1975, Ted's first year, and we're playing an exhibition game in Denver, and I'm viewing it as a competition between Bert Jones and me for the starting quarterback job. Bert's playing a tentative game, which is a retrogression for him. Late in the game, I'm standing on the sideline next to Marchibroda, and I hear him saying to Jones, "Listen, Bert, don't worry about anything. Just play. You're my man, and you're going to be the man I win or lose with."

The impact of those words at that moment was dramatic on my psyche. You think you're competing for the same job and you realize you are overhearing—not even being told directly—the fact that you're not going to be the starter. For me, it created a very poignant emotional reaction. I remember it as if it was yesterday.

After a 1 and 4 start, we won nine in a row, and I was clearly the backup to Bert. Bert was a great talent, a good leader. He was responsible for making the team better. We had a very solid, tough offensive line, and the defense was a good group. Bert took them as far as they could go. It just was not as good a team as the Pittsburgh Steelers in those days.

The process of gelling into a solid team that was capable of winning became evident in a game at Miami. We were down, 17–3, and ran to a 33–17 victory. The contrast with the '74 team was clear in another way.

The year before, at a game in Washington, I remember our guys watching Roy Jefferson and Charlie Taylor and Bill Kilmer and the other Redskins warming up on the field. I said to myself, "Look at Kilmer throw the ball—end over end." Watching our players checking these guys out, my impression was that they were kind of in awe, like it's a privilege just to be on the same field with them.

A year later, as things were snowballing and we began winning each week, the braggadocio that was manifested in the locker room and other places had completely overcome that mentality. Now we went out with the attitude that people should be watching us warming up. The swagger was on our side of the field, and that element of confidence in sports—individual or team—is so important.

Preparing for the playoff game against Pittsburgh, I played the part of Terry Bradshaw running their pass patterns at half speed in practice all week. On the day of the game I wasn't ready to play, but Bert got hurt in the first quarter. Now it's my turn to play. I didn't do well. I threw one pass to Roger Carr that Mel Blount picked off. Then Andy Russell recovered a fumble and ran it back 95 yards.

On the bus going home, I apologized to Marchibroda. "Coach, I wasn't ready to play. It'll never happen again."

It didn't. I was traded to San Francisco.

I learned a lesson in life when I was traded: don't burn bridges. I was in training camp at Goucher when they called me off the field and told me the news. I went into the office and slammed the door and told Joe Thomas, "Now the team's competitive and I'm getting traded when I have a chance to be on a winning team."

Joe said, "I didn't have anything to do with it. It was the owner."

I went out screaming and swearing. Later Thomas was fired, and he wound up with the 49ers, and wanted me to take a significant pay cut out there.

Although I had a bad experience with him, I would say that Joe Thomas was a legitimately nice human being. I wouldn't say that for the owner of the Colts at the time. I've heard conflicting reports about Joe's abilities, but if you judge him by the players he drafted in Baltimore, he must have had an eye for talent. I've heard stories that contradict that, but I think he was a knowledgeable guy.

I was a backup to Jim Plunkett in San Francisco one season, then played my last year with the Jets in 1977. Jim Plunkett got killed in New England, played two years in San Francisco, then went to the Oakland Raiders, absolutely shot psychologically, and got a second life. He was not a graceful athlete, did not have a great arm, but he was smart, and when he got a chance to play with a good team whose abilities were greater than his own, he could take advantage of their abilities and match up the plays. He wound up MVP in the Super Bowl.

I know I could probably go out now and throw the ball better than I did in my last year in pro football, because at that time I was so self-conscious and lacking in confidence. That's why I admire Earl Morrall. I asked him once, "How did you keep your confidence all those years of moving around?"

He said, "I had a few bad stops, but then I got sent to good places like Baltimore and Miami, where I had good teams, and all I had to do was what I was capable of."

In 1981, after my career was over and I was a stockbroker for Alex Brown, I watched Bert Jones in his last year in Baltimore. If you remember that season, you knew he didn't want to be part of the Colts anymore. Watching his mannerisms on the field, you could see that he was unhappy.

I went over to his house and asked him if I could talk to him for a few minutes. I said, "Bert, you know you're not going to be here after this season. But it's one thing for you to leave people with a bad taste in their mouth here. Besides that, you don't know what the impact is on your teammates. It's obvious to everyone that you're not happy. If you are not 'up' relative to how you conduct yourself during the game, it's a bad reflection on you, not just as a leader of the team, but to the fans as a sportsman.

"I'm telling you this because it's important to you. Just get through the season and don't manifest the disappointment that you have, or your feeling of being cheated by being part of the organization here in Baltimore. Do your best to get through the season."

I don't know how much impact it had on him, compared to the impact it had on me when I overheard Ted Marchibroda telling Bert he was going to be the quarterback. But I could see how he had gone full circle; his confidence was no longer what it had been.

Bert was a terrific quarterback. But there were fans in Baltimore who liked him and those who didn't. Everybody thinks John Unitas is the greatest quarterback ever, and everybody else is measured against him.

Looking at some other quarterbacks, Bart Starr didn't have the physical presence that Unitas had on the field, but he did the right things and made few mistakes.

Marty Domres. Photograph by Vince Bagli

Terry Bradshaw had unbelievable physical abilities. Had a great arm. After his third season in the league, they were saying he was not smart enough to play quarterback in the NFL. He was obviously smart enough.

Dan Marino doesn't have Bradshaw's legs, but he's got the arm and sense. He's a fierce competitor.

Then there's Joe Montana, who took his teams to four Super Bowls, making big plays. He flawlessly orchestrated those offenses. It's a tribute to his greatness that he could go to the Kansas City Chiefs with the limited skills he had at that point in his career, and have such command of the offense that he could get so much out of them and himself.

Which one of them is the best? It would be unfair to say. No one is clearly better than the others.

The most telling aspect of the continuing 49ers' success is that they have such a solid environment to play in. Most of them probably think that they can walk on water. They believe that they are champions and they play like it. That's the household, family feeling that they are part of.

On top of that, they have as good an offensive team as any ever put together. When they match up against defenses that can't physically dominate them, they make it look easy, as they did in the Super Bowl. It isn't that easy, but when you have that exceptional talent, and everybody knows his role, their execution percentage is unbelievable.

Their defense is not that super. If you could put the Steelers' defense of the '70s with the 49ers' offense, I don't think any team could ever beat them.

I stayed in the NFL for nine years under eleven head coaches. In retrospect, I wouldn't say I played for nine years. I reflect on that time more now than I did then, because when I go out and play golf, and it's the eighteenth hole and the adrenaline's running and I'm excited about winning $2, and you have to make that clutch shot, and you do it and win, it makes you feel terrific.

The thing I feel bad about is that when I played professional football, I don't think I ever had a chance to be in charge and have my own set of circumstances to operate, where a coach said to me, "It's your team. Here's how we're going to run the show. You've got these abilities, we've got these players, and we're going to put this thing together."

From a player's standpoint, if you get in the right circumstances, you have a lot more chance to succeed than if you are in a constant state of flux, not knowing which end is up. That can work on you over a period of time.

I didn't have a five- or a ten-year career with the same head coach in the same environment, and have that same satisfaction of walking off the field and feeling good, the way I can playing golf today.

Photograph by Bob Miller

Bruce Laird

Born: 5-23-50
Lowell, Massachusetts
American International
Defensive Back

6′ 1″, 198 lbs.
Drafted: #6, 1972
Colts: 1972–1981

"I played the same aggressive, intense, hard-hitting football when I was thirty-six that I did when I was twenty-one. Stan White says that's why I'm all beat up now, because I played like an animal."

I was a Big Man on Campus from a real small school. American International University had 1,800 students. We played Division II football. The biggest crowd I ever played before was 10,000, when we played Springfield in my senior year, 1971. I had a great day, over 260 yards rushing, scored all three touchdowns in a 21–7 win.

We played Amherst every year and never beat them. They had three guys who made the pros. One of them was Jean Fugett, a tight end and wide receiver for the Cowboys and Redskins. He caught fourteen balls against us one day.

I weighed only 180, and didn't have blazing speed. I started out as a monster back, the strong side safety playing opposite the tight end. The next year I played both ways, because we had a tailback who could run, but we didn't have a fullback who could block for him and get out of his way. They just couldn't get to the hole fast enough. So they tried me as a dummy to get in people's way.

Milt Piepul, who played for the Detroit Lions in 1941, was my coach in my senior year. He had the biggest hands I've ever seen. He told me, "No more defense for you. I'm going to teach you how to run the ball and make you a tailback."

So I did a lot of things in college. But I never thought I was going to get even a sniff at the NFL, even though our PR guy, Mike Tragisi, got me a mention in the Boston *Globe* almost every week. Then he got me a chance to play in the North-South Shrine Game in the Orange Bowl in Miami, in front of a lot of scouts. It was the biggest crowd I ever saw, and playing with guys from all those big schools—Notre Dame, Ohio State, Iowa —all those teams I had seen on TV like everybody else, I was scared to death.

But while I was there I realized for the first time that it didn't matter where you played. Some athletes can do it and some can't. After that week, I felt better about my chances of being drafted.

Bruce Laird (40), aggressive defender, good return man. Photograph © 1995 TADDER/Baltimore

I was the Colts' sixth pick in 1972. Because of my size and lack of speed, I thought I would have to fit into a defensive scheme as a back. Being a monster back helped me. I knew how to hit people and was very aggressive.

I started out as a safety, although Jerry Logan and Rick Volk were safeties. They had been around a long time and were very knowledgeable. I had to do well to make the club, because I was the kind of athlete they didn't know what to do with, where to use me. Tom Matte convinced coach McCafferty that he had to do something with me.

Joe Thomas switched me to left cornerback, because he didn't like Charlie Stukes at that position. Charlie wouldn't hit people. I played two games, made one interception, hit some people, came up to support the run, and recovered a couple of fumbles. So Joe starts thinking, "Ah, the next Roger Wehrli." [Wehrli was an outstanding defensive back for the St. Louis Cardinals at the time.]

And in the last pre-season game, McCafferty put me in to return kickoffs. I was scared to death the first time. My main concern was just to catch the ball, then try to find a peripheral lane somewhere, make my one move, and hit it. I didn't have the great speed where I could do a lot of right and left kind of stuff. I had to go north and south, and then I had to be able to get up enough speed and make the cut at full speed and find a lane. If it was crowded, I jumped and spun over it.

So in 1973 I was returning kickoffs and punts, and playing cornerback. As I progressed on kick returns, I began to catch the ball on the run. You see players today—they're back there on their back foot when the ball comes down. I never did that. I had taken two or three steps forward when I got the ball, then got into a full speed mode, found the angle, and went for it. I think that was the key to my success. I had a lot of 40- or 50-yard returns. I also left my feet a lot. If guys wanted to throw real low at me, I'd try to hurdle over the piles of people.

But we had no pass rush, and I was not really a cornerback. Then I twisted my knee and they had to sit me down. I just couldn't go any more. It was a combination of a bad leg, and the fact that the corner was not my spot in life. I really got smoked.

I became a defensive back, but I had to learn to read my keys and understand what these NFL schemes were all about. I didn't have any of that knowledge; I had to be taught.

Fortunately for me, Maxie Baughan came along with Ted Marchibroda in 1975. Maxie Baughan is one of the greatest all-time persons I ever met. I was surprised he never got a head coaching job. He taught me how to be a football player. Years later, we were all together for a reunion, and I went up to him and hugged him and told him how much I appreciated the tutelage he gave me.

Baughan taught me to read and understand what an offense was doing to you. You know how all of a sudden a big light comes on in your head? In my second year under Maxie, that light went slowly from a

50-watt bulb to a 75 to a 150. Then during a stretch of six straight years where I didn't miss a game, I had a big 250-watt bulb in there. I saw the whole picture all the time. I never would have had that unless he had given me the tools.

Marchibroda and Baughan were products of the George Allen system, which I believe in. To me, Allen was a defensive genius. Forget Buddy Ryan and all that stuff. Allen started what you see now in modern football. Under his philosophy, you start your team with, number one, your quarterback; then number two your defensive line; third your cornerbacks; then your offensive line. I think maybe the offensive line belongs higher than that, otherwise I agree with George.

You win championships with defense, although your number-one player has got to be the quarterback. He's the pitcher, your Jim Palmer. Then you get a powerful defensive line and two great cornerbacks. You can build your defense with six players, and everybody else can fit in.

Offensively, you need your line and one great wide receiver. The running game is important, but it is really part of that offensive line, as O.J. Simpson found out. One of the greatest backs in football history, he didn't do anything for two years, because he had no offensive line.

Ted Marchibroda brought us together as a football team in 1975. He carried the philosophy that talks about making it to the playoffs from the first day of training camp, then winning those games and making it to the Super Bowl. He told us, "This is the way you win football games." I loved that about Ted.

We had been together for a few years, a group of young players behind the arm and leadership of Bert Jones. We won the opener in Chicago, then lost four in a row, then won nine in a row.

The day we turned it around in Buffalo on November 9, the sun was shining, and it was the most beautiful day I ever saw in that city. But in the first half, O.J. went for about 170 and we were down, 28–7.

At half-time Teddy got us all together and said, "Guys, we're going to win this football game. Defense, do what you have to do. Shut down their running game."

We went out, got the ball, scored. Three and out for them. We scored again. All of a sudden, we're rolling, doing all we can. We end up winning, 42–35, and never looked back. It was a coming together; we realized collectively that all forty-seven of us together can win.

To me, Bert Jones was the pinnacle of a quarterback. My rookie year was John Unitas's last in Baltimore. Unfortunately for Bert, he had to follow John, whose aura was always there. I heard stories from guys who played with Unitas. In the huddle he was The Man. You did something wrong, you got cursed out when you got back in the huddle. But John blasted people only in the huddle. He was never as flamboyant outside of it.

Bert had a different personality. He was always yelling, screaming, getting mad and showing his emotions outside the huddle. People said,

"Aw, he's a crybaby." But he was just fiery about the game, took it personally that he was going to go out there and win games. He was outspoken, flamboyant, and openly emotional. He also had an arm that was as good as any, and a mentality like a defensive football player.

On our offensive line, Robert Pratt, Kenny Huff, and Elmer Collett were three fine athletes.

Stan White was the defensive captain of the Sack Pack. He was our leader, but he was not the emotional leader. The emotional leaders were John Dutton and me. Between our two mouths out there, nothing else had to be said. It got wild sometimes during those five years we played together. Stan had to referee more than he had to call defenses.

On the defensive line, Joe Ehrmann at inside left tackle played the most physical game. He was the nose-up kind of guy, swinging, biting, scratching, kicking. Mike Barnes was extremely quick off the ball. He had the Randy White type quickness; Joe had the White muscle. Freddie Cook played finesse.

Don McCauley was my best friend on the Colts. There's no finer person, no finer football player. The word "class" is Don McCauley.

Don McCauley. Photograph by Vince Bagli

Marty Domres was a great prankster. In 1975 we picked up Howie "Mighty Mite" Stevens in a trade with New Orleans. Howie was only 5-foot-5, a little halfback. Right after the trade, we're all sitting on the ground getting ready to do calisthenics, and Marty stands up in front, puts his helmet on the ground, and says, "Quiet, everybody. I have an announcement. I'd like you to meet Howard Stevens."

He points down to his helmet on the ground and says, "Howie, meet the guys."

Everybody's rolling around laughing and Stevens comes strutting out. Marty says, "Wait a minute. He's a little bigger than I thought he was."

We also had good trainers. The all-world Eddie Block, Mike O'Shea, and John Lopez and Dave Berringer, and all the young assistants; they were wonderful. They knew everybody's nuances. I know they kept me healthy for a long time.

We had the team in '77 and should have gone all the way. We were committed. We lost one game in Denver because we just didn't do the job. Their quarterback, Craig Morton, was immobile, and we had the pass rush. They weren't going to do anything against us offensively. We held them to less than 200 yards. But they had a pretty good defense at the time, and we just couldn't put it together.

Bert threw a pick [interception] to Tom Jackson early in the game and we never came back.

That double overtime championship game against Oakland in Memorial Stadium on Christmas Eve was one of my finest in a big game. I ran an interception back for six points. Marshall Johnson ran a kickoff back for six. Bert was moving the football, and we had the game plan to keep Oakland where we wanted them.

Then we lost Lyle Blackwood to an injury toward the end of the third period, and Timmy Baylor came in with not much experience. We were rotating our man-to-man coverages according to down and distance and formations, taking things away from them that they liked to do. Their quarterback, Ken Stabler, was adjusting, going to his second and third receivers.

The lead changed hands six times. We went ahead, 31–28, halfway through the fourth period. Then we gave the offense the ball two consecutive times with three and out, and they never gave us another first down. I'll never forget those last few minutes. I was standing next to John Dutton during the whole time we had the ball.

There are two trains of thought about what happened, the offense and defensive trains. Bert had been throwing the ball well up and down the field all day. We thought he should continue attacking, but it looked to us as if he had been told not to throw the football. Then, with twenty-six seconds left, Oakland kicked a 22-yard field goal to tie it. And forty-three seconds into the second overtime, Stabler threw a 12-yard touchdown pass to Dave Casper to beat us, 37–31.

Looking back at 1978, the team's concept and method of handling the injury to Bert Jones in the last pre-season game was not professional. Everything was handled from the point of view: "Let's not make mistakes. We're going to play, not to win, but not to lose." We weren't proactive about ourselves.

We had two young quarterbacks, Mike Kirkland and Bill Troup. Mike Kirkland started the first game in Dallas and we got killed, 38–0. He was totally over his head. But I felt the coaching staff took the wrong approach by not going with him and letting him make his mistakes. Instead of patting the kid on the back and telling him to "go out there and wing this thing all over the place. . . no pressure on you," Teddy told him, "Don't make mistakes. Let's try to be conservative."

That's baloney. You don't do that to a young quarterback. Troup started most of the games after that. They were both gone after that season.

A year later Ted Marchibroda was gone, too. Unfortunately, he didn't have a strong front office, and when Joe Thomas left, Ted and the players lost their buffer between them and Bob Irsay. Whether or not you cared for Joe, to me and the guys who came after me in the next four or five years, he was a football guy and we loved him. A straight shooter, he let you know where you stood with him. If you were a mealy-mouthed guy, going to play one week and take two or three weeks off, Joe Thomas didn't forgive.

When Marchibroda had to deal directly with the Irsay-Chernoff echelon, I don't think he was ready for that, and something was lost. Sure we knew Bob Irsay. He'd come into the locker room with his entourage after the games, and we'd let him hang out with us. Then he was supposed to go back to Chicago and leave Joe in control. Joe paid our checks; he was the man. Then all of a sudden we don't have Joe.

We thought Teddy would be strong enough to keep everything going, but it wasn't so. There was constant change and bickering as Irsay got more and more involved in football operations. We were seeing players not getting signed and moves happening, and tension was building that we had never had before. And Teddy didn't support us. I think he was in over his head. He was given the opportunity to step up to the forefront and become coach and general manager, and he didn't take it. He stayed as coach for one more year, and Dick Szymanski came in as general manager and keeper of the peace.

Mike McCormack replaced Marchibroda in 1980. He was a great player's coach, but you can't be fighting two battles, and he did not have any help from the front office.

McCormack was volatile. He could chuck some things. He'd come in at half-time and throw some garbage cans. After his half-time tirades, the offense would go their way, the defense their way. Maxie Baughan and I probably gave them more half-time entertainment than anybody. I'd yell and scream and get on them to step it up a notch, but real businesslike.

McCormack's greatest explosion came when we were watching a special teams reel after a loss. A lot of times after losses, the whole team would watch special teams films together. On this occasion, he was so mad he yelled, "This is what's wrong with this football team!" and hit the projector with his hand so hard, the whole thing just blew apart. Just disintegrated.

At the end of ten years under the Robert Irsay regime, I really wanted to leave. I saw what they did to Mike McCormack; then Frank Kush came in. I knew I had a lot of football ability left in me. I wanted to go somewhere and just play football and get away from all the garbage that was going on the way Irsay ran the club.

We had seven guys who had operations and needed to use the Jacuzzi, but Mike Chernoff, Irsay's V-P, said our budget for the off-season was too high, and they cut off the electricity. We got guys rehabing, we got this beautiful complex, we got this eight-man Jacuzzi, and we can't run it because we were spending too much money. It's little things, but it's stupid.

I went to San Diego, where Don Coryell was the coach and Dan Fouts was the quarterback. It was a great experience. I found what I had been missing since 1977, because I hadn't really been with a professional team since then. Our defense wasn't the greatest, but we were averaging 38 points a game. And I got hooked up with my all-time best friend in football, Tim Fox.

We had all hated Fox desperately on the Colts when he was a New England free safety, because he was a flamboyant, loudmouthed little son of a gun. He loved to grind you in the dirt, and laughed and had fun doing it. When we first met, we told each other what we thought of each other. Then we decided to room together, and we spent the next two years playing together. When you're on the same side, you admire a guy like Fox for being a great competitor. After all, Lyle Blackwood was the same kind of player for the Colts.

The most punishing runner for me to defend against has got to be Earl Campbell. Earl loved to run the football. He had great speed, and his thighs seemed to grow as he came closer to you. The only time I ever closed my eyes at the point of impact was when I had to tackle Campbell. When he got out in the open with his great speed and moves, you had to take down and get in position to wrap him up or you would miss him, and you knew you were going to take a beating.

One time Houston was playing at Memorial Stadium, and Maxie Baughan and Stan White came up with a way to stop Campbell. We went to an eight-man front; they moved me up late in the cadence into a linebacker's position. I must have had twenty-five tackles that day—I don't know how many solos on Earl—but I couldn't walk until the following Thursday. I was totally beat up, between hitting the fullback and hitting Campbell all day long.

John Riggins was the same kind of back, not as quick, but he was 4.6 for the 40-yard dash. He weighed 240 and loved to run over you. Dropped his shoulder like Walter Payton. In that situation, where it's hit or be hit, they want to be the one to deliver the blow.

Without a doubt, John Hannah was the toughest pulling guard for me. He was 6-foot-1, weighed 275, built like a tank. The only way to deal with big people is by leverage, and I could never get the leverage on John. I not only took on the interference, but I tried to make the tackle, too. The best I could do with Hannah was to meet him and stay in the same place and not get knocked on my tail.

Early in my career, Joe Namath was the best quarterback, best at reading defenses and picking up blitzes. The term you use to disguise what you're doing on defense is "window dressing." We were just learning our system, and sometimes it was very difficult to fool Joe with our window dressing.

Later on I had a lot of respect for Terry Bradshaw of the Steelers. He was a winner, like Bert Jones. He got a bad rap about not being intelligent. That's a bunch of baloney. He trusted his arm more than he trusted what he was reading. I could see that, but he got away with it. Did he throw the ball into double coverage? Sure. Did they come up with some plays for him? They sure did.

Bruce Laird. Photograph by Vince Bagli

The biggest thrill I ever had in football was not in the NFL. It was playing for George Allen and the Arizona Wranglers in the United States Football League in 1984. We played Jim Kelly and Houston for the chance to go to the championship game. Kelly used the run and shoot offense, and was averaging over 38 points a game. We beat them, 13–9.

I'm glad I had a chance to play for Allen. What George Halas was to the 1950s and 1960s, George Allen was to the 1970s and 1980s. A great mind, a great gentleman to play for, he was absolutely without a doubt the best I ever played for.

I played till I was thirty-six years old, over 240 football games. I got everything out of myself that I possibly could. Never had a regret that I left anything on the football field. I played the same aggressive, intense, hard-hitting football when I was thirty-six that I did when I was twenty-one. Stan White says that's why I'm all beat up now, because I played like an animal. But that's how I loved to play. When a guard was coming by who was in my way, I was going to destroy him and make the play.

I still watch some films of me taking on guards and tackles and knocking them on their asses, and 2 yards down, making the spin and making the play on the running back.

I still have football dreams occasionally. They don't come as often as they once did. They bring back pleasant moments, being with the guys, not necessarily on the field. You miss the camaraderie more than the game.

Let me tell you something. I'll never forget what it was like playing in Baltimore. We had this town in the palm of our hands. We were winning. It probably wasn't the football everybody wanted to see, but it was winning football that hadn't been seen in Baltimore for a while.

We had a great mixture of black and white players. We'd have our Halloween parties and everybody was there. We'd go out for our Friday afternoon beer things, fifteen or twenty guys together. We were all young and single, a great bunch of fun-loving guys having a good time. And we gave a lot of ourselves back to the community. We were all over the place. Joe Ehrmann and his crew were big in Fells Point. I and some of the others were big around Towson, Parkville, Pikesville, that whole area. We were rolling as a football team and as a group of guys. We loved it.

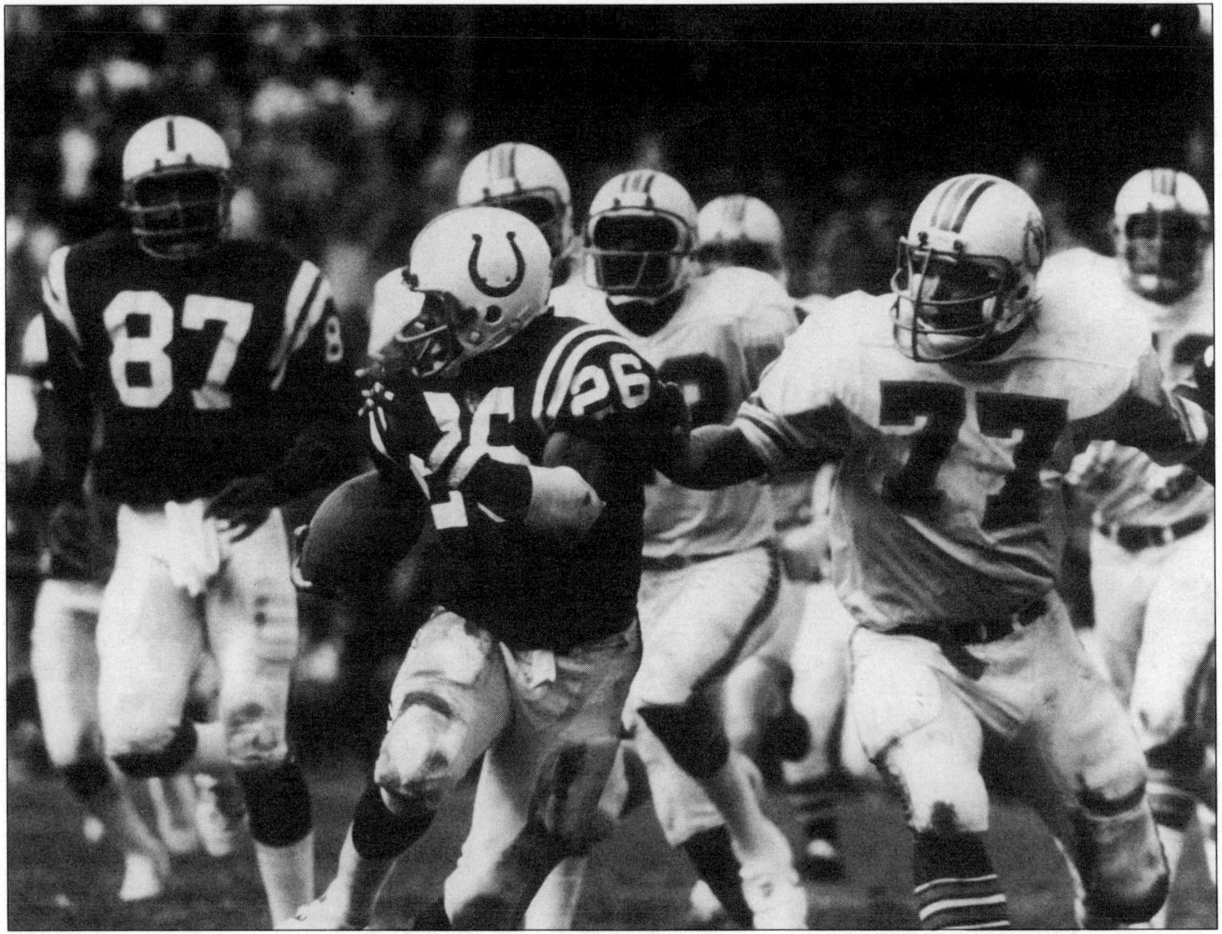

Lydell Mitchell, always among the total yardage leaders. Photograph © 1995 TADDER/Baltimore

LYDELL MITCHELL

Born: 5-30-49
Salem, New Jersey
Penn State
Halfback

5′ 11″, 195 lbs.
Drafted: #2, 1972
Colts: 1972–1977

"I always envisioned myself playing in Baltimore forever, being part of those alumni groups that came back."

Everything I ever knew about football was taught to me by my high school coach, Sam Venuto, who played for Washington in 1952. When I got to college and pro ball, I didn't learn anything that he hadn't shown me. All I needed was experience.

My top three choices of colleges were the University of Maryland, because a girl I knew lived in Washington and I wanted to be close to her; Ohio State, because my grandparents lived in Columbus and I had spent my summers with them when I was a kid, and I was going to be an All-American and have a buckeye tree planted for me, like they do for their All-Americans; and Penn State, my third choice.

Then the day before you had to sign your intent to go somewhere, Penn State coach Joe Paterno walked into the guidance office at my school and asked to speak to me. They called me down there, and we started talking about signing, and I said, "I made up my mind. I'm going to Ohio State."

When Joe got nervous, he started to sweat. He put his head down, then looked up at me and said, "You're afraid to go to Penn State because we have Charlie Pittman there, and you don't think you can play."

I'll say this for him: he knew which button to push.

I looked him in the eye and said, "You know what? I'm coming to Penn State. I'm going to break all of Charlie Pittman's records."

And I did. That was my sole reason for going there.

To this day, I probably owe my philosophy of life to Joe Paterno. We went into college as kids and came out as men, and we did it through discipline. Joe was tough on people; he didn't believe in giving you many chances. My job as a running back was to score touchdowns. If you were a defensive player, it was to stop runs and get sacks. I had played against Franco Harris in high school, and we both went to Penn State. That began a long bond between us that continues to this day. Franco never really wanted to play football. Even in college, his mindset was always to get into business. But he is one of the few people who showed up in every big game. He was one of the best money players I've ever seen. A lot of running backs have good careers, but what happened to them in the crunch time? They dropped a pass or fumbled the ball in crucial situations. Sometimes in football they measure a guy by the yardstick instead of by his ability and what's inside of him. Franco always came through. I think that measures a player more than anything.

In his senior year, Franco got hurt, and it gave me an opportunity to carry the ball more. I scored 29 touchdowns that year, and had the best year of anybody. I probably should have won the Heisman Trophy, but Ed Marinaro [Cornell] and I split the eastern votes, and Pat Sullivan [Auburn] won it. I finished fifth.

To this day, the most significant thing I remember about Baltimore was as a rookie in 1972, when the alumni came back and the guys ran out through the goal posts to the middle of the field. That was exciting to me. When I saw that, I said, "Man, I hope I have a long career here, and do that." Already I'm thinking about retiring years from then and coming back and being a part of that.

I was disappointed that I didn't start my first year. I thought I should have been playing. I think politics influenced who made the team. I had heard that in the past Baltimore didn't want that many black running backs. Charlie Pittman was here in 1971 and didn't make it. Pittman was better than Don Nottingham or Tom Nowatzke. Don McCauley, the Colts' number one draft pick in 1971, was an in-betweener, too small to be a fullback, and not quick or fast enough to be a halfback. John Cappelletti of the Rams was the same type.

And they had some old guys around. I think back then the Colts had been a cliquish type team, which happens when you have guys who have been around and played on a championship team. Unfortunately, the reason a lot of teams go down is that they allow the team to get old. It's tough to tell a guy he can't play anymore, especially when he's been an integral part of the team. That's what I found myself when I first came here.

Coming out of the College All-Star game and a great year in college, you expect to play and contribute. You try to assess the players you are competing against—Matte and Nowatzke and Bulaich and Nottingham and McCauley. I looked at them and I thought I was the better player.

When you have a situation like that and you have an older team, you just kind of go with the flow and say, "Everything's going to be all right. These guys will take the pill the next day and get ready to play the game and there will always be magic." But it's not like that.

I'd rather have a young player who comes from a sound background than an older player with experience who used to be good.

I started one preseason game, against Kansas City, and we won. John Unitas said to me, "Hey, you can play; you're pretty good." But after that I didn't play anymore, and I think the reason was that they didn't want to put pressure on anybody.

So one day coach McCafferty called me in and told me he was putting me on the taxi squad. We didn't have a heated argument, but I did tell him that I thought he was wrong, and I should be playing. Maybe that sounds brash coming from a rookie, but it was to no avail. Then he got fired after five games, and the new coach, John Sandusky, played me. I averaged 4.8 yards on 45 carries and caught 18 passes. It bothered McCauley when they benched him and played me, because they all want to play.

At the Colts' year-end party, McCafferty said to me, "You can play."

I said, "I told you I could."

That's always been the kind of cockiness I've had about my ability. I don't think it's being overconfident. It's just that you go out and work hard and give 100 percent and try to produce, and let things fall where they may.

I hated practice, but I guarantee you I practiced as well as anybody on the team, because I believe you play the way you practice. I looked at practice as going to work every day, and football as a job. If I never had a bad game, it was because of the way I practiced. Nobody else did it my way. A lot of guys get the ball, they run 5 yards and stop. That's not practice to me. I'd run 40 yards during a play, and turn around and jog back. We kept continuously running plays, and I'd do this on every play to build up my endurance. I wanted it to be like a game. It took discipline. I wanted to be one of the best at doing what I was doing. So I was serious and worked hard at it. If you do nothing all week, when it comes game time you're not going to be able to be as successful as you should be.

At Penn State we had been sure of ourselves. We knew we could win. Sometimes you get with a team where you say, "I think we can win." With the Colts, we were at the point where we knew we couldn't win.

We were just not a good team in 1972, '73, and '74. When you have a bad team, you can be competitive with a great team for the first part of a game, then all of a sudden everything starts going downhill, even though you go out there and give 100 percent. We all wanted to be a winning team, but we were a laughingstock. We did fairly well in practice, but we were short a few players we needed to make the difference.

Then Ted Marchibroda came in in 1975 and we turned it around. We always said the reason was that Joe Thomas took our beer away after games, saying, "If you guys win, you can have beer." We always laughed about it; when we won the championship, first thing the guys wanted was their beer back.

We opened the season in Chicago. It was Walter Payton's debut and he was getting all the publicity. That fired up our defense and we won. That got some people talking about how the Bears had made a mistake, drafting him number one from a small school, Jackson State. How wrong they were.

We lost our next four games, then won nine in a row. After the Buffalo win, we didn't really know how good we were. We just kept getting better and having fun.

We went to Miami for a key game on November 23. We had never beaten the Dolphins in the Orange Bowl. We were down, 14–2, in the second quarter when Jones aggravated a rib injury and had to come out. At one time during the season Marchibroda had made a statement that we couldn't win without Bert. I thought that even if he felt that way, don't say it. But Marty Domres came in and did a great job, and we won, 33–17. In one stretch, we ran the exact same play seven times in a row from different formations: the I, the T, split backs, one back, man in motion—all kinds of things. Bert didn't have the ability to do that.

We ran into the Steelers in the AFC playoff. They took us a little lightly during the first half, and maybe we played over our heads, but the second half was men against boys. They were the most dominating team I ever saw, especially on defense. They didn't need much offense; as long as they didn't make any mistakes, they could lean on the defense. Not that they didn't have an offense. With Swann, Stallworth, Bleier, Bradshaw, and Harris, they had all the firepower. They didn't use half of it because they didn't have to. Their defense was great because they were all great athletes. Jack Ham, Ernie Holmes, L.C. Greenwood, Andy Russell—they could play other sports as well.

Even though my first year with the Colts was John Unitas's last, I think he was the greatest quarterback who ever played football. People say Joe Montana is, but you have to remember the rules have changed. When we played, defenses played a lot of man to man. It was bump and run all over the field. Now a guy gets 5 yards upfield and you can't touch him. It's easy to catch a football when a defender can't put his hands on you.

Bert Jones had the greatest arm in football when it came to throwing the ball. He could beat you with every down. If you took the jersey off John Elway and put him in the same uniform as Bert, you couldn't tell them apart. They both threw very hard.

In every great athlete you always have a weakness—except Michael Jordan—and in Bert's case it would be that he couldn't throw the long ball because he never put any air under it. Everything was like a line drive. It was awful hard sometimes to catch up with a ball thrown like that. But if you were down in a game, you knew that every single time you came up to the line of scrimmage, you had an opportunity to win the game because of his great arm.

I caught a record 13 straight passes the day Bert threw 17 in a row. It was fun because Bert could call his own plays. He would say to me, "Worm, what do you have?" Raymond Chester pinned that nickname on me. "Where do you want to run?" he'd ask me, or "How's your man playing? What can you run on him?"

I appreciated that rapport we had; we appreciated each other's abilities. I was one of the first backs to start catching passes out of the backfield. We never really planned it; it just happened by accident. We did it a few times and it worked. I hadn't caught more than 16 or 17 passes my whole time at Penn State. Our approach was: if the linebackers backed off, then we threw to the backs. If the linebackers came up, that would open things up for the wide receivers.

Roger Carr and I helped each other. He was on one side and I was on the other. When I drew attention, it helped him.

To me, everything was cliquish on the Colts at that time. There was some black-white hanging out together, but I never hung out with the guys.

We had two backs, Roosevelt Leaks and me. Leaks was the blocking back for me on most of my runs. Leaks rarely ran the ball, but once when he did, I took the day off [on that play]. Of course, the defensive guy made the play on him. We were watching the game film and a coach, Whitey Dovell, sitting next to me, saw it was obvious I didn't feel like blocking on that play. He says to me quietly, "Hey, that's the guy that takes care of you. You should try to help him, too."

From that day on, I made sure I tried to block and help him.

My greatest thrill was being able to break Lenny Moore's rushing record for the Colts. Our relationship was so good, I felt that he wanted me to break it, although he never said it. I never got to see him play except on film, and I know how great a player he was. If I could be recognized in the same breath with a player as great as he was, that is a real thrill.

I was not considered fast, couldn't outrun O.J. or Tony Dorsett in a race. My best time for the 40 on grass was 4.6 seconds, which is not bad. I had a running style I didn't realize until George Young said to me, "If you ran in a straight line, you'd probably be able to run the 40 faster." My running style was side to side. I was running 44 yards when I ran the 40-yard dash. But he told me, "Don't change."

That's why nobody hit me solid in a game. Whenever I ran toward people, it was never in a straight line. So no one ever got a clean shot on me. Just at impact I was able to turn a little bit away from the hit, like a boxer rolling with the punch. It looked as if I got hit significantly, but I didn't. I guess it had something to do with vision, too. Whatever it was, it was a God-given gift.

But that doesn't mean I didn't get some hard hits. The hardest I remember was on a third and short play. I dove over the pile and Jack Tatum dove at me and we met in midair. It was like hitting a rock. My knees buckled, and I felt like I went partially blind for a minute. I stumbled back to the huddle.

I think Tatum's been knocked as a dirty player, but I thought he played clean. He just hit hard. When Tatum hit Darryl Stingley, who became paralyzed, that was a clean hit. I always defend it as a good hit, and it was.

Willie Lanier was another guy who, when he hit you, you felt it through your whole body. He was a stocky guy, and he had a big extra piece to his helmet to prevent concussions. It must have weighed 40 pounds. When he put that hat on you, man, you were woozy.

Most offensive players are passive. They try to avoid the hits. Walter Payton was aggressive. He played like he was playing defense. Jim Brown, too. Brown was the best running back I've ever seen. Watching him on TV when I was a kid made me want to play pro football.

In our era, O.J. Simpson was the best running back. Big heart. Time and time again he'd get hit and get up and do his thing. But he never blocked, because he was never called on to block, and he didn't catch the ball that much.

It's unfortunate sometimes that players are one-dimensional. It's the difference between being a football player and being an athlete. Charlie Pittman was a football player. I've seen him play basketball; he stinks. Other guys were football players, not athletes in the sense of playing other sports.

Barry Sanders is the best runner today, but Emmett Smith is the best all-around back.

I led the NFL in receptions in 1974, and the AFC in '75, and finished second to O.J. in rushing in '76.

I'll never forget what the general manager, Dick Szymanski, said to me in training camp in 1977. I never liked to work out during the off-season. I stretched a lot and stayed loose, but I never had a good preseason, because I was working myself into shape and it didn't mean anything.

I was having my usual lousy preseason, when Szymanski said to me, "You know your contract's up next year. You got to get going."

I looked at him. "Hey, man, it's only preseason," I said.

I led the NFL in receptions that year, and finished a close third in rushing, behind Mark van Eeghen and Franco Harris, with 1,159 yards. I was twenty-nine.

After the season, I heard nothing from the Colts. My attorney, Lee Goldberg, called them and said, "Let's sit down and talk about a new contract."

They never called him back. June rolled around and I got the standard registered letter that they have to send you to keep you from becoming a free agent. They were extending my contract with a 10 percent raise. That's all I hear from them.

Szymanski came from the old school; you didn't make much money. Everybody talks about how tough Harry Hulmes had been to negotiate with when he ran the club for Rosenbloom. Dick was the same type. He could never deal with the modern players.

Preseason came and we still hadn't negotiated. I wouldn't go to camp without a contract, so we finally had a meeting. We're sitting there with Mr. Irsay and Mike Chernoff (often referred to as Irsay's "Hatchet Man") and Ernie Accorsi, and it's so ironic. Dick says, "Isn't it wonderful. Walter Payton just signed a new contract today." He didn't say for how much, but I wasn't asking for as much as Walter got, although I'd had a better year than he did.

Lydell Mitchell.
Photograph by Vince Bagli

I said, "You know, it's really sad. Do you think Walter Payton's worth two times what I'm asking for?"

I went on and on, and we broke for lunch, and when we came back, Ernie Accorsi was sitting on the floor in the hallway. Ernie and I go back all the way to Penn State. He shook his head and said, "Lydell, I told them not to do this to you."

We went back in and Mr. Irsay said, "I'll tell you what we'll do. We're going to pay you $250,000; $300,000; and $350,000 for the next three years."

I hadn't asked for that much, so I said, "What's the catch?"

"The catch is that you play out your option."

I had been making $99,000, so that meant I would get a 10 percent raise, then they could drop me if they wanted to at the end of the year. They would be getting me for $109,000 instead of $250,000 that year, then they could release me and let me move on.

I sat there. Finally I said, "You know, this is crazy. It's unacceptable. Maybe I should just move on somewhere else."

Dick said to me, "What are you worried about? You're the highest-paid black on the team."

I said, "I guess we don't have anything more to talk about."

It was over in five minutes.

Later I took him before the board of owners for saying what he did. He claimed he had said "back," not "black," but he didn't. Bert Jones was the highest-paid back, and I was second. Dick was always cracking his black-and-white jokes; he thought they were funny. I told him I didn't think it was funny. Why did he do it? You have to consider the era in which people grew up.

The next day I got a phone call from Irsay: everything's worked out. Come into training camp and we'll have a new contract. Lee Goldberg and I and Calvin Hill, who is also Lee's client, are in Washington that night, and we go out to a Chinese restaurant to celebrate. I'll never forget it. After dinner I opened a fortune cookie and it said, "A change in venue is best for you." Sometimes those fortune cookies are right.

I got back to my room and got a phone call from Irsay. He changed his mind. No contract. The next day I was traded to San Diego.

It hurt. It hurt so much when I couldn't get a contract. I had given my guts on the field. I didn't want to leave. I had always envisioned myself playing in Baltimore forever, being part of those alumni groups that came back. I was comfortable here, an integral part of the team and the community, and all of a sudden you're somewhere else and have to change all your ways. It's tough.

That's what happened to me. Some people say you have to move on, but I've never forgotten to this day, and it bothers me. It didn't turn me against Baltimore. The people had nothing to do with it. I don't even look on Bob Irsay as a bad person. They just started letting a lot of players go because of money. It was ridiculous.

At one time I thought I had a chance to go to the Hall of Fame, although Chuck Foreman from Minnesota told me we probably wouldn't get in because we didn't specialize in one thing. We did it all; we ran, caught passes, and blocked. But when you get disrupted, and they take your spirit from you—and that's what they did to me—it throws you off track. I got more money in San Diego than I asked for in Baltimore, and I had a couple good years there, but I wasn't happy. I played with my mind and body there, but my soul wasn't really into playing where I was.

Tommy Prothro was the coach; then he got fired and Don Coryell came along. He was a fiery guy who battled down the line for his players. But I thought the practices were too demanding, and there were too many meetings. We'd get there sometimes at 7:00 A.M. and get home at five or six in the evening.

They had Dan Fouts at quarterback and he threw a lot, but I didn't get many catches. Once I went in to talk to Coryell about it. He looked at you with those piercing eyes—it wasn't easy to look him in the eye. I said, "Coach, I'd like to run the ball more."

He said, "You don't run the ball that much. But you're healthier, aren't you?"

I had to admit that I was. I got the point, and didn't pursue it anymore.

I was at San Diego two years, then played a little with the Rams in 1980. The day I got released, Franco Harris was the first person who called. We had stayed in touch since our Penn State days in 1968. Franco cared. He's probably the most humble, down-to-earth person I've ever met. We operated the Extra Point Lounge on Monroe Street across from the Coliseum, and we're still in business together, manufacturing baking products for schools. The main office is in Pittsburgh. I concentrate on sales, looking to develop new markets and making sure we keep the business we have.

I don't like the showboating of the players today. I was taught that when you score a touchdown, you should act like you've been there before. You don't have to do all those dances and gyrations. Walk over to an official and hand him the ball. Don't even toss it to him; hand it to him. That's what we did, in college and in my professional career.

All these gyrations and the taunting is just acting. It's irresponsible. Kids who do it are undisciplined. Times have changed. If the coach hollers at a player today, they can get the coach fired.

Times change, coaches have to change, but I don't think values change.

Stan White

Born: 10-24-49
Dover, Ohio
Ohio State
Linebacker

6′ 1″, 225 lbs.
Drafted: #17, 1972
Colts: 1972–1979

"I was the Colts' seventeenth and last draft pick in 1972. . . It's a blow to the ego to be drafted so low. I was so depressed, I actually sat in the closet in my room."

I think I enjoyed my professional football experience more than college. I went to Ohio State as a three-sport all-state in high school, and tried to play all three at Ohio State. I wasn't really successful at any of them for the first two years.

I also got on the bad side of Woody Hayes from the start. I was a radical sort of non-conformist, but even worse, I was a kicker who missed a lot of extra points one year. I earned my way back into favor by leading the team in tackles in my junior year.

We went to the Rose Bowl one year and got beat by Jim Plunkett and Stanford. But one of my most vivid memories is the Ohio State-Michigan game in my junior year. We were both undefeated at that point. I intercepted a pass and ran it back inside the 10-yard line to set up the winning touchdown.

I was a 6-foot-1, 225-pound linebacker, which was a little small. I wasn't big, wasn't fast, wasn't strong, and had just average abilities. Still, when I became the Colts' seventeenth and last draft pick in 1972, it was a blow to the ego to be drafted so low. I was so depressed, I actually sat in the closet in my room. My girlfriend—now my wife—and a couple friends who had been drafted before me, came and pulled me out of the closet.

I joined Don Nottingham on the Colts. He had been their last draft pick the year before, from Kent State.

Don McCafferty was the coach, and he was the reason I was drafted at all. He had gone to Ohio State, and had coached at Kent State, and I was from Kent. The general manager who signed me was "the Duke," Don Klosterman. But by the time we got to training camp, Bob Irsay had bought the team, and Joe Thomas was in charge.

The team had trained in Westminster before then; now they were training in Tampa for the first time. Carroll Rosenbloom made that deal.

Stan White (53), durable, heady linebacker for thirteen pro seasons.
Photograph © 1995 TADDER/Baltimore

He was trying to move the team down there before he sold it. It was a mistake. Tampa was a party atmosphere, and the players treated training like it was a lark. They thought they could win anyhow.

McCafferty believed in letting them be adults. That's the way he treated players, and they took advantage of it. He was an easy rider, easy to play for. He had replaced Shula in 1970. For the first year or two, the guys were just happy to be away from a disciplinarian, but then they started to take more and more advantage. They would tell him they weren't going to be in by curfew, and he could take the hundred-dollar fine out of their checks. Joe Thomas saw all those guys going out "cotton spottin" all night long.

From Tampa, we went out to Golden, Colorado, for a few weeks, right next to the Coors brewery. When the season started, the team just wasn't ready to play, and it cost all those guys their jobs.

The next year we trained at Towson State.

I think Joe Thomas was glad in a way. He wanted to remake the team in his own way. He might have been able to transition it, but he felt it was just as good, if not better, to tear it apart and start over. He did what he had to do. The guys he let go just couldn't play anymore. They had seen their best days. They had gone to the Super Bowl in 1969, and it seemed like they had all reached that stage of life where other things were more important. Joe rebuilt the team.

We started with nothing in 1972 and built our way up. Ted Marchibroda took over in 1975. Thomas had a big ego, and he and Ted had some arguments. Joe ran the draft by himself, and Ted thought he should have some input. Once the training camp began, there were arguments over who to cut, and who to bring up if somebody got hurt.

You knew Joe was capable of knifing anybody in the back, and he would get rid of you in a second. There was no loyalty factor there at all. You also knew that if you were playing well, Joe would pay you well.

Maxie Baughan, who came with Marchibroda, was by far the biggest help in developing me as a pro player. A nine-time all-pro linebacker, he taught me all there was to know about that position. He made it possible for me to play thirteen years.

Nothing tops that 1975 season. The three most memorable games were the comeback in Buffalo and the two against Miami. We beat Miami down there when Marty Domres came in after Bert Jones was hurt. Then in December it was head to head with Miami in the game in the fog. We had to win that game; a tie would have hurt us. We held that great Miami team to one touchdown, and Bert led a late drive to tie it. Then Toni Linhart kicked a field goal in overtime for a 10–7 win.

During those years Bert Jones was the best quarterback in the league, and that included Bradshaw, Stabler, all those guys. Nobody was better until he got hurt in the 1978 preseason, and it was a shame. Here was a Hall-of-Fame quarterback. But he never won in the playoffs. We ran into Pittsburgh in 1975 and '76, and the Oakland Raiders in '77. Like

Archie Manning, you can be a great quarterback, but if you don't win it all, you don't win.

We just were not quite as good as Pittsburgh and Oakland. We had the quarterback you had to have, the wide receiver in Roger Carr, the defensive front to pass rush, and the linebackers who could make the plays. Tom McCloud was a good left linebacker, but he didn't have the football mentality. He just didn't like the game. He retired once and they brought him back. He's a fireman now, and he likes it. We lacked a better secondary and a big, sturdy middle linebacker.

As the right linebacker, I would pick up late information sometimes on the cheating that was going on while the quarterback was calling the signals. That was the George Allen system that Ted and Maxie brought with them. You put smart guys on the field who might not match up athletically, but were smart enough to make defensive changes on the field and stay a step ahead of everybody else.

So if I saw something that told me what the play was going to be, I'd audible to a defense that would stop the play. If I saw a tendency toward a certain receiver they liked to go to in that formation or that situation, I would audible the defense to double-team that guy. If we had a blitz call, and the quarterback noticed it or we gave it away, and he started to audible to something else, I would get out of the blitz and go into a coverage. We changed at the line of scrimmage maybe 60 percent of the time.

I had my best years while I was going to law school on Monday and Wednesday nights during the season from 1974 through 1977, and full-time during the off-season. I didn't tell the coaches. I liked the mental challenge of law school, and it kept me mentally sharp for playing NFL football.

My wife and my daughter, who was born in 1975, didn't see much of me during that time. But I made the commitment that the most important job I'd have is being a father, and everything else I do is so I can be a father first.

When Joe Thomas left, there was no insulation from Bob Irsay and everybody lost. Irsay got involved in every situation and the team went down the tubes. That's when Freddie Scott left, Raymond Chester left, Lydell Mitchell left. He wouldn't pay them.

Irsay realized that everybody in the NFL game gets the same amount of money. They sell 90 percent of their tickets, and the television money is all split evenly. So your revenues are going to remain constant whether you win or lose. If you cut expenses, then you have a higher level of profit. Irsay wanted to win, but he didn't want to pay to win. Lydell was among the best backs in the league, but Irsay didn't want to pay him. He wanted to take the money out of the franchise.

I left in 1980 when Mike McCormack came in, and they decided to go with younger linebackers, Sanders Shivers and Mike Woods. They were faster, bigger, and stronger than I was. But the game consists of making the plays. The Colts decided I wasn't good enough, and they

Stan White. Photograph by Vince Bagli

traded me to Detroit for an eighth-round draft choice. When that happens to you, you begin to wonder if they're right. But I thought I could still play as well as ever. I just needed the confidence of the coaches.

I had worn 53 in Baltimore. At Detroit, somebody else had that number, so I figured I was starting new, so I'd wear a new number. I played well there for three years, wearing number 52.

One of the best games I ever had was my first against the Colts in 1980. A little bit of my success in that game was due to my knowledge of the team, but I think more of it was due to the intensity with which I played. You want to make every play in a game like that. Bert and I had a little bit of a chess game going between his offensive calls and my defensive calls. We had done that in practice all the time, and now it was for real. They took it down for a touchdown the first time they touched the ball, but then they didn't move it the rest of the game. We lost, 10–9.

I had started with Woody Hayes at Ohio State, and I ended up with George Allen in the United States Football League. I think Allen was a step above the other coaches I played for. They were really about the same, Woody and George. Just the methodology was different. One patted you on the back; one kicked you in the butt. Both expected you to do the job. Both made it known they cared about you, and that's what the players reacted to. I was about thirty-three when I got to play for Allen as a rookie. He was a defensive coach who put defense first, and for a defensive player, you like to have that opportunity once in a lifetime.

But I found it harder to play in the U.S. Football League than in the NFL. I couldn't figure out what they were doing, because *they* didn't know what they were doing. It was more a game of ability versus ability, and I was at a disadvantage. In the NFL I knew what every team was going to do, and all their tendencies. They were more professional, but they also cheated to get things done, like the way they would line up, and I could pick up those things. In the USFL, those guys didn't even know how to cheat. They had a lot of college coaches running a lot of college plays, so it was much more difficult for me than in the NFL.

I played thirteen years, and of the two hundred games I was eligible to play in, I missed only four. I was hurt in the opening game of the 1978 season and missed the next four. Luck had something to do with my escaping serious injuries. But I always set records for flexibility and stretching whatever team I was on.

The key to avoiding injury is not getting out of position so you get blindsided, and not getting hit in places you shouldn't get hit, where you don't even know you're going to get hit. That's when you get hurt–when you're out of position and can't protect yourself. Playing a mental game, I always had to be in the right position to be successful.

Nothing in Maryland football–high school or college–comes close to the level of interest in Ohio, but Colts fans were at least as fanatical as the Browns fans in Cleveland, and they still are. The guys who stayed in Baltimore are still looked at as part of the people here.

Photograph by Bob Miller

Bert Jones

Born: 9-7-51
Ruston, Louisiana
L.S.U.
Quarterback

6′ 3″, 215 lbs.
Drafted: #1, 1973
Colts: 1973–1981

"My place and my time in Baltimore was not to replace John Unitas. It was to play quarterback for the Baltimore Colts."

I don't think there's any question that my father, Dub Jones–the greatest father there is—and my mother were as important an influence over my career as anything that ever touched me.

We lived a somewhat schizophrenic life, as professional sports require you to do. My father was offensive coordinator for the Cleveland Browns, so during the fall he would be in Cleveland and we were living in Ruston, Louisiana. We would visit him whenever we could. When my brothers and I played ball, my mother would chart every game, then write it all out in a letter and send it to my father, so he could reenact what we had done.

The first play book I ever saw was one that he wrote. Once, as a kid, I got to go to a Browns training camp in Hiram, Ohio. Paul Brown, Otto Graham, Dante Lavelli, and Mac Speedie were also influential in my youth.

I was not a very highly recruited athlete coming out of Ruston High School. Genetically, we are what you would characterize as late bloomers. My father had gone to LSU, then transferred into the wartime V-12 program at Tulane, where he gained 50 pounds and grew a few inches. I wasn't much different.

I played every year against Joe Ferguson, who was probably the most highly recruited quarterback in the country the year we both graduated. Later, while I was in the NFL, we had Ferguson, Terry Bradshaw, James Harris, Doug Williams, and me, all starting quarterbacks, who grew up within forty miles of each other.

Ferguson was a groomed and polished player. He was probably a deterrent as far as someone recruiting me. I wanted to play at the biggest and best school that I could, but Joe and I felt it was not a good idea to go to the same school. He went to Arkansas.

I didn't have many offers: Tulane, LSU, and that was about it. I think Notre Dame would have entertained the thought of inviting me simply

Bert Jones unloading before the hit!
Courtesy Transcendental Graphics

because the coach there, Ara Parseghian, was a good friend of my father. It began to look like LSU was the only real choice I had, but I put off signing.

My father and I were great friends with Eddie Robinson, the coach at Grambling. One Saturday I was working at the family lumberyard—in the Jones family, if you wanted some money to spend on Saturday night, that's how you earned it—and Eddie came by and told me, "Bert, if you don't hurry up and sign, I'm going to have to offer you a scholarship."

I said, "Coach, don't do that unless you want me to come there."

I probably would have been the first white player at the school.

I went to LSU, where "conservative" is an okay way to describe their system. I really didn't become well-versed in a pro-type throwing situation. They liked to play more than one person at each position. There was an option quarterback and there was me, a thrower. So we did split time.

In my junior year, we had a good win over Notre Dame. I was still the second-string quarterback and played when needed, like third and long situations. In that game, I think we threw eighteen times; I'm not sure—I've been hit in the head so much I don't recall. But we won decisively. I threw two touchdown passes, one to my first cousin, Andy Hamilton, and I ran for one. It was a big win for us, and the first time I was the "star of the day."

One of the most enjoyable wins was 17–16 over Ole Miss, one of our primary rivals. You don't often have the opportunity in any sport where your destiny can be determined by yourself. If you get it done, you win. In that game, we were six points behind with two minutes left and the ball on our own 17, with one time-out left. We knew it would be the last time we would have the ball. We decisively marched downfield, picking up a few first downs on fourth-down passes. With just one second left on the clock, I threw a touchdown pass to tie it, and we kicked the extra point to win it. Winning that game as we did was truly exciting. Later I would have a similar experience with the Colts.

As a result, I have an NCAA Division 1A record that may never be broken. I'm the only second-string quarterback on his own team to be named consensus All-American.

The Colts had a first-round draft pick as a result of a trade with New Orleans, and they picked me. I came out of the box starting. Howard Schnellenberger was the coach, and I think he was hoping that physical assets would overcome mental inadequacies. Howard gave me a great basis. I just wasn't capable of grasping it at the time. It was too much.

Marty Domres had come over from San Diego and taken John Unitas's place. I had assumed that he was the heir apparent to John, but when I came in that seemed to change. With 20-20 hindsight, it probably was not very good that I was playing that early. I had gone to the College All-Star game and come in two weeks after the opening of training camp, and lo and behold, here I am playing. I just barely knew my own signals, much less what the defense was theoretically doing.

Those first two years were discouraging, with our 4–10 and 2–12 records in 1973 and '74. In order to compete at the level that professional athletes do, I don't think you can ever lose faith that you can win, and go on from there. It was not out of the realm of possibility that we could win.

To this day, I still believe that I was the best there was when I was there, and I don't think I could have competed had I not felt that way. That's not slighting any other player. It's just the way that we as competitors have to feel.

By that time I had a pretty good knowledge of what the coaches wanted us to do. Then Ted Marchibroda came in, a young coach with a vast knowledge of how to utilize talent. He brought it all together in 1975. He had some weapons, including a player in me who believed everything he said, and tried to enact his theories. To this day, I think it was as good a relationship as a coach and player—and players—could have. As far as formulating a true knowledge and philosophy of how to get something done, he was the most influential person in my football career.

I think the turnaround in Buffalo was circumstantial. We had done a lot of good things in the four early losses. We had competed, the first time we had done that. I know I was finally understanding what, in theory, was supposed to happen. As a team, we started maturing physically and mentally.

The game in Buffalo was a major turning point because we had been losers whenever we got behind. The games we had won, we had been ahead during the game. This time we established ourselves as a team that was competing to win at all times.

We were down 21–0, then 28–7, and wound up winning. It was one of those things that doesn't happen very often. You get out of a bad situation and make something positive out of it. After the last touchdown, I spiked the ball, and we had a wild bus ride to the airport.

But I was hurting. I got stove in by Victor Washington; every rib on my left side was broken. Was I ever hurting the rest of the year!

After that game, the will to win and the belief that we could win became commonplace. Ted would say, "Let's get to the playoffs. If you win, you can be there," and you begin to believe.

Physically and man for man, we were not that talented a football team. We were not bad, but we didn't match up to half the teams we played. We had only one explosive weapon in Roger Carr. Lydell Mitchell was a great running back, but he ran a 5-flat 40. I could almost outrun wide receiver Glenn Doughty, but he was a great pass receiver because he was able to get inside and catch possession-type passes.

We had a young Sack Pack in John Dutton, Joe Ehrmann, Mike Barnes, and Fred Cook. Without question, they came together and molded and matured as a unit. Dutton had the most raw talent. You had quickness in Barnes, strength and quickness in Ehrmann, and a good outside rusher in Cook. And we were able to get ahead in games, which made them even more valuable. Once you get a team into a passing position, it's a lot easier and a lot better to be able to rush them. The Sack Pack was a fun group; they called it the Looney Tunes Group.

That game in the fog against Miami at Memorial Stadium was one we had to win to make the playoffs. Late in the overtime it was 7–7, and Larry Seiple kicked out of bounds at our 4-yard line. It was one of those situations like the Ole Miss game in college. It was the last chance we had. If we got it done, we won. If we did not, we tie or lose, and we needed a win. Hero or goat.

We got to third and long. I was thinking first down, not deep. Miami had a tendency with Jake Scott to come to the back side and play in and out with Roger Carr, which in turn left Raymond Chester in single coverage. After I had seen that earlier, we had thrown to Roger into that coverage a couple times. Even knowing that they were in double coverage, I had been in a position where I could get the ball to him anyway.

But on this play I saw that I could not do that. Coming back around and seeing that Raymond had the position, I just stuck the ball in there and he made a great catch for the first down. That was a key play.

When we got down close enough, it was time to kick the field goal, because I had been spent. I was hurting pretty bad. All my ribs were in pretty tough shape. Linhart's kick gave us a 10-7 win.

Two years later, the double-overtime game against Oakland was sort of like the end of the rainbow. For the first time, we competed in the playoffs. Pittsburgh had drubbed us two years in a row. Now we were playing as good a team as there was, and competing to the bitter end. It was just a situation where maybe there's time, maybe we can do it. But we just didn't get it done.

They were a talented defensive team, and it was not as if we were overwhelming on offense. We got two cheap touchdowns on a Bruce Laird kickoff return and a Marshall Johnson punt return. Still, we had a three-point lead in the fourth quarter. Then we got conservative. Well, I don't know if we got conservative, or if we had just run out of plays that would work.

I second-guess myself to this day. Every night I still think about one pass to Raymond Chester going into the corner. Had I thrown it right to him instead of leading him and overthrowing it just off the ends of his fingers, we probably would have won the game in regulation time.

In a preseason game in August 1978 at Detroit, Bubba Baker got in and rolled me over. I fell on my right shoulder. That was the end of me and the Colts. I knew it was bad at the time, but I did not know how bad. I think we all made a tactical error at that point by my not sitting down for that year. Roger Staubach and others have done it. But kids are dumb. I was pretty weird—about half a bubble off [level]. That was my life at the time—to compete.

My father never injected what he thought I should do, or how it should be done, but he was always there, supportive and watching. I think he probably wished that I would just sit down and go see some good doctors and get well. But he also knew that I was a half-bubble off and that was not the option I was going to take. I was going to play when I could. In hindsight, it was not a good decision. But at the time, it was what I wanted to do. If I had it to do over again, I probably would be stupid again and play just as soon as I could.

Every time I played that year, it was one of those games we had to win. Crazy as it sounds, I really think down deep, that's the reason I came back and played as much as I did. For example, the Monday night 21–17 win over Washington was important to Ted, because that was the team he had coached for before he came to the Colts. I wanted to play for that reason. It was a feather in both our caps to beat his former coaches.

Greg Landry, a quarterback who came over from the Lions in '79 to back me up, was a good player, but he was put in a very precarious, no-win situation. He had to prepare every week, but he did not know when he would play. By the time I had figured out that the only way I was going to get well was to give it enough time, it was a lost cause. If I played, we won, and if I didn't, we lost. It didn't make any difference anyhow; we weren't going to make it to the playoffs, and the coach was going to be fired, and the players were going to be traded, and nobody was going to get signed.

Teddy getting fired in January 1980 affected me, but that's a reality we all face. All of a sudden, my perspective became to get well, and I did. After that, I performed equally as well, if not better, than I had in the previous years.

My last two years with the Colts were my best performing years in Baltimore. It just so happened that we were a horrible football team. Mike McCormack became the coach, and he had less feel of the game than anybody I've ever seen. It was really embarrassing.

I went to the Rams in 1982 with great hopes and expectations. Then we had that big strike, the first time a strike ever interfered with regular season play. The week after the strike ended, I sustained a neck injury that ultimately forced me to retire. I had ruptured a disc at roughly C-5, C-6, and fractured cervical 6. I had to have an anterior cervical fusion, where they take a piece of bone out of your hip and put in into your neck.

This time I let my head rule my heart and retired.

Today I'm in the pressure-treated lumber business with my brother, Bill, in Ruston, and I have a planer and molder and millworks operation. I just finished a six-year term as a commissioner for the state wildlife and fisheries department. I enjoy the outdoors, like to hunt and fish when I can. We have four children: twins Tram (Bertram, Jr.) and Molly, Stephanie, and Beau.

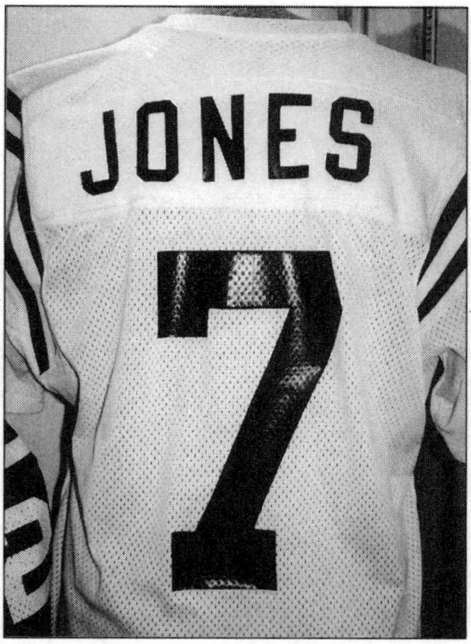

Photograph by Bob Miller

Photograph © 1995 TADDER/Baltimore

The Ruston Rifle

As I reflect back, the one thing I would like Baltimore and its community to understand is that I admired John Unitas as much as they did. I hold him in reverence as they do. John was without question one of the greatest players to ever play in the NFL. To me, he was one of the half-dozen greatest quarterbacks. Otto Graham, Joe Namath, Roger Staubach—as true and fine a player as ever was—Sonny Jurgenson—whom people probably wouldn't regard as much as I do—and Joe Montana measure right up there.

My time and my place in Baltimore was not to replace John Unitas. It was to play quarterback for the Baltimore Colts. I did not dislike the comparisons to John—whether I was or was not as good—because, whether they knew it or not, in my eyes, even when they told me that I was not as good as John, they were complimenting me.

John was a help because he was there, and he had established a mark with the Colts that could never be erased, but could only be aspired to attain.

Baltimore and the people I met are a fixture in my life and I enjoyed it.

Joe Ehrmann (76) sheds the block as Kenny Stabler cranks up.
Photograph © 1995 TADDER/Baltimore

Joe Ehrmann

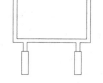

Born: 3-29-49
Buffalo, New York
Syracuse
Defensive Tackle

6′ 4″, 255 lbs.
Drafted: #2, 1973
Colts: 1973–1980

"I'd say I spent the whole first part of my professional football career trying to earn my father's love and respect."

I grew up on the streets, hard and fast, in a tough environment in Buffalo, New York. My father was an ex-boxer, and I really didn't know him until I was in high school. We didn't have a good relationship. I found most of my worth in my toughness and ability to dominate and control situations.

When I got to Syracuse, I thought I was under emotional control, but I really wasn't. I manifested an awful lot of things, and had a lot of personal problems and pain. I held on to the bleak psychology that if I could only get into the NFL, I'd find real purpose in my life. It only added to the confusion, because just playing ball isn't going to add a lot of depth or dimension to your life.

In Buffalo, I was an American Football League fan. I didn't really follow the NFL or the Colts. If I watched the NFL, it was the Cleveland Browns. I rooted for the Jets in the 1969 Super Bowl against the Colts.

Buffalo had told me they were going to draft me, so I was really disappointed when Baltimore drafted me in the first round, number ten overall, after they had picked Bert Jones. I came here with tremendous doubts, not knowing anything about the city or what I was getting into.

We struggled those first few years. I had come from Syracuse, where we were very competitive and anticipated winning all the time. You have to remember the turmoil this franchise was in at the time. Everybody was disgusted that Irsay had gotten rid of Unitas and dismantled the team. Baltimore fans were up in arms because Joe Thomas was getting rid of all the old legends. And here we were, a bunch of college kids who were not connected to what the history had been here, just a bunch of young guys happy to have an opportunity to play. We were naive about how you treat veterans. I think ignorance was bliss for us. But I do think they should have kept some of those older players to help teach us younger guys. For myself, it would have been very helpful to have a veteran pro show me, "This is how a pro works . . . this is what a pro does . . ."

Our front four was good, but how much better we would have been if they had kept around a Fred Miller, somebody of that character and experience. We had to learn on our own.

I think there was also a bit of resentment over why the town continued to talk about those guys of the past when here we were; we were the team now. I think it was very difficult for Bert Jones to come in and be compared all the time to John Unitas.

And in the midst of all that, we were losing. But Joe Thomas was putting together a group of guys who really liked each other and played off each other. I think we had tremendous harmony and camaraderie in the midst of all that losing and fans' anger. We learned to stick together, because we really couldn't go out in the city all that much.

To add to the turmoil, Irsay fired the coach, Howard Schnellenberger, right on the field during the third game of the 1974 season, at Veterans Stadium in Philadelphia. Schnellenberger was playing Marty Domres and refused to put Bert Jones in, so Irsay fired him right there. I'll never forget it. You come off the field to the sidelines during the game and you hear the coach got fired.

We got killed in that game, 30–10, and afterwards Joe Thomas stood up in the dressing room and said, "We fired Schnellenberger, and I'm going to coach the team the rest of the year." Mike Curtis stood up and said something to the effect of, "That's an impossible task!" Only he said it a little rougher than that.

The rest of that year was utter chaos. We won two games all year.

But during that time, Joe Thomas was doing a terrific job of assembling players through trades and the draft. He had taken apart a team that was coming apart from age and injuries anyhow, and made it a winner in a short time. Thomas was always good and nice and kind to me. I liked him a lot. He brought in Ted Marchibroda to coach in '75, and Ted did a lot to solidify us. I have a lot of respect for him as a coach and outstanding human being.

That 1975 season was an exciting sports experience, having come from only knowing losing, and then it looked like that was going to happen again when we got off to a 1 and 4 start. Then we started winning one game and then another. I give a lot of credit for the turnaround to Thomas and Marchibroda. They took the pressure off us by saying, "We're rebuilding. Let's just focus on next week's game."

The hardest thing in a sports franchise is to turn around a loser. You get conditioned to losing. The only way to do it is by winning one week at a time, until you begin to expect to win instead of expecting to lose.

I think we reached that point after the Buffalo game. I'll never forget the way O.J. ate us up, especially on pass receiving. Then we came from far behind to win.

At that point we began to get acceptance by the Baltimore fans. There was a tremendous amount of spirit, and people connected us to the old glory days of the Colts. We played some good football, and we had an awful lot of fun. There was a radio contest to name our front foursome. The Sack Pack won out over the Stone Coneys. For three years we were first or second in the league in sacks.

Now we were well liked in the city. Mike Barnes grew up in the same kind of blue collar area as I did. I was always much more comfortable in the areas of town that were like where I grew up. So when we got to Baltimore, Barnes and I found Dundalk and Fells Point, where people really embraced us coming in and being part of those communities. At that time, a lot of the action had shifted to the northern Baltimore and Towson areas.

When you first get into the playoffs, you have to learn to handle the timing and the pressure. Those first two years we were a little young, and we lost to the Steelers. In '77 we should have gone to the Super Bowl, but we lost to Oakland in the six-quarters game.

Among the people I played against during those years, John Hannah was a great offensive guard for New England. I had a great deal of respect for him as a player and a person. He was classy; always handled himself well on the field, with no cheap shots, no trash talk. He was consistent and gave everything he had whether his team was winning or losing.

One guy who always had my number was Randy Rasmussen of the Jets, an old whooped-up kind of guy. He just matched me up perfectly.

Among the Colts, I always thought Robert Pratt was a terrific guard who was very much underrated and underappreciated.

In the 1978 preseason game when Bert Jones got hurt, I got knocked out, too, and was out cold for quite a while. When I came to in the locker room, there was a giant fight going on. Irsay came in and started screaming all kinds of names at various players. It developed into a big eruption. Stools were thrown, and it got really heated. I was sitting there, still disoriented, and I started hyperventilating from the chaos that was going on between Irsay and the players.

We had a strong core to really build a winning tradition, and I think it was more than Bert getting hurt that pulled us down. The NFL is like any other business; you're only as good as you are up top. The owner didn't add the players we needed, and didn't maintain any relationship with the players. That's when Lydell Mitchell went into those heavy negotiations, and it broke out racially at that point. John Dutton had the same kind of issue.

I think there was a sense among the players that the ownership was not committed to us and to winning. That's what broke down the fabric. I think we would have struggled in '78 anyhow; we certainly needed Bert to win. But there was a moral decay, a kind of leukemic spirit that flowed from the office to the players.

But 1978 was a different kind of turning point for me. My brother Bill was ten years younger than me and getting ready for his freshman year in college when he visited our training camp that summer. In the second week of camp, he came down with terminal cancer. His dying process would last until a couple days before the last game of the season. That caused tremendous emotional problems for me, trying to balance a career and football responsibilities with my brother dying in a hospital a couple miles away. I'll be eternally grateful to Ted Marchibroda for giving me permission to take care of my number one priority—my brother. Ted gave me total freedom to take care of my family first and deal with football when I could. I had great support from the city and my teammates as well.

Joe Ehrmann. Photograph by Vince Bagli

When Bill was dying, I had a profound spiritual awakening, where I saw things from an entirely different perspective and reevaluated my life as to what matters and what doesn't. After he died, I started going to Dallas Theological Seminary six months and playing football six months a year.

Through the support of the Colts players, including some older ones from the earlier eras, we opened the Ronald McDonald House on Baltimore Street that is dedicated to Bill. My father came down for the dedication ceremony.

In '79 the controversy between Marchibroda and Thomas erupted. Most of the players were naive. We didn't understand the politics of past relationships of the Unitas-era guys with management and the city. I'm sure Joe Thomas had hired Ted on the basis that Thomas would be running every aspect of the operation. Once we were winning, and Ted had the backing of the players, he wanted more control over his destiny. It became a typical power struggle. The players got the brunt of it, and the bottom line was the whole franchise lost.

Whether you liked him or not, Joe Thomas was a football man. We were okay until he left, and Irsay became a hands-on owner, involved in everything. He brought in his own people, and non-football decisions started entering into the locker room.

When Mike McCormack came in in 1980, I think it was a coach's graveyard at that point. The morale and the nucleus had been so broken down that it was very difficult for any coach to come in and win. Then they brought in a strong-arm guy like Frank Kush to try to make up for what was going on between the front office and the players, and you're not going to win that way. It takes a commitment and a relationship between the ownership and players, and mutual respect. From '78 on, we had lost that.

But I was gone by the time Kush came in. I played for Detroit 1980–1981, then three years in the U.S. Football League.

I've had a rough decade physically since I retired in 1985. I've had three operations on my ankle, and finally had it fused. It took me almost three years to get over the fusion. Then my hip went, and I struggled with that for a few years before getting it replaced. The ankle was the result of injuries late in my career. The hip was just from general wear and tear over the years. The Astroturf has some part in it.

I played thirteen years, and in retrospect I should have played less. They always say the athlete is the last one to know when he's losing it, and I think that's true.

You pay a tremendous price. Every decade the players are bigger, faster, and stronger, and the rate of collision increases. When I came in in '73, I was a 6-foot-4 270-pounder and ran a 4.9 40. I was considered a big, strong, fast guy. By the time I retired I was smaller than the average player. Players' muscles and body frames are bigger, but the ligaments and tendons stay about the same size.

I think it's inevitable: if you play X number of years, you're going to get beat up. The generation before me is a beat-up generation; everybody's getting parts replaced. It's happening with my contemporaries, and it will with the next generation as well.

I have two boys, and I told them I'd let them play high school football, but not little league—if they chose to. I wouldn't encourage it. They play lacrosse and soccer; those are good sports. I don't want them to play like I did. The cost is too great.

If I were to look over my career, I would say the number one common denominator among pro football players is that they have a tremendous father–son dysfunction. What separates a really good college player from a professional is often that dysfunction. It's always striving to prove your masculinity, your worth, your value—much of it to their fathers, much of it to themselves.

I got into football for a lot of pathological reasons that motivated me, that weren't necessarily about Joe Ehrmann. It goes deeper than just wanting to hit somebody. I'd say I spent the whole first part of my professional football career trying to earn my father's love and respect.

Bottom line—that was my deepest motivation for what I was doing out there. I think that is true of a lot of players, being able to attain certain levels so that their fathers will walk back into their lives and say, "I love you and accept and embrace you," which an awful lot of people from my generation never received from their dads. It's not just in football. I think you'll find the same thing in boardrooms of corporate America and all the way through this country.

I would hope my kids are a little healthier in understanding who and what they are, and they don't need to prove it. Let them play ball because they enjoy it and really want to; that would be terrific. But not to do it out of some other reasons.

With all the issues of poverty that we deal with at The Door [Joe's ecumenical ministry headquartered in East Baltimore], to me the greatest crisis in this country has to do with issues of masculinity—what it is to be a man—and I don't think you can define that in athletic ability or economic success or in sexual areas. It has to be a value system that's much deeper than that.

We try here to define masculinity based on relationships: what kind of husband or father or friend a man is. That ought to count. Then I think every man ought to have some cause or purpose in his life that's bigger than he is. Then you can start defining what a real man is.

We don't bring a lot of professional athletes down to talk to kids, because what the kids wind up seeing is the size of their contracts and the power and prestige that goes with it. These kids don't need some pie in the sky hopes and dreams. They need to learn about values. There are an awful lot of unhappy, miserable professional athletes who had dedicated their lives and climbed the mountain of success, and they get destination sickness. That's why the drugs and alcohol are so prevalent, not only in sports, but in high-income professions. Their success doesn't meet their basic needs.

We serve about two hundred people a year with a staff of twenty, and we're in locations all around the metropolitan area. When I was playing football and going to the seminary, people would ask me, "How can you be in two such different worlds, the NFL and seminary?" To me, they were really complementary. The key on a football team is to figure out how to galvanize forty men from all kinds of backgrounds, get them to set aside personal goals so they can achieve the goal of the team. That's what I feel is needed in the religious community. How do you galvanize all the people from different denominations and beliefs, and get them to set aside their personal agendas for the good of all mankind? We ought to be about the least and the lost of this city.

It's team building. I end up not coaching in the NFL, but doing a lot of coaching here. It's just a different play book.

I don't hold out a lot of hope for an NFL team coming here. I thought we had a good shot the last time, but I learned a long time ago that, in the NFL, logic doesn't always apply.

One thing that amazes me about the league is that everything is structured for parity. The worst teams get the top draft picks. They have an easier schedule. Yet the same owners win decade after decade. Those owners are committed to winning. Some owners are never going to win no matter how much parity there is.

Joe Ehrmann

I think having a professional football team does two things; it creates civic pride—makes people proud of where they live—and when you're proud of your city, you tend to invest in it more. You give it time and money and lip service. Second thing the Colts did was provide a forum that allowed people from different ethnic and economic groups to come together on a common point of interest. Losing that did much to the detriment of the city. There's less to talk about for a large segment of the year.

I love Baltimore. It's a lot like Buffalo, but the weather's better. I love the quality of the people. It's a big city with a small town mentality.

I had so much instability coming into my rookie year in pro football, I think I would have gotten eaten up in a New York or Los Angeles, caught up in the fast lane. Coming to Baltimore gave me an opportunity to be with some real genuine folks. I think Baltimore helped shape some of its athletes. If you look at the history of some of them, they've been molded and shaped by this city and its fans. It kept them honest and humble and connected to the realities of life.

I think that's why so many Orioles and Colts have made so many significant contributions to this city, because this city helps keep people grounded. It's a real slice of Americana for a big city.

One of the great contributions of the Colts to Baltimore can be found in the history of so many nonprofit institutions here. You'll often find an involvement of the Colts. They added a tremendous amount to the good will that takes place here. They helped me personally in my ministry.

Everywhere you go, you see the fingerprints of those people.

Marty Domres holds for Toni Linhart.
Photograph © 1995 TADDER/Baltimore

Toni Linhart

Born: 7-24-42
Vienna, Austria
Technical Institute of Vienna
Kicker

5′ 11″, 180 lbs.
Free Agent, 1972
New Orleans
Colts: 1974–1979

"You make them and you miss them, and you've got to be able to handle both."

I was born in Vienna, Austria, during World War II. My dad was in the German army. When the Allies invaded on D-Day, he was somewhere in France. Three days later he was captured. They sent him to Colorado where he worked on a farm for two years as a prisoner of war. That was fortunate for him. If he had been captured on the eastern front, he would have been sent to Russia. About 30 percent of those captured by the Russians never came back. They were just bundled up in camps like the Jews, with no food or water. Most of them froze to death.

After the war, Vienna was divided into four zones, each section occupied by one of the Allies. I was seven years old. Our area was occupied by the Russians, and they had less than we did. When I went to visit my grandmother in the American zone, I could get some fruit and chocolates. The American army really liked the kids. That's the first time I saw baseball.

Growing up in Europe I never saw football. I played soccer for the Vienna Sport Club and the Austrian National team. In 1972 the coach for the New Orleans Saints, J.D. Roberts, was scouting in Europe, and he was impressed when I kicked a ball right into his hands, like a pass, as he was running down the sidelines. I did it three times in a row. He talked me into signing a contract with them, and I went to New Orleans as a kicker.

It was a disaster. I had grown up on grass, and could never adjust to Astroturf. In practice, my left foot was always hurting from the sudden stopping when I landed on the hard surface. I preferred a softer field. The muddier it was, the better I liked it.

New Orleans had a good quarterback, Archie Manning, but no offensive line. I didn't really understand it at the time, but I did later. I understood what I had to do, but very little of the defense. I worked with the offensive line and I lifted weights.

I was just starting to speak English. There was nobody I could talk to on the field. And nobody knew how to adjust from a soccer player to football to help me. I read the play book a little, but I couldn't read the language much.

Renata and I had been married for two years when we came here. We went shopping in the grocery store, and everything we bought we threw out. It wasn't the right stuff, and it didn't taste the way it was supposed to.

I got cut in the second year when they changed the coach. The new one didn't believe in a soccer-style kicker. When Roberts got fired, I was the first player to go. I went back to Austria and played soccer.

I liked America. I went to college for nine years during my pro career, and I was very opinionated about politics and all that stuff. I had a very high mind about Americans as a whole. It was the only country in the world to help everybody and never get anything back. They just keep on giving.

I was trained as an architect at the Technical Institute of Vienna, and I intended to go back to New Orleans to work as an architect. I didn't think about football anymore.

Before I had left the United States, I told Russ Thomas of the Detroit Lions that I would come to the Lions' training camp, but I thought no more about it. Then, two days before I was to leave for New Orleans, I heard there was a guy in Vienna scouting for a soccer-type kicker and his name was Thomas. So I thought it was the man from Detroit. I went to the hotel and it was not the same Thomas. It was Joe Thomas, from the Colts.

Joe asked me if I could still kick, and I said I could. So we went out to the stadium, where Austria and Hungary were going to play that evening. There were already about 10,000 people standing around out there, and they watched us. It was a beautiful sunny day, almost no wind. I had some old American footballs in my car that I had brought back from New Orleans, and they really flew. Older balls will go about 10 yards farther; they give a little more than the new ones. It was fun. Joe couldn't believe how far I could kick the ball. He was so excited he signed me.

I didn't model myself after anybody; I didn't know anybody. The most I would practice was in April, May, and June. Then I stopped kicking until training camp began in mid-July. I looked at films a couple times. And I ran at least 3 miles every day, sometimes as much as 10 miles.

I learned how to physically train myself to be fit when I was training for the Austrian Olympic skiing team. We had no coaches. You had to do your own training. In skiing, you have to sit back. All the weight is in your knees. You're going downhill 50 to 70 miles an hour and you have to see everything ahead of you. Everything is relaxed except your legs, so they really have to be in shape. That's probably where I got the strength to kick the ball farther than most of the guys playing soccer.

I was probably 5 seconds away from making the Olympic team.

Toni Linhart. Photograph by Vince Bagli

Things really changed when I came to the Colts in 1974. I made friends on the team and had a good time. I thought it was a lot of fun. I played on a soccer team in Vienna for twelve years, and sixteen of the twenty-two of us were together the whole time. It was like a family. I had the same feeling here.

Wind or rain or people didn't bother me when I was kicking. Defenses tried at first to rattle me by yelling at me, but they soon quit because they knew I couldn't speak English and it didn't bother me. When people are talking so quick or saying things you don't understand, it's like a wall is hitting you.

The crowds here didn't affect me; I had played in front of 152,000 people in Glasgow, Scotland. I was one of the older guys on the team, and I can't remember ever being nervous. Maybe a little bit on the kickoff to start the game, but once we were in it, I just followed my routine.

I took a few hits as a kicker, but I gave a lot of them, too. I was pretty tough from playing soccer in Europe. I loved to play soccer against the English especially. They were the straightest-forward players you could find. They were honest and hard and tough, and I liked to play that way. So when somebody hit me in the NFL, I didn't mind.

The only time I got hurt was after I was cut by the Colts, and went to New York to replace Pat Leahy on the Jets till he got well again. A guy hit me in the back after a kickoff and I got a stress fracture in my hip. That's what made me retire in 1980.

On a kickoff, the kicker is the last safety. I had to come down one side, and if the returner broke loose, I had to try to tackle him. Sam Cunningham of the New England Patriots broke through one time on a Monday night game in the rain, and I tried to tackle him like I was supposed to. The guy didn't break stride, not even a stutter step. He just ran right through me. I only weighed 185 or 190.

I made two tackles, but they hurt so much, after that I started tripping runners. I never got called for it. I remember once, in a preseason game against the Saints, Howard Stevens really broke one and was wide open and I just clipped him a little bit. He remembers it, too. I didn't have to swing at him to trip him, just kick his feet a little. I got him good twice that way.

When the game was on my shoulders to kick a field goal after a long battle, the key to it is to prepare yourself. You already know what to do; you can't get any better. I had done my thing in Friday practice: start at the 50, kick two kicks, then move closer to the goal line. I'd make 10 out of 10, and I couldn't get any better.

During a long drive late in the game, I didn't want to get too excited, jumping up and down and yelling, and then all of a sudden have to go out and kick a field goal or extra point. I tried to tune it out and stay calm. After I kicked the field goal to beat Miami, 10–7, in overtime in 1975, Marty Domres, my holder, was jumping around and I was trying to shake his hand, but ordinarily I kept a pretty even keel. You make them and you miss them, and you've got to be able to handle both.

In Cleveland one day in 1979, I missed three field goals in a 13–10 loss. I was kicking in the infield part of the baseball diamond, and the sand was just giving way. I couldn't get under the ball. I thought I was going to get axed that day.

Of all the holders I had, Marty Domres had the most relaxed hands. In that Miami game, we scored late in the game. When I had to kick the extra point to tie it, the snap from center was high. When that happened, I had to give Marty time to get down. I couldn't start until he was in a certain spot. He was always good at recovering, so I knew he would get the ball down.

I had told him, "If you don't have time to get the laces facing forward, don't bother with it." But he would get them up front if he could. If you meet the ball nice and clean, it doesn't matter where they are, anyhow. The big thing is the timing.

You don't feel the same every day. If I had trouble with the kickoffs, I would get in a position I felt comfortable with and shorten them by 10 yards.

The best memory I have is the double overtime game against Oakland, even though we lost, 37–31. It was a great game. There was not one player on the whole field who had a bad day.

I never applied for an architect's license in this country. When I retired from football in 1982, I got involved in a direct mail service company, and we are now one of the biggest on the East Coast.

Baltimore has been good to me and I try to give back whatever I can. I like living here. My son played here at Loyola High School and went to LSU as a walk-on. He played a few games in 1994. His best friend is the son of the long-time Colt punter, David Lee.

I still see Roger Carr, and visit with Bert Jones about four times a year. I think it's very unusual for those friendships to last so long.

Nesby Glasgow

Born: 4-15-57
Los Angeles, California
University of Washington
Defensive Back

5′ 11″, 185 lbs.
Drafted: #6, 1979
Colts: 1979–1983

"I'll never forget the Colt Corrals and the people there who bled Colt blue, like Loudy."

My high school coach in Los Angeles, Ralph Vidal, was the most influential coach in my career. He did a great job of trying to prepare his players for life. He had the successful players come back and talk to us, but only the ones with great character whom we could look up to. He gave us a great foundation.

Vidal always taught us to play as hard as we could. There were games where we beat people, but we played poorly, and he ran our butts off. He wouldn't put up with a mediocre performance.

When you are as fortunate as I was to play for a coach you really respect, you don't want to do anything to disrespect him. So you play as hard as you can, and do your best to beat the guy in front of you. "Win your individual one-on-one battle," he said. "If enough of us do that, we'll win the game."

I still keep in touch with him.

At the University of Washington, Don James was a great coach, a molder of men. A great psychologist, he let his assistant coaches coach, but he ran things, and knew how to deal with the players.

Growing up in Los Angeles, my childhood fantasy was to be on that train that brought teams to play in the Rose Bowl. They always showed the teams arriving on television. I recall in the early '70s seeing the Ohio State team at Disneyland waving to people, and I wanted to do that. It was real exciting when it happened, and we arrived to play Michigan. We beat them.

I was one of the top cornerbacks eligible for the 1979 draft, but I broke my ankle in the Senior Bowl. My draft prospects looked like a stock market crash after that happened. The head coach of the Bengals came out to see me. They wanted to take me but they weren't sure about my ankle.

I wasn't very excited when the Colts drafted me in the eighth round, but I was surprised. Fred Schubach had come out to work me out,

Nesby Glasgow (25) had five Baltimore Colt years to start an outstanding pro career.
Photograph © 1995 TADDER/Baltimore

apparently not realizing that I was still on crutches. I thought if they didn't even know about my injury, they couldn't be very serious about picking me.

The Colts had taken two other defensive backs from the PAC 10, Kim Anderson and Larry Braziel, ahead of me. Kim told me that, having seen me play and talked to some of the guys on our team, he felt he had to get to training camp and start working if we were going to be competing for a position. When your peers think that highly of you, it makes you feel better.

Maybe it was arrogance or self-assurance, but I knew that if I stayed healthy, I'd have a good chance to play in the NFL. After the Colts drafted me, I was talking to Ted Marchibroda and he told me, "Don't worry about the first year." They didn't think I'd be able to play because I really couldn't do anything when I showed up at mini-camp. But I went in with the attitude that I would try to play as soon as I could. Dealing with the pain and adversity was part of the game of football. John Lopez would ice my ankle down before and after every practice.

I remember when I was a kid and the Steelers were a real bad team, I thought that meant that all the guys on the Steelers were bad football players. Then, after being on winners, I came to Baltimore, where they had a poor team, and I was put in that situation.

I played in Baltimore for five years, and I'll never forget the Colt Corrals and the people who bled Colt blue, like Loudy. Everything was on the upside with the downtown renovations, and the city was turning itself around. But I continued to live in the northwest.

In the spring of 1983, I was talking contract with Ernie Accorsi, who wanted me to move to Baltimore. I told him, "If you give me a decent contract, and tell me the team's not going anywhere and you're not leaving, I'll move there and be part of the community year-round."

And Ernie said, "I'm not going anywhere." That's all he said.

I had a good contract and we moved to Reisterstown. There were not many players living in Baltimore year-round at that time. A year later the team moved out.

Indianapolis people were hungry for a pro football team and we fit the bill. We could have been 0 and 80 and it would have been all right with them. The people embraced us. It died down for a while, but it's coming back. The team is better now.

I played my last five years back in Seattle with the Seahawks. I love that part of the country, and have a business out there, installing appliances for a major retailer. Of all the coaches I played for in pro football, Chuck Knox did the best job of managing players, motivating and pushing the right buttons. I ran back a lot of kickoffs. I did that wherever I played, and had a lot of opportunities, because we were scored on a lot.

I played with and against Steve Largent. Other players might have had more potential with their skills, but he produced more. I don't think people realized how quick he was. He could come out of breaks and get separated quickly. He had enough bursts to get by you and stay in front of you long enough to catch the ball. And he had the knack of making big plays at the most opportune times.

Dave Krieg is an old warrior who was one of the most productive quarterbacks, although people get caught up in his bad games. The negative things are always magnified. He has so much confidence, he can go out there and throw five interceptions and it won't prevent him from throwing the winning touchdown. A lot of guys talk about it, but Dave has done it. He's resilient, and can let a bad play run down his back.

I played fourteen years, until 1993. I'm thirty-eight and I came out of it in great shape physically. I wanted to stay involved in the game; I knew I was not one of those people who can say they don't want anything more to do with it after they stop playing. I called around, and the Colts invited me to training camp for ten days, then offered me a job. So I packed up my family and moved back to Indianapolis.

I scout all the guys in the NFL, so if somebody becomes available, we know if he can help us. With the free agents and the salary cap today, you're putting so much money up front, you have to be sure they can come in and improve us at a position. Once you go out and get a guy, you're stuck with him, because of the economics. You bite the bullet and hope he comes around.

When I was with the Colts, in Baltimore or Indianapolis, we were never on national television. But the Seahawks were, so fans know me as a Seahawk, but people in football know me as a Colt.

Ernie Accorsi

Born: 10-1-41
Hershey, Pennsylvania
Wake Forest
Public Relations Director,
1970–1975

NFL Front Office, 1976
Assistant General
Manager, 1977–1981
General Manager,
1982–1983

"When it's all done, the thing that will mean the most to me will be that I was a Baltimore Colt."

The first Colts regular season game I saw was November 22, 1953, when they lost to the Rams, 21–13 in the fog. I remember George Taliaferro filled in at quarterback because the regular, Fred Enke, and the backup, Jack DelBello, were both hurt.

But the Colts really captured my heart in Hershey, Pennsylvania, when they came up there and beat the Eagles, 10–0, in a 1954 preseason game.

One day in 1956 I had to double caddie at the golf course to get the money to buy a ticket to the next game. Then I read the Colts were going to start a guy named John Unitas at quarterback in place of George Shaw, who had been Rookie of the Year in '55. I remember how upset I was that I was going to be watching some guy off the sandlots in Pittsburgh, and I thought I was being cheated.

I was an assistant public relations guy at Penn State when I came here in 1970 to run the PR operation, and my first year we go to the Super Bowl. It was great fun. Not only did I catch the tail end of the great Colt teams—Unitas, Mackey, Matte—I also caught the tail end of the great writers: Jimmy Cannon, Red Smith, Harold Rosenthal, Dick Young, Cooper Rollow of Chicago, who was the first to describe Memorial Stadium as "the world's largest outdoor insane asylum." They were all here for our championship game against the Raiders January 3. I remember looking around the press room at the Hilton Hotel. I had grown up reading all those people, and there they were, covering our game. That was a thrill.

Beating the Raiders that day gave me my biggest kick, more than beating Dallas in the Super Bowl. They had come in here with their trunk all packed to go to Miami. We beat them up front, and won, 27–17.

That '70 team will not go down in history as one of the great teams, but it may go down as one with the greatest people. Bill Curry and Ray Perkins became head coaches; John Mackey was president of the players' union. In the front office, there were four people other than the general manager who became GMs in the NFL.

The best assistant coach I ever saw was John Sandusky. It's a shame he never had a head coaching opportunity, except for filling in in 1972, when he did an outstanding job. He and Marty Schottenheimer and Bud Carson were the three best I was ever around.

One of the finest people I have ever been around in sports is Earl Morrall. Not only for the type of person he is, but the way he handled the most difficult role in sports, the backup quarterback. And to be the MVP in 1968. Then he came back and had a big year in 1971, and got replaced again, by Marty Domres, then went on to Miami. He's at the top of my list.

Another guy who was thrilling to be around was John Mackey. John just exuded leadership qualities. He lifted everybody, though he may not be recognized so much for that. Facing a tough road game, you'd see John get on the bus and you knew things were going to be all right. Like Phil Rizzuto talking about seeing Joe DiMaggio out in center field in the seventh game of the World Series; you knew everything would be all right. On top of Unitas, when Mackey got on the bus, you said, "Okay, we got him on our side."

In 1970 we traded for wide receiver Roy Jefferson, who had a reputation for trouble in Pittsburgh. He showed up wearing a German World War II combat helmet, and I think he was the first guy to carry some kind of purse. Coach Don McCafferty told Dick Bielski, "Run him. I want to see how fast he is." I was in McCafferty's office when Dick came back.

"What did he run?" Don asked.

"He wouldn't run. He told me to go to hell."

About three minutes later, Mackey walked in and said, "Coach, room him with me. I want him to realize how we do things here."

We wouldn't have smelled Super Bowl without Jefferson. He was a warrior on the field, blocking and receiving.

I remember Thanksgiving weekend 1971 at Oakland. We had lost to Miami the week before, and we had to win to keep a chance for the playoffs. When John Unitas walked off the field, the score was Baltimore 31, Oakland 0. To me, that was John's last game.

Not long ago, Leslie Visser, the television commentator, said that undoubtedly Joe Montana was the greatest quarterback of all time. I asked her, "Did you ever see John Unitas play?"

She said, "No."

The franchise-turning game was the Buffalo game in 1975. Later Ted Marchibroda told me, "My mother told me one time, 'Ted, if you take this job, realize there's going to be a day when you're going to be humiliated.' When O.J. Simpson ran for the second touchdown that day, I said to myself, 'Ma, this is the day.' "

When you study that 1975 team, you realize how great Bert Jones was. It wasn't that good a team. Defensively, after the front four, it was marginal. We had a few weapons in Lydell Mitchell and Roger Carr. Glenn Doughty was a good player. But it was not a Super Bowl team. That's a testimonial to Bert's greatness.

Ernie Accorsi

Physically, he was like John Elway, but there was a strain of toughness about Bert. You talk about performances; the performance he put on against New England in the last game of the 1977 season included two plays I'll never forget.

The Colts were down 24–16. On a third and 18 double safety blitz, he threw to Raymond Chester for a touchdown. That cut it to 24–23. Later they punted the ball out of bounds at our 1 yard line. On the first play of the winning drive, Bert threw a 50-yard out to Doughty that I can still see. He had great protection, stepped back into the end zone; Doughty ran a deep, deep cut, ran to the sidelines, and Bert drilled it right at him. A great player can throw a 15-yard out. He threw a 50. That was one of the most memorable games I ever witnessed.

Another was the night they retired Unitas's jersey, October 9, 1977. We were losing to Miami, 28–10; he cut it to 28–24 at the half, and went on to win, 45–28. Jones threw four touchdown passes.

I think Bert would have been one of the great players in the history of the game. For three years he was as good as they come. I recently told him, "Bert, every year I'm in the league, I appreciate you more. Every year, I watch a new cast of players, and I think you were better."

But when he went to Detroit in 1978, his career was essentially over. The injury to his right shoulder was one of the tragedies of this franchise's history. What made it so bad was that after he got hurt he kept playing. We won almost every game he played, and lost every one he didn't play in 1978 and '79. Those years were sprinkled with games where he kept playing hurt and suffering injuries. I remember the game where he came out of the dugout—I think it was against Cincinnati—and the crowd cheered as he ran to the huddle against Dr. McDonnell's orders and sent Landry to the sidelines.

Mike Flanagan told me something in 1994 that applies to Bert. I was watching Mike Mussina pitching against Roger Clemens. Clemens got stronger as the game went on. Mike said, "The problem with Mussina is his heart's too big for his arm."

I think Bert's heart was too big for his body. He should have sat out but he wouldn't, because he knew he meant so much to the team.

The most satisfying thing for me was to be the general manager of the Colts after we had gone winless during the strike year 1982, and almost having a big year in '83, going 7–9. At one point we were 6–4, playing for first place. To have it turn around that quickly with all we had to go through that year was very satisfying.

I drafted John Elway in 1983 because I felt that to not draft him would be to sell the franchise down the river. I felt we had to stay with that until he decided to play football, which I think he would have done, no matter what he ever said. But he wouldn't sign with the Colts.

Of course, with the benefit of thirteen years' hindsight, Dan Marino is the one I should have picked. He's a better quarterback. I think he would have played here. But there were so many questions about him—his shoulder, his poor season as a senior—it would have taken an incredible amount of courage to take him in.

If Elway had signed with the Colts, it would have boosted interest. But something else would have happened. No one player could have kept the franchise from moving. It was inevitable.

The Irsay years were terrible. You never had any stability. You cannot win without continuity and stability, and it was impossible to have that. When Elway was traded to Denver after the draft for offensive tackle Chris Hinton, it wasn't necessarily the fact that it was Elway and we made a bad trade. It was the idea that there was not a total commitment to win at all costs. I knew from that point on, I wouldn't stay here. Then there were rumors of the team moving, and I wasn't going to be part of that, either.

I don't think the name Colts or the logo belong in Indianapolis. It doesn't seem right when I sit there and watch the team. They are not the Baltimore Colts. And the characters that played here! To me, they were very comparable to the Brooklyn Dodgers. They captivated a town. As the Dodgers captivated Brooklyn in baseball, the Colts took Baltimore in football.

A few years ago, I was on Tom Matte's radio show with Bruce Laird and Earl Morrall. I said, "The essence of the Baltimore Colts history is the bond between Laird and Morrall—and they never played together." That says it all. They both played for other teams, too. But if you ask them what they were in the NFL, they say, "Colts."

I still think of Morrall as a Colt, even though he killed us in other uniforms. I would love to ask him what uniform he would want to be seen in if he were in the Hall of Fame. I bet it would be Baltimore.

This sounds corny, and maybe it happens in other places, but these guys played for the town.

I've worked for three historical franchises: the Colts, Browns, and Giants. When it's all done, the thing that will mean the most to me will be that I was a Baltimore Colt.

Chuck Thompson

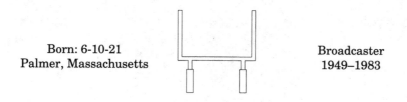

Born: 6-10-21
Palmer, Massachusetts

Broadcaster
1949–1983

"When we went into overtime [in New York in 1958] it was my turn to work again. That's as big a break as any broadcaster could care for."

I came to Baltimore to broadcast Orioles baseball in the International League in 1949. I had done some Eagles games when I was in Philadelphia. Bert Bell was the commissioner. In his time, when you were broadcasting or televising a game, there were no such things as fights on the field. No serious injuries; a player was just "shaken up a little bit." That's all.

We're in Little Rock, Arkansas, the Eagles and the Bears, and we picked up a young man to work color for me and to fill in at half-time. At the end of the first half a scrap breaks out on the field. I know how to ignore it and just say, "Well, there seems to be a little misunderstanding down there, but at the end of the first half. . . ."

I left the booth to grab something to eat, and this young man was so taken with the fight that he described it on the air. I didn't know it. I came back and did the second half and we flew home. The next morning my phone rang.

"Thompson."

It was Bert Bell.

"Yes, sir."

He let me have it up one side and down the other. All I could do was apologize. I should not have left the booth. If I had stayed, it would not have happened. Finally he said, "Well, kid, let's not have it happen again."

I assured him that it would not.

I got to know Bert Bell well while I was working at a radio station in Philadelphia. There was a place at 15th and Walnut called Curly Perry's Moravian Dining Club. A lot of sports people hung out there. Bell would come in for dinner a few times a week. If I was in there on a break from the station, he'd come over and sit down, and we'd have dinner together. He did that for a reason. He knew that not many people in there knew who I was; therefore, he knew they weren't going to bother him while he was sitting with me.

Three broadcasters in 1959: left to right, Chuck Thompson, Bailey Goss, and Vince Bagli. Courtesy National Brewing Company

The first Colts game I did was at Soldier Field in Chicago with Bill Dyer in 1949. Dyer was THE sports man here, a true promoter of sports in this city. Doing baseball, he'd talk about "walking around the little red chair" to see if he couldn't change the team's luck, and people remembered that. He did that when he was recreating games, and he knew that something good was going to happen before he walked around the chair. Smart showmanship on his part.

Soldier Field lighting was not as good as it is now. I recall the Colts had the misfortune of dropping quite a few passes in the first part of the game. I turned it over to Dyer at half-time, and he expounded on some theories he thought were important to the broadcast about dropping footballs, and his summation was something to the effect that with all the magnificent medical brains and the Johns Hopkins Hospital and all in Baltimore, it's a shame they have not invented a serum that could be injected into our players to keep them from dropping the ball.

I began a long association with the Colts in 1953. Then, in the summer of 1954, Pat Roche and Norman Almony took me down to the National brewery and introduced me to Jerry Hoffberger. We talked for maybe forty-five minutes, then Jerry said in so many words, "Kid, we got a deal." With that, he stood up and extended his hand. I stood up and shook hands with him. That handshake lasted twenty-three years. I never signed a contract. It's a shame business can't be done that way today. It's something I'm very proud of. To have anyone have that much faith in you that he didn't have to have something written down gives me a good feeling when I talk about it.

I was strictly a play-by-play man. I didn't do any studio work. It took a lot more individual preparation in the old days. The team PR departments didn't supply the broadcasters with pages of notes and statistics. I kept my own. There was an old cliché: "If you didn't bring it with you, you're not going to find it here." That was true then; it's not true today. It's all done for you now.

Football ran into basketball which ran into baseball, and that's the way you spent your years. If I had it to do over, I would do the same, but I think I would try to spend more meaningful time with my children as they grew up, which was difficult to do. I think I was one for three in graduations. They never had a summer vacation with their dad. Thanksgiving days I was never there, but out doing football games somewhere.

The one that really hurt was trying to explain to an eight-year-old why you had to leave the house on Christmas day. I only had to do it a few times.

The advantage to football was they only played one day a week, and at that time I thought it was an excellent game. The all-out violent contact of professional football contrasted with the lack of contact in baseball, even before they wore face masks and rib protectors. I remember Art Donovan began to take the cases from adhesive tape cartons and he'd tape them around his shins for protection.

The game was played so differently then. It was really a demanding physical game. I look at telecasts today and I see the offensive linemen using their hands to protect the quarterback. That was not allowed in the days of Unitas and Donovan and Marchetti and Mutscheller and Parker and Moore. Parker had to fend off those guys who were trying to get Unitas just on tremendous agility, balance, determination, and skill. If he could have used his hands, there would have been nobody getting Unitas on the blind side, that's for sure.

In those days, the quarterback was considered to have a better idea of what was going on than the guys on the sidelines or the coaches up in the press box. He called his own game. Today they have headsets with radios in them to tell the quarterback exactly what to do. I wonder what Bobby Layne would have to say about that.

My recollections of general manager Don Kellett are all good. When it came time to sit down and negotiate a contract with a player, Kellett was tough. One year I think he and John Unitas ended up going in front of Carroll Rosenbloom to plead their cases. Kellett mentioned the amount of money John was asking for. "We don't pay guys that much money for playing ten years," he said.

John responded, "Are you interested in longevity or the ability to get the job done?"

And Rosenbloom said to Kellett, "I think he's got you."

The 1958 championship game turned out to be a good break for me. I was working NBC television with Chris Schenkel, a good guy and solid pro. We went into the commissioner's office in New York the day before to determine who would do the first half and who the second. We flipped a coin and the guy who won the toss would naturally pick the second half. Schenkel won and chose to do the second half.

I was happy to do the first half, and then suddenly we realized that something was happening down there that had never happened in the history of pro football. So when we went into overtime, it was my turn to work again. That's as big a break as a broadcaster could care for.

The thing that terrorized Baltimore fans was right after Unitas hit Mutscheller and he was a yard from scoring and went out of bounds, NBC lost its picture. There might have been fifteen or twenty NBC people in the booth with us. When that picture went blank, I looked around and everybody was running to get out of there and we were left with Schenkel and me and our two spotters. They knew the problem was not in the booth, and they were trying to make sure that everybody was doing whatever they could to eliminate the problem.

It turned out not to be a very difficult problem, but they tell me when people in Baltimore were watching that telecast and all of a sudden the picture goes blank, people were throwing their beer mugs and dishes and things at their television sets and running around trying to remember where their radios were.

That night we came back into Baltimore on the National Brewing Company plane. Cars were parked on both sides of the BWI parkway all the way into the airport, and the crowd was unrestrained to say the least. It's one of those things you look back on and you don't really pick out any single incident that occurred, but you know darn well that you were so happy you were there.

I think that game was my broadcasting highlight; even more, I think that telecast of that game from Yankee Stadium had more to do with selling the NFL to television than any other game that's been played. From that game on, the NFL became a very important part of television. It's a nice feeling to have been a part of that.

Weeb Ewbank was a deliberate, methodical coach who took nothing for granted. In preparation and attitude on the sideline, Weeb and Earl Weaver were much alike. Weeb was extremely careful about information that you might pass along to another newspaper guy or radio guy. You could ask him a question, and if there were only a few of us in there and he knew us, you'd get an exact answer. But with other people around, he would walk around it.

But he was the most nervous coach during a game I've ever seen. Now you see the deadpans, the television look. No expression. With Weeb, his shoulders would be going, he'd be up and down and get so excited he'd forget a guy's name. Some of the Colts told me they'd go over to him and say, "Weeb, relax. Sit down. Everything's all right." That was his nature.

I never saw a football player wear sunglasses until Raymond Berry did it one day in the fourth quarter in San Francisco. In Kezar Stadium,

Chuck Thompson (*left*) and Vince Bagli in 1977. Photo: Ed Thomas

if you were going east at that time of day and you turned to look west at your quarterback, that sun would hit you right in the eyes. Raymond decided maybe sunglasses would help, and they obviously did.

He had a pretty good sense of humor, and he did unusual things that people in those days never heard of. When we were going to go out to the West Coast, we would be out there ten days. He'd start living on the West Coast time—eating, sleeping on West Coast time—before we went out there, so his body was attuned to California before the rest of the people were.

Gino Marchetti had everything a defensive end needed. He had tremendous takeoff speed, was quick and strong, and had the ability to go either way. I've always felt sorry for the guys who tried to handle him. He was probably the most agile defensive end I have ever seen. He found a way to fool that blocker and get around him by the direct route. Today they tend to use speed more to run around the blocker.

The Colts of the 1970s with Bert Jones were popular, but you're talking about a different generation of fans. In the 1950s, if the Colts were playing at home, you could go to almost any country club in the area on Sunday night, and there would probably be four or five football players and their wives attending a dinner. That was the way the club members celebrated. They went to the game, then came back to the club and you'd find Colt players and their wives mixing with everybody. I don't think that was true of the 1970s.

Robert Irsay's conduct as an owner left a lot to be desired. When Ernie Accorsi left, that told me right there and then there was really something amiss; nobody in this town loved football more than Ernie, and he saw fit to step aside.

Irsay said he moved because the fans didn't support him. Well, it was the other way around. He didn't support them. He let a wonderful football franchise completely deteriorate. And he thinks the Baltimore football fans were going to thank him for that? I wouldn't.

This is one of the best football areas anywhere in the country. We had a lot of good teams here until the wrong guy came in and took over. If I never broadcast another game, I would hope a franchise comes back here. But they're looking at television markets. They don't care much about the fans.

But would I want one owned by Bob Irsay? No.

THE BALTIMORE COLTS' BAND

The 1947 Baltimore Colts' Band dressed in their green and silver jockey cap and cape marched for the All America Conference Baltimore Colts. Photograph from the collection of John Ziemann

The Baltimore Colts' Band was founded when Baltimore first played in the All America Conference in 1947. The Colts joined the NFL for one year in 1950; then the team's owner turned the franchise back to the league.

Although without a team for two years, the band stayed together, playing in other NFL half-time shows.

When the Dallas Texans were transferred to Baltimore in 1953, the band's efforts to keep the Colts' name alive resulted in the rechristening of the Texans with the old name.

In 1984 the band once again lost its team, but they continued to keep their tradition alive, performing at NFL games, in parades, at the Hall of Fame game and induction ceremonies, and at other events. The Band has served as the official Preakness band at Pimlico for thirty-three years.

The band's musical director is Harry Wacker; its president is John Ziemann. The Colts' Band can be contacted at (410) 557-8335.

The band that never gave up: The 1995 Baltimore Colts' Band wearing their new uniforms that were a gift from Baltimore Football Club owner Jim Speros. No organization in the state of Maryland has been more dedicated in their support of professional football for the city of Baltimore.
Photograph by Rick Preski from the collection of John Ziemann

THE COLTS DRAFT STORY

FIRST-ROUND DRAFT CHOICES

1953 — Billy Vessels, HB, Oklahoma
1954 — Cotton Davidson, QB, Baylor
1955 — George Shaw, QB, Oregon (bonus)
Alan Ameche, FB, Wisconsin
1956 — Lenny Moore, HB, Penn State
1957 — Jim Parker, T, Ohio State
1958 — Lenny Lyles, HB, Louisville
1959 — Jackie Burkett, C-LB, Auburn
1960 — Ron Mix, T. Southern Cal
1961 — Tom Matte, HB, Ohio State
1962 — Wendell Harris, HB, LSU
1963 — Bob Vogel, T., Ohio State
1964 — Marv Woodson, HB, Indiana
1965 — Mike Curtis, FB-LB, Duke
1966 — Sam Ball, T, Kentucky
1967 — Bubba Smith, T, Michigan State
Jim Detwiler, RB, Michigan
1968 — John Williams, G, Minnesota
1969 — Eddie Hinton, FI, Oklahoma
1970 — Norm Bulaich, RB, TCU
1971 — Don McCauley, RB, North Carolina
1972 — Tom Drougas, T, Oregon
1973 — Bert Jones, QB, LSU
Joe Ehrmann, DT, Syracuse
1974 — John Dutton, DE, Nebraska
Roger Carr, WR, Louisiana Tech
1975 — Ken Huff, G, North Carolina
1976 — Ken Novak, DT, Purdue
1977 — Randy Burke, WR, Kentucky
1978 — Reese McCall, TE, Auburn
1979 — Barry Krauss, LB, Alabama
1980 — Curtis Dickey, RB, Texas A & M
Derrick Hatchett, DB, Texas
1981 — Randy McMillan, RB, Pittsurgh
Donnell Thompson, DE, North Carolina
1982 — Johnie Cooks, LB, Mississippi State
Art Schlichter, QB, Ohio State
1983 — John Elway, QB, Stanford

1953

1—Billy Vessels, HB, Oklahoma; 2—Bernie Flowers, E, Purdue; 3—Buck McPhail, FB, Oklahoma; 4—Tom Catlin, C, Oklahoma; 5—Jack Little, T, Texas A&M; 6—Jim Sears, HB, USC; 7—Bill Athey, G, Baylor; 8—Jim Prewett, T, Tulsa; 9—Bob Blair, TE, TCU; 10—John Cole, HB, Arkansas; 11—Gene Rossi, HB, Cincinnati; 12—Kaye Vaughn, G, Tulsa; 13—Bobby Moorhead, HB, Georgia Tech; 14—Frank Continetti, G, George Washington; 15—Buddy Sutton, HB, Arkansas; 16—Jim Currin, E, Dayton; 17—George Rambour, T, Dartmouth; 18—LeRoy Labat, HB, LSU; 19—Bill Powell, HB, California; 20—Pete Russo, T, Indiana; 21—Frank Kirby, T, Bucknell; 22—Merlin Gish, C, Kansas; 23—Mike Housepian, G, Tulane; 24—Monte Brethauer, E, Oregon; 25—Joe Szombathy, E, Syracuse; 26—Scott Prescott, C, Minnesota; 27—Ray Graves, HB, Texas A&M; 28—Joe Sabol, HB, UCLA; 29—Jack Allessandrini, G, Notre Dame; 30—Tom Roche, T, Northwestern.

1954

1—Cotton Davidson, QB, Baylor; 2—Larry Grigg, B, Oklahoma U.; 4—Thomas Allman, B, W. Virginia; 5—Don Ellis, B, Texas A&M; 7—Glenn Turner, B, Georgia Tech; 8—Dennis McCotter, G, Detroit U.; 9—Robert Adams, G, Shippensburg St. Tchrs.; 10—Robert Schoonmaker, B, Missouri; 11—Robert Leberman, B, Syracuse; 12—Donald Chelf, T, Iowa; 13—David McMillan, B, John Carroll; 14—Ordell Braase, T, S. Dakota State; 15, Joseph D'Agostino, G, Florida U.; 16—Alex Sandusky, C, Clarion St. Tchrs.; 17—Thomas Adkins, C, Kentucky; 18—Richard Shinault, B, Texas Western; 19—Charles Wenzlau, C, Miami (Ohio); 20—Raymond Berry, E, S.M.U.; 21—Robert Lade, G, Nebraska St. Tchrs.; 22—Robert Meyer, T, Ohio State; 23—Leon Hardeman, B, Georgia Tech; 24—Donald Kerlin, B, Concordia; 25—Pepper Rodgers, B, Georgia Tech; 26—Jesus Esparza, T, New Mexico A&M; 27—William Sennett, C, Georgia Tech; 28—Raymond Ecstrom, C, Westminster; 29—Claude Taliaferro, B, Illinois; 30—Patrick Abruzzi, B, Rhode Island.

1955

Bonus Pick—George Shaw, QB, Oregon; 1—Alan Ameche, B, Wisconsin; 2—Richard Szymanski, C, Notre Dame; 3—L.G. Dupre, B, Baylor; 4—Jack Patera, G, Oregon (traded by New York); 5—George Preas, G, V.P.I.; 6—Leo Lewis, B, Lincoln University (Missouri); 7—Frank McDonald, C, Miami (Florida); 8—Dale Meinert, G, Oklahoma A&M; 9A—Walter Bryan, B, Texas Tech; 9B—William Evans, G, Miami (Ohio) (traded by New York); 11—Emil Radik, B, Omaha; 12—Dick Cherovich, T, Miami (Ohio) 13—Pat Abbruzzi, B, Rhode Island; 14—John Lee, B, Georgia Tech; 15—Gerald Peterson, T, Texas; 16—Dick Laswell, T, T.C.U.; 17—Wesley Clark, T, Mississippi Southern; 18—Charles Shepherd, B, North Texas State; 19—James Cobb, T, Abilene Christian; 20—Charles Cianciola, C, Lawrence College; 21—Nick Manych, C, Michigan State Normal; 22—Jerry Welch, B, South Dakota State; 23—Dick McNamara, B, Minnesota; 24—Alex Esquivel, B, Mexico City College (Mexico); 25—Richard Grann, T, Rhode Island; 26—Marion Minker, T;

Bucknell; 27—James Locke, T, V.P.I.; 28—Robert Myers, T, Ohio State; 29—Bill Waters, T, Austin College.

1956

1—Lenny Moore, HB, Penn State; 2—Dick Donlin, E. Hamline; 3—Bob Pascal, HB, Duke; 4—B.C. Inabinet, T, Clemson; 5—Herb Gray, E, Texas; 6—Dan Schmidt, HB, Texas Tech; 7—Bill Waters, T, Austin; 8—Bill Koman, G, North Carolina; 9—John Lewis, E, Michigan State; 10—Gene Scott, HB, Centre; 11—Dennis Shaw, E, N. Texas State; 12—Steve Myhra, G, North Dakota; 13—Jack Hill, HB, Utah State; 14—Ted Schwanger, HB, Tennessee Poly; 15—John Polzer, LB, Virginia; 16—Gene Hendrix, HB, Drake; 17—Bill Dannenhauer, E, Emporia; 18—Earl Looman, G, Stetson; 19—Bob Fyvie, T, Lafayette; 20—Bob Hill, FB, Jackson; 21—Jim Harness, HB, Mississippi State; 22—Pat Del Vicaro, G, Mississippi Southern; 23—Al Stephenson, T, Idaho State; 24—Bobby Fox, HB, E, Texas State; 25—Bradley Mills, HB Kentucky; 26—Jim Lohr, G, S.E. Missouri; 27—Herb Hartwell, HB, Virginia; 28—John Shearer, QB, Shepherd; 29—Jim Rusher, E, Kansas State; 30—Terry Sweeney, HB, Middle Tenn. State.

1957

1—Jim Parker, T, Ohio State; 2—Don Shinnick, LB, UCLA; 3—Luke Owens, T, Kent State; 4—Jackie Simpson, HB, Florida; 5—Ron Underwood, HB, Arkansas; 6—Bill Pricer, FB, Oklahoma; 7—Reuben Saage, HB, Baylor; 8—Jack Harmon, HB, East Oregon State; 9—Robert White, T, Otterbein; 10—Joe Grisham, E, Austin Peay; 11—Andy Nelson, QB, Memphis State; 12—Don Simonic, T, Tennessee Poly; 13—John Call, HB, Colgate; 14—Joe Guido, HB, Youngstown; 15—Hall Whitley, C, Texas A. & I.; 16A—Joe Cannavino, HB, Ohio State (in trade for fullback Charles Shepard); 16B—Ed Preelock, T, Kansas; 17—Dan Wisniewski, G, Pittsburgh; 18—Jim Villa, HB, Allegheny; 19—Charles Frochle, T, St. John's of Minn.; 20—Walt Livingstone, HB, Heidelberg; 21—Owen Mulholland, HB, Houston; 22—Chet Van Atta, LB, Kansas; 23—Connie Baird, E, Hardin-Simmons; 24—Harwood Hoeft, E, South Dakota State; 25—Harlon Geach, T, College of Idaho; 26—Joe Unitas, T, Louisville; 27—Len DeMalon, LB, St. Vincent's of Pennsylvania; 28—Walt Schneiter, T, Colorado; 29—Bob Rasmussen, G, Minnesota; 30—Bob Bailey, E, Thiel.

1958

1—Leonard Lyles, HB, Louisville; 2—Bob Stransky, HB, Colorado; 3—Joe Nicely, G, West Virginia; 4—Les Walters, E, Penn State; 5—Raymond Brown, QB-HB, Mississippi; 6—Bob Taylor, E, Vanderbilt; 7—John Sample, HB, Maryland State (in trade from Pittsburgh); John Diehl, T, Virginia; 8—Floyd Peters, G, San Francisco State; 9—Harold Bullard, FB, Lenoir Rhyne; 10—Ray Schamber, HB, South Dakota; 11—Bobby Jordon, HB, V.M.I.; 12—Tommy Addison, T, South Carolina; 13—Jerry Richardson, E, Wofford; 14—Ken Hall, HB-FB, Texas A & M; 15—Les Carney, HB, Ohio; 16—Arch Matsos, G-LB, Michigan State; 17—James Reese, QB, Minnesota; 18—Dale Lloyd, C, Georgia; 19—Tim Murnen, G, Bowling Green; 20—Tom

Forrestal, QB, Navy; 21—Jim Faulk, HB, Texas Christian; 22—Bob McKee, E, Monmouth; 23—Phil Parslow, HB, UCLA; 24—Bobby Sandlin, HB, Tennessee; 25—Jim Roundtree, HB, Florida; 26—Bob Grimes, G, Central Michigan; 27—George Dintiman, HB, Lock Haven Teachers; 28—Jim Murphy, T, East Tennessee State Teachers; 29—Doug Padgett, E, Duke; 30—Gary Lund, G, Utah State.

1959

1—Jackie Burkett, C, LB, Auburn; 2—Dave Sherer, E, S.M.U.; 3—traded to Detroit for Ray Krouse; 4—Zeke Smith, G, LB, Auburn; 5—Hanson Churchwell, G, LB, Mississippi; 6—Palmer Pyle, T, Michigan State; 7—Harold Lewis, HB, Houston; 8—Tom Coffey, HB, West Texas State; 9—Tom Brown, G, Minnesota; 10—Don Stewart, E, S.M.U.; 11—Tom Stephens, HB, Syracuse; 12—Richard Wood, QB, Auburn; 13—Rudy Smith, G-T, Mississippi; 14—Ferdie Burket, HB, Southeastern Oklahoma; 15—Ted Foret, T, Auburn; 16—Morris Keller, T, Clemson; 17—Leroy Bergen, T, South Dakota State; 18—Opie Bandy, E-LB, Tulsa; 19—Milton Crain, C-LB, Mississippi; 20—Paul Balonick, C-LB, North Carolina State; 21—John Hernstein, FB, Michigan; 22—Lonny Leatherman, T, T.C.U.; 23—Bob Davis, HB, Houston; 24—Bob Novogratz, G-LB, Army; 25—Ed Kieffer, HB, Syracuse; 26—Rene Lorio, HB, Mississippi Southern; 27—Thurman Terry, T, Rice University; 28—Fred Long, FB, Iowa; 29—Perry McGriff, E, Florida; 30—Blair Weese, FB, West Virginia Tech.

1960

1—Ron Mix, T, U.S.C.; 2—Don Floyd, T, T.C.U.; 2—Marvin Terrell, G, Mississippi (selection obtained in trade with New York for George Shaw); 3—Jim Welch, HB, S.M.U.; 4—Geerhard Schwedes, HB, Syracuse; 5—Marvin Laster, HB, T.C.U.; 6—Al Bansavage, G, U.S.C.; 7—Harry Beabout, T, Purdue; 8—Jim Colvin, T, Houston; 9A—Bob Hall, T, Kent State; 9B—Don Perkins, HB, New Mexico (selection obtained in trade with Philadelphia for Jimmy Carr); 10A—Ernest Barnes, C, North Carolina College; 10B—Bobby Boyd, QB, Oklahoma (selection obtained in trade with Washington for Hanson Churchwell); 11—Bob Wehking, C, Florida; 12—Bill Bucek, HB, Rice; 13—Jim Nemeth, C, South Carolina; 14—Dale Johannson, T, Augustana College; 15—Larry Grantham, E, Mississippi; 16—George Boynton, HB, East Texas State; 17—Jim Beaver, T, Florida; 18—Dan Sheeham, T, Chattanooga; 19—Bill Carpenter, E, Army; 20—Bob Hogue, T, Shepherd.

1961

1—Tom Matte, HB, Ohio State; 2—Tom Gilburg, T, Syracuse; 3—Jerry Hill, HB, Wyoming; 4—Ken Gregory, E, Whittier; 5A: Ron Osborne, T, Clemson; 5B—Ed Dyas, FB, Auburn; 6—Don Kern, HB, V.M.I.; 7—Ike Grimsley, HB, Michigan State; 8—Paul Terhes, QB, Bucknell; 9—Pete Nicklas, T, Baylor; 10—Bob Clemens, HB, Pitt; 11—Ralph White, T, Bowling Green; 12—Dick Reynolds, T, North Carolina State; 13—Dallas Garber, FB, Marietta; 14—Bob Hunt, T, S.M.U.; 15—E.A. Sims, E, New Mexico State; 16—Tom

Weisner, FB, Wisconsin; 17—Steve Jastrzembski, E, Pitt; 18—Wilson Allison, T, Baylor; 19—Joe Novsek, T, Tulsa; 20—Al Kimbrough, HB, Northwestern.

1962

1—Wendell Harris, HB, Louisiana State; 2—Bill Saul, LB, Penn State; 3—Dan Sullivan, T, Boston College; 4—Jim Dillard, HB, Oklahoma State; 5—Jerry Croft, G, Bowling Green; 6—traded to Green Bay; 7—Fred Miller, T, Louisiana State (future); 8—Pete Brokaw, HB, Syracuse; 9A—Roy Walker, FB, Purdue; 9B—Walt Rappold, QB, Duke; 10—Fred Moore, T, Memphis State; 11—Scott Tyler, HB, Miami (Ohio); 12—Bake Turner, HB, Texas Tech; 13—Charles Holmes, FB, Maryland State; 14—Stinson Jones, HB, V.M.I.; 15—Joe Monte, G, Furman; 16—Ray Abruzzese, HB, Alabama; 17—Bill Knocke, HB, Fresno State; 18—Mel Rideout, QB, Richmond; 19—Fred Gillett, HB, Los Angeles State; 20—Herm McKee, HB, Washington State.

1963

1—Bob Vogel, T, Ohio State; 2A—John Mackey, E-HB, Syracuse; 2B—Butch Wilson, FB, Alabama; 3—traded to St. Louis; 4A—Jerry Logan, HB, West Texas State; 4B—Harlow Fullwood, T, Virginia Union; 5—Bill Ventura, E, Richmond; 6—Jerry Cook, HB, Texas; 7—Willie Richardson, E, Jackson State; 8—Dave Hayes, FB, Penn State; 9—Don Trull, QB, Baylor; 10—Bill Siekierski, G, Missouri; 11—Winston Hill, T, Texas Southern; 12—Butch Maples, C, Baylor; 13—Paul Watters, T, Miami (Ohio); 14—Neil Petties, E, San Diego State; 15—Leon Mavity, HB, Colorado; 16—Dick Quast, E, Memphis State; 17—Kern Carson, HB, San Diego State; 18—Luther Woodruff, T, North Carolina A & T; 19—Steve Berzansky, FB, West Virginia; 20—D.L. Hurd, E, San Francisco State.

1964

1—Marv Woodson, HB, Indiana; 2—Tony Lorick, HB, Arizona State; 3—traded to Green Bay; 4—Ted Davis, LB, Georgia Tech; 5—Ed Lothamer, T, Michigan State; 6—Jim Mazurek, T, Syracuse; 7—Ken Sugarman, T, Whitworth; 8—John Williamson, LB, Louisiana Tech; 9—Vince Turner, HB, Missouri; 10—traded to Detroit; 11—John Paglio, T, Syracuse; 12—Ken Graham, HB, Washington State; 13—Charlie Parker, T, Southern Mississippi; 14—John Case, E, Clemson; 15—Larry Kramer, T, Nebraska; 16—Roger Lopes, FB, Michigan State; 17—Don Green, HB, Susquehanna; 18—Alvin Haymond, HB, Southern U; 19—Owen Dejanovich, T, Arizona State (Flagstaff); 20—John Butler, FB, San Diego State.

1965

1—Mike Curtis, FB-LB, Duke; 2—Ralph Neely, T, Oklahoma; 3A—traded to San Francisco; 3B—Glenn Ressler, G, Penn State (from Vikings); 4A—Dave Johnson, HB, San Jose State; 4B—Martin Schottenheimer, LB, Pitt (from Redskins); 5—John McGuire, E, Syracuse; 6A—Al Atkinson, T, Villanova; 6B—Bob Felts, HB, Florida A & M (from Giants); 7—John Kolocek, T, Corpus

Christi; 8—Roosevelt Davis, T, Tennessee A & I; 9—Tom Bleick, HB, Georgia Tech; 10—George Harold, HB, Allen U; 11—Lamar Richardson, E, Fisk U; 12—Ted Radosovich, G, Cincinnati; 13—Bruce Airheart, HB, North Dakota State; 14—Jerry Fishman, LB, Maryland; 15—Roy Hilton, E, Jackson State; 16—Steve Tensi, QB, Florida State; 17—Rick Reichardt, E, Wisconsin; 18—Charley King, HB, Purdue; 19—Barry Brown, E-LB, Florida; 20—George Haffner, QB, McNeese State; Raymond Johnson, C, Prairie View (from Washington).

1966

1—Sam Ball, T, Kentucky; 2—Butch Allison, G, Missouri; 3—Rick Kestner, E, Kentucky; 4A Rod Sherman, FL, Southern California (from Cowboys); 4B—Hoyle Granger, FB, Mississippi State; 5—traded to Cowboys; 6—Stas Moliszewski, LB, Princeton; 7A—Dave Ellis, T, North Carolina State (from 49ers); 7B—Ray Perkins, FL, Alabama; 8A—Gerald Allen, HB, Omaha (from Vikings); 8B—Jack White, QB, Penn State; 9—Gerald Gross, HB, Auburn; 10—Claude Brownlee, DE, Benedict; 11—Eric Crabtree, HB, Pittsburgh; 12—Jim Carter, G, Tennessee A & I; 13—Bob Hadrick, E, Purdue; 14—Jim Ward, QB, Gettysburg; 15—Lee Garner, LB, Mississippi; 16—Rod Steward, E, Duke; 17—Randy Matson, T, Texas A & M (found ineligible for drafting); 18—Ed Toner, T, Massachusetts; 19—Ken Duke, FB, Morgan State; 20—Tom Carr, T, Morgan State.

1967

1A—Bubba Smith, DE, Michigan State (from Saints); 1B—Jim Detwiler, HB, Michigan; 2—Rick Volk, DB, Michigan; 3A—Norman Davis, G, Grambling (from Saints); 3B—Leon Ward, LB, Oklahoma State; 4—Charles Stukes, DB, Maryland State; 5—Ron Porter, LB, Idaho (from Falcons); 6—Terry Southall, QB, Baylor; 7—Bo Rein, FL, Ohio State; 8A—Lee Anderson, DT, Bishop (from Cardinals); 8B—Cornelius Johnson, T, Virginia Union; 9—Ron Kirkland, HB, Nebraska; 10—Leigh Gilbert, FB, Northern Illinois; 11—Herman Reid, T, St. Augustine's; 12A—Preston Pearson, DB, Illinois (from Steelers); 12B—J.B. Christian, G, Oklahoma State; 13—Marc Allen, DT, West Texas State; 14—Pat Conley, LB, Purdue; 15—Bob Wade, DB, Morgan State; 16—Don Alley, FL, Adams State; 17—traded to Saints.

1968

1—John Williams, T, Minnesota; 2—Bob Grant, LB, Wake Forest; 3—Rich O'Hara, E, Northern Arizona; 4—James Duncan, DB, Maryland State; 5—Paul Elzey, LB, Toledo; 6—traded to Atlanta; 7—Anthony Andrews, HB, Hampton Institute; 8—Tommy Davis, DT, Tennessee A & I; 9—Terry Cole, FB, Indiana; 10A—Ocie Austin, DB, Utah State; 10B—Ed Tomlin, FB, Hampton Institute; 11—Bill Pickens, G, Houston; 12—James Jackson, DT, Jackson State; 13—Howie Tennebar, G, Kent State; 14—Charles Mitchell, TE, Alabama State; 15—Jeff Beaver, QB, North Carolina; 16—Walt Blackledge, FL, San Jose State; 17—Ray Pederson, G, State College of Iowa.

1969

1—Ed Hinton, FL, Oklahoma; 2A—Ted Hendricks, LB, Miami; 2B—Tom Maxwell, DB, Texas A & M; 3—Dennis Nelson, T, Illinois State; 4—Jackie Stewart, FB, Texas Tech; 5—King Dunlap, DT, Tennessee A & I; 6—Bill Fortier, G, Louisiana State; 7A—Gary Fleming, LB, Stanford; 7B—Roland Moss, RB, Toledo; 8—Sam Havrilak, DB, Bucknell; 9A—George Wright, DT, Sam Houston; 9B—Larry Good, QB, Georgia Tech; 10—Marion Griffin, TE, Purdue; 11—Ken Delaney, T, Akron; 12—Butch Riley, LB, Texas A & I; 13—Carl Mauck, LB, Southern Illinois; 14—Dave Bartelt, LB, Colorado; 15—George Thompson, DB, Marquette; 16—Jim McMillan, FL, The Citadel; 17—Joe Cowan, FL, Johns Hopkins.

1970

1—Norm Bulaich, RB, TCU; 2—Jim Bailey, DT, Kansas; 3A—Jim O'Brien, K-WR, Cincinnati; 3B—Ara Person, TE, Morgan State; 4—Steve Smear, DT, Penn State; 5—Billy Newsome, DE, Grambling; 6—Ron Gardin, FL, Arizona; 7—Gordon Slade, QB, Davidson; 8—Bob Bouley, T, Boston College; 9—Barney Harris, CB, Texas A & M; 10—Dick Palmer, LB, Kentucky; 11—George Edwards, RB, Fairmont State (W. Va.); 12—Don Burrell, FL, Angelo State; 13—Dave Polak, LB, Bowling Green; 14—Tom Curtis, S, Michigan; 15—Phillip Gary, DE, Kentucky State; 16—Jack Maitland, RB, Williams; 17—Alvin Pearman, RB, Colgate.

1971

1A—Don McCauley, RB, North Carolina (awarded from Miami); 1B—Leonard Dunlap, DB, North Texas State; 2—Bill Atessis, DT, Texas; 3—Karl Douglas, QB, Texas A & I; 4—traded to Pittsburgh; 5—John Andrews, TE, Indiana; 6, Ken Frith, DT, Northeast Louisiana; 7—Gordon Bowdell, WR, Michigan State; 8—Willie Bogan, DB, Dartmouth; 9—Bill Burnett, RB, Arkansas; 10—Rex Kern, QB, Ohio State; 11—Dave Jones, LB, Baylor; 12A—Bob Wuensch, T, Texas (from Pittsburgh); 12B—Bill Triplett, WR, Michigan State; 13—Tom Neville, LB, Yale; 14—Mike Mikolayunas, RB, Davidson; 15—Mike Hogan, LB, Michigan State; 16—Rich Harrington, DB, Houston; 17—Don Nottingham, RB, Kent State.

1972

1—Tom Drougas, T, Oregon; 2A—Jack Mildren, S, Oklahoma (from Oakland); 2B—Glenn Doughty, WR, Michigan (from Washington); 2C—Lydell Mitchell, RB, Penn State; 4—Eric Allen, WR, Michigan State; 5—Don Croft, DT, Texas El Paso; 6—Bruce Laird, S, American International; 7—John Sykes, RB, Morgan State; 8A—Al Qualls, LB, Oklahoma (from San Diego); 8B—Van Brownson, QB, Nebraska; 9—Gary Hambell, DT, Dayton; 10—Dave Schilling, RB, Oregon State; 11—Fred DeBernardi, DE, Texas El Paso; 12—Gary Theiler, TE, Tennessee; 13—Herb Washington, WR, Michigan State; 14—John Morris, C, Missouri Valley; 15—Robin Parkhouse, LB, Alabama; 16—Gary Wichard, QB, C.W. Post; 17—Stan White, LB, Ohio State.

1973

1A—Bert Jones, QB, LSU (from New Orleans); 1B—Joe Ehrmann, DT, Syracuse; 2—Mike Barnes, DE, Miami; 3A—Bill Olds, RB, Nebraska (from Denver through Houston); 3B—Jamie Rotella, LB, Tennessee; 4A—Gery Palmer, T, Kansas (from Chicago through Philadelphia); 4B—Ollie Smith, WR, Tennessee State (from San Diego); 5—David Taylor, G, Catawba; 8A—Ray Oldham, DB, Middle Tennessee (from San Diego); 8B—Bill Windauer, G, Iowa; 11—Dan Neal, C, Kentucky; 12—Bernard Thomas, DE, Western Michigan; 13—Tom Pierantozzi, QB, West Chester; 14—Ed Williams, RB, West Virginia; 15—Jackie Brown, DB, South Carolina; 16—Marty Januskiewicz, RB, Syracuse; 17—Guy Falkenhagen, T, Northern Michigan.

1974

1A—John Dutton, DE, Nebraska; 1B—Roger Carr, WR, Louisiana Tech (from Los Angeles); 2A—Fred Cook, DE, Southern Mississippi; 2B—Ed Shuttlesworth, RB, Michigan (from Philadelphia); 3A—Glen Robinson, LB, Oklahoma State; 3B—Robert Pratt, G, North Carolina (from Denver); 4—Tony Bell, S, Bowling Green; 5—Doug Nettles, CB, Vanderbilt (from Minnesota); 6—Danny Rhodes, LB, Arkansas (from New England); 7A—Noah Jackson, G, Tampa; 7B—Dan Dickel, LB, Iowa (from Denver); 7C—Freddie Scott, WR, Amherst (from Buffalo); 8A—Greg Latta, TE, Morgan State; 8B—Paul Miles, RB, Bowling Green (from Denver); 10A—Bob Van Duyne, G, Idaho; 10B—Glenn Ellis, DT, Elon (from Los Angeles); 11—Tim Rudnick, DB, Notre Dame; 12A—Dave Simonson, T, Minnesota; 12B—Bob Bobrowski, QB, Purdue (from Washington); 13—Randy Hall, S, Idaho; 14—Ed Collins, WR, Rice; 15—Pat Kelly, LB, Richmond; 16—Dave Margavage, T, Kentucky; 17A—Tim Berra, WR, Massachusetts; 17B—Buzzy Lewis, DB, Florida State (from Washington).

1975

1—Ken Huff, G, North Carolina (from Atlanta); 3A—Mike Washington, DB, Alabama; 3B—Dave Pear, DT, Washington (from Chicago); 4A—Marshall Johnson, RB, Houston; 4B—Paul Linford, DT, Brigham Young (from N.Y. Jets); 5—Roosevelt Leaks, FB, Texas; 6—Don Westbrook, WR, Nebraska (from N.Y. Giants); 7A—Kim Jones, FB, Colorado State; 7B—Steve Joachim, QB, Temple (from Chicago); 7C—Derrel Luce, LB, Baylor (from N.Y. Jets through Chicago); 8A—John Bushong, DE, Western Kentucky; 8B—Greg DenBoer, TE, Michigan (from Chicago through Denver); 8C—Mario Cage, RB, Northwestern (La.) State (from Green Bay); 9—Royce McKinney, DB, Kentucky State; 10—Phil Waganheim, P, Maryland; 11—Dave Hazel, WR, Ohio State; 12—Brad Storm, LB, Iowa State; 13—John Roman, G, Idaho State; 14—Mike Smith, C, SMU; 15—John Goodie, FB, Langston; 16A—Bill Malouf, WR-DB, Mississippi; 16B—Mike Evavold, DT, Macalester (from San Francisco); 16C—Bob Smith, DB, Maryland (from Oakland); 17A—David McKnight, LB, Georgia; 17B—Mike Bengard, DE, Northwestern (Iowa) (from San Francisco); 17C—Frank Russell, WR, Maryland (from Oakland).

1976

1—Ken Novak, DT, Purdue; 2—Choice to Pittsburgh; 3A—Ed Simonini, LB, Texas A & M; 3B—Ron Lee, RB, West Virginia (from Tampa Bay); 4—Choice to Pittsburgh; 5A—Sanders Shiver, LB, Carson-Newman (from Chicago through Miami and Chicago); 5B—Mike Kirkland, QB, Arkansas; 6—Choice to Buffalo; 7—Choice to New Orleans through Chicago and Oakland; 8—Ricky Thompson, WR, Baylor; 9—Stu Levenick, T, Illinois; 10—Tim Baylor, DB, Morgan State; 11—Rick Gibney, DT, Georgia Tech; 12—Frank Stavroff, K, Indiana; 13—Choice to Oakland; 14—Jeremiah Cummings, DE, Albany (Ga.) State; 15—Gary Alexander, T, Clemson; 16A—Mike Fuhrman, TE, Memphis State (from Washington through Baltimore and San Francisco); 16B—Steve Ludwig, C, Miami (Fla.); 17—Choice to Oakland.

1977

1—Randy Burke, WR, Kentucky; 2—Mike Ozdowski, DE, Virginia; 6—Calvin O'Neal, LB, Michigan; 7—Blanchard Carter, T, Nevada-Las Vegas; 8—Kenneth Helms, T-C, Georgia; 9—Glen Capriola, RB, Boston College; 10—Ron Baker, G, Oklahoma State; 11—Brian Ruff, LB, The Citadel; 12—Bill Deutsch, RB, North Dakota.

1978

1—Reese McCall, TE, Auburn; 2—Mike Woods, LB, Cincinnati; 5—Frank Myers, OT, Texas A & M; 6—Ben Garry, RB, Southern Mississippi; 7—Jeff Logan, RB, Ohio State; 8—Monte Anthony, RB, Nebraska; 9—Dave Studdard, OT, Texas; 10—Dallas Owens, DB, Kentucky; 11—Henry Mason, WR, Central Missouri; 12—Bruce Allen, P, Richmond.

1979

1—Barry Krauss, LB, Alabama; 3—Kim Anderson, DB, Arizona State; 5—Larry Braziel, DB, USC; 6—Jim Moore, OT, Ohio State; 8A—Steve Heimkreiter, LB, Notre Dame; 8B—Nesby Glasgow, DB, Washington; 9—Russ Henderson, P, Virginia; 10—Steven Stephens, TE, Oklahoma State; 11—John Priestner, LB, Western Ontario; 12—Charles Green, WR, Kansas State.

1980

1A—Curtis Dickey, HB, Texas A & M; 1B—Derrick Hatchett, DW, Texas; 2A—Ray Donaldson, C, Georgia; 2B—Tim Foley, OT, Notre Dame; 3—no choice; 4—Ray Butler, WR, U.S.C.; 5—no choice; 6—Chris Foote, C, U.S.C.; 7—Wesley Roberts, DE, Texas Christian; 8—Ken Walter, OT, Texas Tech; 9—Mark Bright, FB, Temple; 10—Larry Stewart, OT, Maryland; 11—Ed Whitley, TE, Kansas State; 12A—Randy Bielski, K, Towson State; 12B—Marvin Sims, FB, Clemson.

1981

1A—Randy McMillan, FB, Pittsburgh; 1B—Donnell Thompson, DT, North Carolina; 3—Randy Van Divier, OT, Washington; 4—Tim Sherwin, TE, Boston College; 6—Bubba Green, DT, North Carolina State; 7— Obed Ariri,

K, Clemson; 8A—Ken Sitton, S, Oklahoma; 8B—Hosea Taylor, DT, Houston; 9—Tim Gooch, DE, Kentucky; 10A—Gregg Gerken, LB, North Arizona University; 10B—Trent Bryant, CB, Arkansas; 11—Holden Smith, WR, Cal-Berkeley; 12—Eric Scoggins, LB, U.S.C.

1982
1A—Johnie Cooks, LB, Mississippi State; 1B—Art Schlichter, QB, Ohio State; 2A—Leo Wisniewski, NT, Penn State; 2B—Rohn Stark, P, Florida State; 3—James Burroughs, CB, Michigan State; 4—Mike Pagel, QB, Arizona State; 5—Terry Crouch, OG, Oklahoma; 6—Pat Beach, TE, Washington State; 7—Fletcher Jenkins, NT, Washington; 8—Tony Loia, OG, Arizona State; 9—Tony Berryhill, C, Clemson; 10—Tom Derry, S, Widener; 11—Lamont Meacham, CB, Western Kentucky; 12—Johnny Wright, RB, South Carolina.

1983
1—John Elway, QB, Stanford; 2—Vernon Maxwell, LB, Arizona State; 3—George Achica, NT, U.S.C.; 4—Phil Smith, WR, San Diego State; 5—Sid Abramowitz, OT, Tulsa; 6—Grant Feasel, C, Abilene Christian; 7—Alvin Moore, RB, Arizona State; 8—selection traded to Denver; 9A—Jim Mills, OT, Hawaii; 9B—Chris Rose, OT, Stanford; 10—Ronald Hopkins, CB, Murray State; 11—Jim Bob Taylor, QB, Georgia Tech; 12—Carl Williams, WR, Texas Southern.

Colts All-Time Results

ALL-AMERICA FOOTBALL CONFERENCE

1947
Won 2, Lost 11, Tied 1
Fourth in Eastern Division
Coach: Cecil Isbell

S	7	Brooklyn Dodgers	W	16-7
S	14	at San Francisco 49ers	L	7-14
S	21	at Cleveland Browns	L	0-28
S	28	New York Yankees	L	7-21
O	5	San Francisco 49ers	T	28-28
O	12	at Buffalo Bills	L	15-20
O	19	Los Angeles Dons	L	10-38
O	26	at Los Angeles Dons	L	0-56
N	2	at New York Yankees	L	21-35
N	7	at Chicago Rockets	L	21-27
N	16	at Brooklyn Dodgers	L	14-21
N	23	Buffalo Bills	L	14-33
N	30	Chicago Rockets	W	14-7
D	7	Cleveland Browns	L	0-42

1948
Won 7, Lost 7
Tied First Eastern Division
Coach: Cecil Isbell

S	5	New York Yankees	W	45-28
S	10	at Chicago Rockets	L	14-21
S	16	at New York Yankees	W	27-14
S	26	Brooklyn Dodgers	W	35-20
O	5	Cleveland Browns	L	10-14
O	10	San Francisco 49ers	L	14-56
O	15	at Los Angeles Dons	W	29-14
O	24	at San Francisco 49ers	L	10-21
O	31	at Buffalo Bills	L	17-35
N	7	at Cleveland Browns	L	7-28
N	14	Chicago Rockets	W	38-24
N	21	Los Angeles Dons	L	14-17
N	28	at Brooklyn Dodgers	W	38-20
D	5	Buffalo Bills	W	35-15

EASTERN DIVISION PLAYOFF GAME

D	12	Buffalo Bills	L	17-28

1949
Won 1, Lost 11
Seventh in Conference
Coach: Cecil Isbell (4 games)
Walt Driskill (8 games)

A	28	at San Francisco 49ers	L	17-31
S	2	Los Angeles Dons	L	17-49
S	11	at Cleveland Browns	L	0-21
S	16	at Chicago Hornets	L	7-35
S	25	Cleveland Browns	L	20-28
O	2	at Buffalo Bills	W	35-28
O	16	Brooklyn New York Yankees	L	21-24
O	23	Chicago Hornets	L	7-17
O	30	at Brooklyn New York Yankees	L	14-21
N	16	San Francisco 49ers	L	10-28
N	20	Los Angeles Dons	L	10-21
N	27	Buffalo Bills	L	14-38

NATIONAL FOOTBALL LEAGUE

1950
Won 1, Lost 11
Seventh in National Conference
Coach: Clem Crowe

S	17	Washington Redskins	L	14-38
S	24	Cleveland Browns	L	0-31
O	2	at Chicago Cardinals	L	13-55
O	15	Philadelphia Eagles	L	14-24
O	22	at Los Angeles Rams	L	27-70
O	29	at San Francisco 49ers	L	14-17
N	5	Green Bay Packers	W	41-21
N	12	at Pittsburgh Steelers	L	7-17
N	19	New York Giants	L	20-55
N	26	at Washington Redskins	L	28-38
D	3	Detroit Lions	L	21-45
D	10	New York Yanks	L	14-51

1953
Won 3, Lost 9
Fifth in Western Conference
Coach: Keith Molesworth

S	27	Chicago Bears	W	13-9
O	3	Detroit Lions	L	17-27
O	11	at Chicago Bears	W	16-14
O	18	at Green Bay Packers	L	14-37

O	25	Washington Redskins	W	27-17
O	31	Green Bay Packers	L	24-35
N	7	at Detroit Lions	L	7-17
N	15	at Philadelphia Eagles	L	14-45
N	22	Los Angeles Rams	L	13-21
N	29	San Francisco 49ers	L	21-38
D	5	at Los Angeles Rams	L	2-45
D	13	at San Francisco 49ers	L	14-45

1954
Won 3, Lost 9
Sixth in Western Conference
Coach: Weeb Ewbank

S	26	Los Angeles Rams	L	0-48
O	2	New York Giants	W	20-14
O	10	at Chicago Bears	L	9-28
O	16	at Detroit Lions	L	0-35
O	24	Green Bay Packers	L	6-7
O	31	at Washington Redskins	L	21-24
N	6	Detroit Lions	L	3-27
N	13	Green Bay Packers at Milwaukee	L	13-24
N	21	Chicago Bears	L	13-28
N	28	San Francisco 49ers	W	17-13
D	4	at Los Angeles Rams	W	22-21
D	11	at San Francisco 49ers	L	7-10

1955
Won 5, Lost 6, Tied 1
Fourth in Western Conference
Coach: Weeb Ewbank

S	25	Chicago Bears	W	23-17
O	1	Detroit Lions	W	28-13
O	8	Green Bay Packers at Milwaukee	W	24-20
O	16	at Chicago Bears	L	10-38
O	23	Washington Redskins	L	13-14
O	29	Green Bay Packers	W	14-10
N	5	at Detroit Lions	L	14-24
N	13	at New York Giants	L	7-17
N	20	Los Angeles Rams	T	17-17
N	27	San Francisco 49ers	W	26-14
D	4	at Los Angeles Rams	L	14-20
D	11	at San Francisco 49ers	L	24-35

1956
Won 5, Lost 7
Fourth in Western Conference
Coach: Weeb Ewbank

S	30	Chicago Bears	W	28-21
O	6	Detroit Lions	L	14-31
O	14	Green Bay Packers at Milwaukee	L	33-38
O	21	at Chicago Bears	L	27-58
O	28	Green Bay Packers	W	28-21
N	11	at Cleveland Browns	W	21-7
N	18	at Detroit Lions	L	3-27
N	25	Los Angeles Rams	W	56-21
D	2	San Francisco 49ers	L	17-20
D	9	at Los Angeles Rams	L	7-31
D	16	at San Francisco 49ers	L	17-30
D	23	Washington Redskins	W	19-17

1957
Won 7, Lost 5
Third in Western Conference
Coach: Weeb Ewbank

S	29	Detroit Lions	W	34-14
O	5	Chicago Bears	W	21-10
O	13	Green Bay Packers at Milwaukee	W	45-17
O	20	at Detroit Lions	L	27-31
O	27	Green Bay Packers	L	21-24
N	3	Pittsburgh Steelers	L	13-19
N	10	at Washington Redskins	W	21-17
N	17	at Chicago Bears	W	29-14
N	24	San Francisco 49ers	W	27-21
D	1	Los Angeles Rams	W	31-14
D	8	at San Francisco 49ers	L	13-17
D	15	at Los Angeles Rams	L	21-37

WORLD CHAMPIONS
1958
Won 9, Lost 3
First in Western Conference
Coach: Weeb Ewbank

S	28	Detroit Lions	W	28-15
O	4	Chicago Bears	W	51-38
O	12	Green Bay Packers at Milwaukee	W	24-17
O	19	at Detroit Lions	W	40-14
O	26	Washington Redskins	W	35-10
N	2	Green Bay Packers	W	56-0
N	9	at New York Giants	L	21-24
N	16	at Chicago Bears	W	17-0
N	23	Los Angeles Rams	W	34-7
N	30	San Francisco 49ers	W	35-27
D	6	at Los Angeles Rams	L	28-30
D	14	at San Francisco 49ers	L	12-21

WORLD CHAMPIONSHIP GAME

D	28	at New York Giants	W	23-17 (OT)

WORLD CHAMPIONS
1959
Won 9, Lost 3
First in Western Conference
Coach: Weeb Ewbank

S	27	Detroit Lions	W	21-9
O	3	Chicago Bears	L	21-26
O	11	at Detroit Lions	W	31-24
O	18	at Chicago Bears	W	21-7
O	25	Green Bay Packers	W	38-21
N	1	Cleveland Browns	L	31-38
N	8	at Washington Redskins	L	24-27
N	15	Green Bay Packers at Milwaukee	W	28-24
N	22	San Francisco 49ers	W	45-14
N	29	Los Angeles Rams	W	35-21

D	5	at San Francisco 49ers	W	34-14
D	12	at Los Angeles Rams	W	45-26

WORLD CHAMPIONSHIP GAME

D	27	New York Giants	W	31-16

1960
Won 6, Lost 6
Fourth in Western Conference
Coach: Weeb Ewbank

S	25	Washington Redskins	W	20-0
O	2	Chicago Bears	W	42-7
O	9	at Green Bay Packers	L	21-35
O	16	Los Angeles Rams	W	31-17
O	23	at Detroit Lions	L	17-30
O	30	at Dallas Cowboys	W	45-7
N	6	Green Bay Packers	W	38-24
N	13	at Chicago Bears	W	24-20
N	26	San Francisco 49ers	L	22-30
D	4	Detroit Lions	L	15-20
D	11	at Los Angeles Rams	L	3-10
D	18	at San Francisco 49ers	L	10-34

1961
Won 8, Lost 6
Third in Western Conference
Coach: Weeb Ewbank

S	17	Los Angeles Rams	W	27-24
S	24	Detroit Lions	L	15-16
O	1	Minnesota Vikings	W	34-33
O	8	at Green Bay Packers	L	7-45
O	15	at Chicago Bears	L	10-24
O	22	at Detroit Lions	W	17-14
O	29	Chicago Bears	L	20-21
N	5	Green Bay Packers	W	45-21
N	12	at Minnesota Vikings	L	20-28
N	19	St. Louis Cardinals	W	16-0
N	26	at Washington Redskins	W	27-6
D	3	San Francisco 49ers	W	20-17
D	9	at Los Angeles Rams	L	17-34
D	16	at San Francisco 49ers	W	27-24

1962
Won 7, Lost 7
Fourth in Western Conference
Coach: Weeb Ewbank

S	16	Los Angeles Rams	W	30-27
S	23	at Minnesota Vikings	W	34-7
S	30	Detroit Lions	L	20-29
O	7	San Francisco 49ers	L	13-21
O	14	at Cleveland Browns	W	36-14
O	21	at Chicago Bears	L	15-35
O	28	Green Bay Packers	L	6-17
N	4	at San Francisco 49ers	W	22-3
N	11	at Los Angeles Rams	W	14-2
N	18	at Green Bay Packers	L	13-17
N	25	Chicago Bears	L	0-57
D	2	at Detroit Lions	L	14-21
D	8	Washington Redskins	W	34-21
D	16	Minnesota Vikings	W	42-17

1963
Won 8, Lost 6
Third in Western Conference
Coach: Don Shula

S	15	New York Giants	L	28-37
S	22	at San Francisco 49ers	W	20-14
S	29	at Green Bay Packers	L	20-31
O	6	at Chicago Bears	L	3-10
O	13	San Francisco 49ers	W	20-3
O	20	at Detroit Lions	W	25-21
O	27	Green Bay Packers	L	20-34
N	3	Chicago Bears	L	7-17
N	10	Detroit Lions	W	24-21
N	17	at Minnesota Vikings	W	37-34
N	24	at Los Angeles Rams	L	16-17
D	1	at Washington Redskins	W	36-20
D	8	Minnesota Vikings	W	41-10
D	15	Los Angeles Rams	W	19-16

1964
Won 12, Lost 2
First in Western Conference
Coach: Don Shula

S	13	at Minnesota Vikings	L	24-34
S	20	at Green Bay Packers	W	21-20
S	27	Chicago Bears	W	52-0
O	4	Los Angeles Rams	W	35-20
O	12	St. Louis Cardinals	W	47-27
O	18	Green Bay Packers	W	24-21
O	25	at Detroit Lions	W	34-0
N	1	San Francisco 49ers	W	37-7
N	8	at Chicago Bears	W	40-24
N	15	Minnesota Vikings	W	17-14
N	22	at Los Angeles Rams	W	24-7
N	29	at San Francisco 49ers	W	14-3
D	6	Detroit Lions	L	14-31
D	13	Washington Redskins	W	45-17

NFL CHAMPIONSHIP GAME

D	27	at Cleveland Browns	L	0-27

1965
Won 10, Lost 3, Tied 1
Tied for First in Western Conference
Coach: Don Shula

S	19	Minnesota Vikings	W	35-16
S	26	Green Bay Packers at Milwaukee	L	17-20
O	3	San Francisco 49ers	W	27-24
O	10	Detroit Lions	W	31-7
O	17	at Washington Redskins	W	38-7
O	24	Los Angeles Rams	W	35-20
O	31	at San Francisco 49ers	W	34-28
N	7	at Chicago Bears	W	26-21
N	14	at Minnesota Vikings	W	41-21
N	21	Philadelphia Eagles	W	34-24
N	25	at Detroit Lions	T	24-24
D	5	Chicago Bears	L	0-13
D	12	Green Bay Packers	L	27-42
D	18	at Los Angeles Rams	W	20-17

WESTERN CONFERENCE PLAYOFF

D	26	at Green Bay Packers	L	10-13 (OT)

PLAYOFF BOWL

J	9	Dallas Cowboys at Miami	W	35-3

1966
Won 9, Lost 5
Second in Western Conference
Coach: Don Shula

S	10	Green Bay Packers at Milwaukee	L	3-24
S	18	at Minnesota Vikings	W	38-23
S	25	San Francisco 49ers	W	36-14
O	9	at Chicago Bears	L	17-27
O	16	Detroit Lions	W	45-14
O	23	Minnesota Vikings	W	20-17
O	30	at Los Angeles Rams	W	17-3
N	6	Washington Redskins	W	37-10
N	13	at Atlanta Falcons	W	19-7
N	20	at Detroit Lions	L	14-20
N	27	Los Angeles Rams	L	7-23
D	4	Chicago Bears	W	21-16
D	10	Green Bay Packers	L	10-14
D	18	at San Francisco 49ers	W	30-14

PLAYOFF BOWL

J	8	Philadelphia Eagles at Miami	W	20-14

1967
Won 11, Lost 1, Tied 2
Tied for First in Coastal Division
Coach: Don Shula

S	17	Atlanta Falcons	W	38-31
S	24	at Philadelphia Eagles	W	38-6
O	1	San Francisco 49ers	W	41-7
O	8	at Chicago Bears	W	24-3
O	15	Los Angeles Rams	T	24-24
O	22	at Minnesota Vikings	T	20-20
O	29	at Washington Redskins	W	17-13
N	5	Green Bay Packers	W	13-10
N	12	at Atlanta Falcons	W	49-7
N	19	Detroit Lions	W	41-7
N	26	at San Francisco 49ers	W	26-9
D	3	Dallas Cowboys	W	23-17
D	10	New Orleans Saints	W	30-10
D	17	at Los Angeles Rams	L	10-34

1968
Won 13, Lost 1
First in Coastal Division
Coach: Don Shula

S	15	San Francisco 49ers	W	27-10
S	23	at Atlanta Falcons	W	28-20
S	29	at Pittsburgh Steelers	W	41-7
O	6	Chicago Bears	W	28-7
O	13	at San Francisco 49ers	W	42-14
O	20	Cleveland Browns	L	20-30
O	27	Los Angeles Rams	W	27-10
N	2	at New York Giants	W	26-0
N	10	at Detroit Lions	W	27-10
N	17	St. Louis Cardinals	W	27-0
N	24	Minnesota Vikings	W	21-9
D	1	Atlanta Falcons	W	44-0
D	7	at Green Bay Packers	W	16-3
D	15	at Los Angeles Rams	W	28-24

WESTERN CONFERENCE CHAMPIONSHIP GAME

D	22	Minnesota Vikings	W	24-14

NFL CHAMPIONSHIP GAME

D	27	at Cleveland Browns	W	34-0

SUPER BOWL III

J	12	New York Jets at Miami	L	7-16

1969
Won 8, Lost 5, Tied 1
Second in Coastal Division
Coach: Don Shula

S	21	Los Angeles Rams	L	20-27
S	28	at Minnesota Vikings	L	14-52
O	5	at Atlanta Falcons	W	21-14
O	13	Philadelphia Eagles	W	24-20
O	19	at New Orleans Saints	W	30-10
O	26	San Francisco 49ers	L	21-24
N	2	Washington Redskins	W	41-17
N	9	Green Bay Packers	W	14-6
N	16	at San Francisco 49ers	L	17-20
N	23	at Chicago Bears	W	24-21
N	30	Atlanta Falcons	W	13-6
D	7	Detroit Lions	T	17-17
D	13	at Dallas Cowboys	L	10-27
D	21	at Los Angeles Rams	W	13-7

SUPER BOWL CHAMPIONS
1970
Won 11, Lost 2, Tied 1
First in Eastern Division
Coach: Don McCafferty

S	20	at San Diego Chargers	W	16-14
S	28	Kansas City Chiefs	L	24-44
O	4	at Boston Patriots	W	14-6
O	11	at Houston Oilers	W	24-20
O	18	at New York Jets	W	29-22
O	25	Boston Patriots	W	27-3
N	1	Miami Dolphins	W	35-0
N	9	Green Bay Packers at Milwaukee	W	13-10
N	15	Buffalo Bills	T	17-17
N	22	at Miami Dolphins	L	17-34
N	29	Chicago Bears	W	21-20
D	6	Philadelphia Eagles	W	29-10
D	13	at Buffalo Bills	W	20-14
D	19	New York Jets	W	35-20

AFC DIVISIONAL PLAYOFF GAME

D	26	Cincinnati Bengals	W	17-0

AFC CHAMPIONSHIP GAME

J	3	Oakland Raiders	W	27-17

SUPER BOWL V

J	17	Dallas Cowboys at Miami	W	16-13

1971
Won 10, Lost 4
Second in Eastern Division (Wildcard)
Coach: Don McCafferty

S	19	New York Jets	W	22-0
S	26	Cleveland Browns	L	13-14
O	3	at New England Patriots	W	23-3
O	10	at Buffalo Bills	W	43-0
O	17	at New York Giants	W	31-7
O	25	at Minnesota Vikings	L	3-10
O	31	Pittsburgh Steelers	W	34-21
N	8	Los Angeles Rams	W	24-17
N	14	at New York Jets	W	14-13
N	21	at Miami Dolphins	L	14-17
N	28	at Oakland Raiders	W	37-14
D	5	Buffalo Bills	W	24-0
D	11	Miami Dolphins	W	14-3
D	19	New England Patriots	L	17-21

AFC DIVISIONAL PLAYOFF GAME

D	26	at Cleveland Browns	W	20-3

AFC CHAMPIONSHIP GAME

J	2	at Miami Dolphins	L	0-21

1972
Won 5, Lost 9
Third in Eastern Division
Coaches: Don McCafferty (5 games)
John Sandusky (9 games)

S	17	St. Louis Cardinals	L	3-10
S	24	New York Jets	L	34-44
O	1	at Buffalo Bills	W	17-0
O	8	San Diego Chargers	L	20-23
O	15	Dallas Cowboys	L	0-21
O	22	at New York Jets	L	20-24
O	29	Miami Dolphins	L	0-23
N	6	at New England Patriots	W	24-17
N	12	at San Francisco 49ers	L	21-24
N	19	at Cincinnati Bengals	W	20-19
N	26	New England Patriots	W	31-0
D	3	Buffalo Bills	W	35-7
D	10	at Kansas City Chiefs	L	10-24
D	16	at Miami Dolphins	L	0-16

1973
Won 4, Lost 10
Fourth in Eastern Division
Coach: Howard Schnellenberger

S	16	at Cleveland Browns	L	14-24
S	23	New York Jets	L	10-34
S	30	New Orleans Saints	W	14-10
O	7	at New England Patriots	L	16-24
O	14	at Buffalo Bills	L	13-31
O	21	at Detroit Lions	W	29-27
O	28	Oakland Raiders	L	21-34
N	4	Houston Oilers	L	27-31
N	11	at Miami Dolphins	L	0-44
N	18	at Washington Redskins	L	14-22
N	25	Buffalo Bills	L	17-24
D	2	at New York Jets	L	17-20
D	9	Miami Dolphins	W	16-3
D	16	New England Patriots	W	18-13

1974
Won 2, Lost 12
Fifth in Eastern Division
Coaches: Howard Schnellenberger (3 games)
Joe Thomas (11 games)

S	15	at Pittsburgh Steelers	L	0-30
S	22	Green Bay Packers	L	13-20
S	29	at Philadelphia Eagles	L	10-30
O	6	at New England Patriots	L	3-42
O	13	Buffalo Bills	L	14-27
O	20	at New York Jets	W	35-20
O	27	at Miami Dolphins	L	7-17
N	3	Cincinnati Bengals	L	14-24
N	10	Denver Broncos	L	6-17
N	17	at Atlanta Falcons	W	17-7
N	24	New England Patriots	L	17-27
D	1	at Buffalo Bills	L	0-6
D	8	Miami Dolphins	L	16-17
D	15	New York Jets	L	38-45

1975
Won 10, Lost 4
First in Eastern Division
Coach: Ted Marchibroda

S	21	at Chicago Bears	W	35-7
S	28	Oakland Raiders	L	20-31
O	5	at Los Angeles Rams	L	13-24
O	12	Buffalo Bills	L	31-38
O	19	at New England Patriots	L	10-21
O	26	at New York Jets	W	45-28
N	2	Cleveland Browns	W	21-7
N	9	at Buffalo Bills	W	42-35
N	16	New York Jets	W	52-19
N	23	at Miami Dolphins	W	33-17
N	30	Kansas City Chiefs	W	28-14
D	7	at New York Giants	W	21-0
D	14	Miami Dolphins	W	10-7 (OT)
D	21	New England Patriots	W	34-21

AFC DIVISIONAL PLAYOFF GAME

D	27	at Pittsburgh Steelers	L	10-28

1976
Won 11, Lost 3
First in Eastern Division
Coach: Ted Marchibroda

S	12	at New England Patriots	W	27-13
S	19	Cincinnati Bengals	W	28-27

S	26	at Dallas Cowboys	L	27-30
O	3	Tampa Bay Buccaneers	W	42-17
O	10	Miami Dolphins	W	28-14
O	17	at Buffalo Bills	W	31-13
O	24	at New York Jets	W	20-0
N	1	Houston Oilers	W	38-14
N	7	at San Diego Chargers	W	37-21
N	14	New England Patriots	L	14-21
N	22	at Miami Dolphins	W	17-16
N	28	New York Jets	W	33-16
D	4	at St. Louis Cardinals	L	17-24
D	12	Buffalo Bills	W	58-20

AFC DIVISIONAL PLAYOFF GAME

D	19	Pittsburgh Steelers	L	14-40

1977
Won 10, Lost 4
First in Eastern Division
Coach: Ted Marchibroda

S	18	at Seattle Seahawks	W	29-14
S	25	at New York Jets	W	20-12
O	2	Buffalo Bills	W	17-14
O	9	Miami Dolphins	W	45-28
O	16	at Kansas City Chiefs	W	17-6
0	23	at New England Patriots	L	3-17
0	30	Pittsburgh Steelers	W	31-21
N	7	Washington Redskins	W	10-3
N	13	at Buffalo Bills	W	31-13
N	20	New York Jets	W	33-12
N	27	at Denver Broncos	L	13-27
D	5	at Miami Dolphins	L	6-17
D	11	Detroit Lions	L	10-13
D	18	New England Patriots	W	30-24

AFC DIVISIONAL PLAYOFF GAME

D	24	Oakland Raiders	L	31-37 (2 OT)

1978
Won 5, Lost 11
Fifth in Eastern Division
Coach: Ted Marchibroda

S	4	at Dallas Cowboys	L	0-38
S	10	Miami Dolphins	L	0-42
S	18	at New England Patriots	W	34-27
S	24	at Buffalo Bills	L	17-24
O	1	Philadelphia Eagles	L	14-17
O	8	at St. Louis Cardinals	W	30-17
O	15	New York Jets	L	10-33
O	22	Denver Broncos	W	7-6
O	29	at Miami Dolphins	L	8-26
N	6	Washington Redskins	W	21-17
N	12	at Seattle Seahawks	W	17-14
N	19	Cleveland Browns	L	24-45
N	26	New England Patriots	L	14-35
D	3	at New York Jets	L	16-24
D	9	at Pittsburgh Steelers	L	13-35
D	17	Buffalo Bills	L	14-21

1979
Won 5, Lost 11
Fifth in Eastern Division
Coach: Ted Marchibroda

S	2	at Kansas City Chiefs	L	0-14
S	9	Tampa Bay Buccaneers	L	26-29 (OT)
S	16	at Cleveland Browns	L	10-13
S	23	at Pittsburgh Steelers	L	13-17
S	30	Buffalo Bills	L	13-31
O	7	New York Jets	W	10-8
O	14	Houston Oilers	L	16-28
O	21	at Buffalo Bills	W	14-13
O	28	New England Patriots	W	31-26
N	4	Cincinnati Bengals	W	38-28
N	11	at Miami Dolphins	L	0-19
N	18	at New England Patriots	L	21-50
N	25	Miami Dolphins	L	24-28
D	2	at New York Jets	L	17-30
D	9	Kansas City Chiefs	L	7-10
D	16	at New York Giants	W	31-7

1980
Won 7, Lost 9
Fourth in Eastern Division
Coach: Mike McCormack

S	7	at New York Jets	W	17-14
S	14	Pittsburgh Steelers	L	17-20
S	21	at Houston Oilers	L	16-21
S	28	New York Jets	W	35-21
O	5	at Miami Dolphins	W	30-17
O	12	at Buffalo Bills	W	17-12
O	19	New England Patriots	L	21-37
O	26	St. Louis Cardinals	L	10-17
N	2	at Kansas City Chiefs	W	31-24
N	9	Cleveland Browns	L	27-28
N	16	at Detroit Lions	W	10-9
N	23	at New England Patriots	L	21-47
N	30	Buffalo Bills	W	28-24
D	7	at Cincinnati Bengals	L	33-34
D	14	Miami Dolphins	L	14-24
D	21	Kansas City Chiefs	L	28-38

1981
Won 2, Lost 14
Fourth in Eastern Division
Coach: Mike McCormack

S	6	at New England Patriots	W	29-28
S	13	Buffalo Bills	L	3-35
S	20	at Denver Broncos	L	10-28
S	27	Miami Dolphins	L	28-31
O	4	at Buffalo Bills	L	17-23
O	11	Cincinnati Bengals	L	19-41
O	18	San Diego Chargers	L	14-43
O	26	at Cleveland Browns	L	28-42
N	1	at Miami Dolphins	L	10-27
N	8	New York Jets	L	14-41
N	15	at Philadelphia Eagles	L	13-38

N	22	St. Louis Cardinals	L	24-35
N	29	at New York Jets	L	0-25
D	6	Dallas Cowboys	L	13-37
D	13	at Washington Redskins	L	14-38
D	20	New England Patriots	W	23-21

1982
Won 0, Lost 8, Tied 1
Fourteenth in American Conference
Coach: Frank Kush

S	12	New England Patriots	L	13-24
S	19	at Miami Dolphins	L	20-24
S	26	New York Jets	canceled	
O	3	at Detroit Lions	canceled	
O	10	Buffalo Bills	canceled	
O	17	at Cleveland Browns	canceled	
O	24	Miami Dolphins	postponed to 1/2/83	
O	31	Tampa Bay Buccaneers	canceled	
N	7	at New England Patriots	canceled	
N	14	Oakland Raiders	canceled	
N	21	at New York Jets	L	0-37
N	28	at Buffalo Bills	L	0-20
D	5	Cincinnati Bengals	L	17-20
D	12	at Minnesota Vikings	L	10-13
D	19	Green Bay Packers	T	20-20
D	26	at San Diego Chargers	L	26-44
J	2	Miami Dolphins	L	7-34

1983
Won 7, Lost 9
Fourth in Eastern Division
Coach: Frank Kush

S	4	at New England Patriots	W	29-23 (OT)
S	11	Denver Broncos	L	10-17
S	18	at Buffalo Bills	L	23-28
S	25	Chicago Bears	W	22-19 (OT)
O	2	at Cincinnati Bengals	W	34-31
O	9	New England Patriots	W	12-7
O	16	Buffalo Bills	L	7-30
O	23	Miami Dolphins	L	7-21
O	30	at Philadelphia Eagles	W	22-21
N	6	at New York Jets	W	17-14
N	13	Pittsburgh Steelers	L	13-24
N	20	at Miami Dolphins	L	0-37
N	27	at Cleveland Browns	L	23-41
D	4	New York Jets	L	6-10
D	11	at Denver Broncos	L	19-21
D	18	Houston Oilers	W	20-10

The following compilation of Colts alumni includes every player who has ever appeared in a Baltimore Colts uniform during a regular season National Football League Game since 1953.

COACHES

Arnsparger, Bill—Miami (O.)	1964-69
Ball, Herman—Davis-Elkins	1956-62
Baughan, Maxie—Georgia Tech	1975-79
Bielski, Dick—Maryland	1964-72, 77-81
Boutselis, George—North Carolina	1975-81
Boyd, Bob—Oklahoma	1969-72, 81
Bratkowski, Zeke—Georgia	1982-83
Bridgers, John—Auburn	1957-58
Bullough, Hank—Michigan State	1970-72
Callahan, Ray—Kentucky	1973
Carson, Bud—North Carolina	1982
Cumiskey, Frank—Ohio State	1954-56
Cunningham, Gunther—Oregon	1982-83
Doll, Don—USC	1974
Douglas, Otis—William & Mary	1953
Dovell, Whitey—Maryland	1975-78
Ewbank, Weeb—Miami (Ohio)	1954-62
Franklin, Bobby—Mississippi	1973
Hawkins, Ralph—Maryland	1978
Hughes, Tom—Purdue	1955
Hunter, Hal—Pittsburgh	1982-83
Idzik, John—Maryland	1970-72, 80-81
Khayat, Ed—Tulane	1977-81
Kush, Frank—Michigan State	1982-83
Lauterbur, Frank—Mt. Union	1955-56, 74-77
Mann, Richard—Arizona State	1982-83
Marchetti, Gino—USF	1963
Marchibroda, Ted—St. Bonaventure	1975-79
McCafferty, Don—Ohio State	1960-72
McCormack, Mike—Kansas	1980-81
McCulley, Pete—Louisiana Tech	1973-76
Miller, Red—Western Illinois	1971-72
Molesworth, Keith—Monmouth	1953
Murphy, Russ—Davidson	1954
Mutscheller, Jim—Notre Dame	1963
Noll, Chuck—Dayton	1966-67
Pellington, Bill—Rutgers	1963
Powers, Clyde—Oklahoma	1980
Richards, Ray—Nebraska	1953
Rymkus, Lou—Notre Dame	1970
Sandusky, John—Villanova	1959-72
Schnellenberger, Howard–Kentucky	1973-74
Sefcik, George—Notre Dame	1973
Shaw, Bob—Ohio State	1957-58
Shula, Don—John Carroll	1963-69
Smith, Jerry—Wisconsin	1974-76
Symank, John—Florida	1979-81
Szymanski, Dick—Notre Dame	1974
Theder, Roger—W. Michigan	1982-83
Thomas, Joe—Ohio Northern	1954-74
Valesente, Bob—Ithaca	1982-83
Venturi, Rick—Northwestern	1982-83
Voris, Dick—San Jose State	1973
Wasylik, Nick—Ohio State	1953
Weber, Chuck—West Chester State	1980-81
Westhoff, Mike—Wichita State	1982-83
Wietecha, Ray—Northwestern	1980-81
Winner, Charlie—Wash. U. (St. Louis)	1954-65
Young, George—Bucknell	1970, 73
Zwahlen, Ernie—Oregon State	1979

PLAYERS

Abramowitz, Sid (T) Tulsa	1983
Agase, Alex (G) Illinois	1953
Allegre, Raul (K) Texas	1983
Allen, Gerald (B) Omaha	1966
Alley, Don (F) Adams State	1967
Alston, Mack (TE) UMES	1977-80
Ameche, Alan (B) Wisconsin	1955-60
Amman, Richard (DE) Florida State	1972-73
Anderson, Kim (DB) Arizona State	1980-83
Anderson, Larry (DB) Louisiana Tech	1982-83
Andrews, John (TE) Indiana	1973-74
Austin, Ocie (DB) Utah State	1968-69
Averno, Sisto (G) Muhlenberg	1953-54
Bailey, Elmer (WR) Minnesota	1982
Bailey, Jim (DT) Kansas	1970-74
Baker, Ron (OG) Oklahoma State	1978-79
Baldischwiler, Karl (OT)	1983
Baldwin, Bob (B) Clemson	1966-67
Ball, Sam (T) Kentucky	1966-70
Ballard, Quinton (NT) Elon	1983
Barnes, Ernie (NT) Mississippi State	1983
Barnes, Mike (DE) Miami (Fla.)	1973-81
Barwegan, Dick (G) Purdue	1953-54
Baylor, Tim (DB) Morgan State	1976-78
Beach, Pat (TE) Washington State	1982-83
Bell, Mark (DE) Colorado State	1983
Berra, Tim (WR) Massachusetts	1974
Berry, Raymond (E) SMU	1955-67
Bertuca, Tony (LB) Chico State	1974
Beutler, Tom (LB) Toledo	1971
Bielski, Dick (E) Maryland	1962-63
Bighead, Jack (E) Pepperdine	1954
Blackwood, Lyle (S) TCU	1977-80
Blandin, Ernie (T) Tulane	1953
Blue, Forrest (C) Auburn	1975-78
Bieick, Tom (B) Georgia	1956
Bouza, Matt (WR) Cal-Berkeley	1982-83
Boyd, Bob (DB) Oklahoma	1960-68
Braase, Ordell (DE) South Dakota	1957-68
Bracelin, Greg (LB) California	1982-83
Bragg, Mike (P) Richmond	1980
Braziel, Larry (DB) USC	1979-81
Brethauer, Monte (E) Oregon	1953, 55
Brown, Barry (E) Florida	1966-67
Brown, Ed (QB) USF	1965
Brown, Ray (DB) Mississippi	1958-60
Brown, Timmy (RB) Ball State	1968
Bryan, Walter (B) Texas Tech	1955
Bulaich, Norm (RB) TCU	1970-72
Burke, Randy (WR) Kentucky	1978-81
Burkett, Jack (LB) Auburn	1961-66
Burroughs, James (CB) Michigan State	1982-83
Butler, Ray (WR) USC	1980-83
Call, Jack (B) Colgate	1957-58
Campanella, Joe (T) Ohio State	1953-57
Campbell, John (LB) Minnesota	1969
Carr, Roger (WR) Louisiana Tech	1974-81
Cheatham, Ernie (T) Loyola LA	1954
Cherry, Stan (LB) Morgan State	1973
Chester, Raymond (TE) Morgan State	1973-77
Cheyunski, Jim (LB) Syracuse	1975-76
Chrovich, Dick (T) Miami (Ohio)	1955-56
Clemens, Bob (B) Pitt	1962
Cogdill, Gail (E) Washington State	1968
Cole, Terry (RB) Indiana	1968-69
Collett, Elmer (G) San Francisco State	1973-77
Colteryahn, Lloyd (E) Maryland	1954-56
Colvin, Jim (T) Houston	1960-63
Conjar, Larry (B) Notre Dame	1969-70
Cook, Fred (DE) So. Mississippi	1974-80
Cooke, Ed (E) Maryland	1959
Cooks, Johnie (LB) Mississippi State	1982-83
Coutre, Larry (B) Notre Dame	1953
Craddock, Nate (RB) Parsons	1963
Crosby, Cleveland (DE) Arizona	1982
Crouch, Terry (OG) Oklahoma	1982
Cuozzo, Gary (QB) Virginia	1963-66
Curry, Bill (C) Georgia Tech	1967-72
Curtis, Mike (LB) Duke	1965-75
Curtis, Tom (DB) Michigan	1970-71
Davidson, Cotton (QB) Baylor	1954, 1957
Davis, Milt (DB) UCLA	1957-60
Davis, Norman (G) Grambling	1967
Davis, Ted (LB) Georgia Tech	1964-66
DeCarlo, Art (E) Georgia	1957-60
Delaney, Jeff (S) Pittsburgh	1982-83
DeRoo, Brian (WR) Redlands University	1979-81
DelBello, Jack (QB) Miami (Fla.)	1953
Dickel, Dan (LB) Iowa	1974-77
Dickey, Curtis (RB) Texas A & M	1980-83
Diehl, John (T) Virginia	1961-64
Dilts, Bucky (P) Georgia	1979
Dixon, Zachary (RB) Temple	1980-82
Domres, Marty (QB) Columbia	1972-75
Donaldson, Ray (C) Georgia	1980-83
Donovan, Art (DT) Boston College	1953-61
Doughty, Glenn (WR) Michigan	1972-79
Drougas, Tom (T) Oregon	1972-73
Duncan, James (DB) Maryland State	1969-71
Dunlap, Len (DB) North Texas State	1971
Dunn, Perry Lee (RB) Mississippi	1969
Dupre, L.G. (RB) Baylor	1955-59
Durham, Steve (DE) Clemson	1982
Dutton, John (DE) Nebraska	1974-78
Ecklund, Brad (C) Oregon	1953
Edmunds, Randy (LB) Georgia Tech	1972
Edwards, Dan (E) Georgia	1953-54
Eggers, Doug (LB) South Dakota State	1954-57
Ehrmann, Joe (DT) Syracuse	1973-80
Embree, Mel (E) Pepperdine	1953
Enke, Fred (QB) Arizona	1953-54
Feagin, Wiley (G) Houston	1961-62
Feamster, Tom (T) Florida State	1956
Feasel, Grant (C) Abilene Christian	1983
Federspiel, Joe (LB) Kentucky	1981
Felts, Bob (B) Florida A & M	1965
Fernandes, Ron (DE) Eastern Michigan	1976-79
Fields, Greg (DE) Grambling	1979-80

Finnin, Tom (DT) Detroit	1953-56
Flowers, Bernie (E) Purdue	1956
Flowers, Dick (B) Northwestern	1953
Foley, Tim (DT) Notre Dame	1981
Foote, Chris (C) USC	1980-81
Franklin, Cleveland (RB) Baylor	1981-82
Franklin, Willie (WR) Oklahoma	1972
Fultz, Mike (DT) Nebraska	1981
Ganas, Rusty (DT) South Carolina	1971
Gardin, Ron (DB) Arizona	1970-71
Garrett, Mike (P) Georgia	1981
Garry, Ben (RB) So. Mississippi	1979-80
Gaubatz, Dennis (LB) LSU	1965-69
George, Ed (T) Wake Forest	1975
Gilburg, Tom (T-P) Syracuse	1961-65
Ginn, Hubert (RB) Florida A & M	1973
Glasgow, Nesby (DB) Washington	1979-83
Glick, Gary (B) Colorado A & M	1961
Golsteyn, Jerry (QB) Northern Illinois	1979
Goode, Tom (C) Mississippi State	1970
Grant, Bob (LB) Wake Forest	1968-70
Gregory, Ken (E) Whittier	1961
Green, Anthony (DT) North Carolina State	1981
Griffin, Wade (T) Mississippi	1977-81
Griggs, Perry (KR) Troy State	1977
Grimm, Dan (G) Colorado	1969
Gross, Lee (C) Auburn	1979
Hall, Randy (CB) Idaho	1974, 76
Hardeman, Don (RB) Texas A & I	1978-79
Harness, Jim (B) Mississippi State	1956
Harold, George (B) Allen	1966-67
Harris, Joe (LB) Georgia Tech	1982
Harris, Wendell (DB) LSU	1962-65
Harrison, Bob (B) Ohio University	1961
Harrison, Dwight (DB) Texas A & I	1978-79
Hart, Jeff (T) Oregon State	1979-83
Hatchett, Derrick (CB) Texas	1980-83
Havrilak, Sam (B) Bucknell	1969-73
Hawkins, Alex (B) South Carolina	1955-65, 67-68
Haymond, Alvin (DB) Southern University	1964-67
Heimkreiter, Steve (LB) Notre Dame	1980
Hemphill, Darryl (FS) West Texas State	1982
Hendricks, Ted (LB) Miami (Fla.)	1969-73
Henry, Bernard (WR) Arizona State	1982-83
Henry, Steve (DB) Emporia State	1981
Hepburn, Lonnie (CB) Texas So.	1971-72
Herman, Mark (QB) Purdue	1983
Hermann, John (B) UCLA	1956
Herosian, Brian (S) Connecticut	1973
Hickman, Dallas (LB) California	1981
Hill, Jerry (RB) Wyoming	1961, 63-70
Hilton, Roy (DE) Jackson State	1965-73
Hinton, Chris (G/T) Northwestern	1983
Hinton, Chuck (DT) N. Carolina College	1972
Hinton, Ed (WR) Oklahoma	1969-72
Hoaglin, Fred (C) Pitt	1973
Horn, Dick (B) Stanford	1958
Hudson, Nat (OG) Georgia	1982
Huff, Ken (G) N. Carolina	1975-82
Hugasian, Harry (B) Stanford	1955
Humm, David (QB) Nebraska	1981-82
Hunt, George (K) Tennessee	1973
Hunter, James (NT) USC	1982
Huzvar, John (RB) Pitt	1953-54
Hyde, Glenn (OT) Pittsburgh	1982
Jackson, Ken (G) Texas	1953-57
James, Tommy (B) Ohio State	1956
Jefferson, Roy (WR) Utah	1970
Jenkins, Fletcher (DE) Washington	1982
Johnson, Cornelius (G) Va. Union	1968-72
Johnson, Gary Don (DT) Baylor	1980
Johnson, Greg (DT) Florida State	1977
Johnson, Marshall (WR) Houston	1975-78
Jones, Bert (QB) LSU	1973-81
Jones, Ricky (LB) Tuskegee	1980-83
Joyce, Don (DE) Tulane	1954-60
Justin, Sid (CB) Long Beach State	1982
Kaczmarek, Mike (LB) Southern Illinois	1973
Kafentzis, Mark (S) Hawaii	1983
Kalmanir, Tom (B) Nevada	1953
Keane, Tom (DB) West Virginia	1953-54
Kennedy, Jimmie (TE) Colorado State	1975-77
Kerkorian, Gary (QB) Stanford	1954-56, 58
Kern, Rex (DB) Ohio State	1971-73
Kirchiro, Bill (G) Maryland	1962
Kirkland, Mike (QB) Arkansas	1976-78
Kirouac, Lou (T) Boston College	1964
Koman, Bill (G) North Carolina	1956
Kostelnik, Ron (T) Cincinnati	1969
Kovac, Ed (B) Cincinnati	1960
Krahl, Jim (DT) Texas Tech	1979-80
Krauss, Barry (LB) Alabama	1979-83
Krouse, Ray (DT) Maryland	1958
Kunz, George (T) Notre Dame	1975-77, 80
Laird, Bruce (DB) American International	1972-81
Landry, Greg (QB) Massachusetts	1979-81
Langas, Bob (E) Wayne	1954
Lange, Bill (G) Dayton	1953
LaPointe, Ron (TE) Penn State	1980
Larson, Lynn (T) Kansas State	1971-72
Laskey, Bill (LB) Michigan	1971-72
Leaks, Roosevelt (RB) Texas	1975-79
Leberman, Bob (B) Syracuse	1954
Lee, David (P) Louisiana Tech	1966-78
Lee, Monte (C) Texas	1965
Lee, Ron (RB) West Virginia	1976-78
Lesane, Jimmy (B) Virginia	1954
Lewis, Harold (B) Houston	1959
Lewis, Joe (T) Compton	1961
Linhart, Toni (K) Austria Tech	1974-79
Linne, Aubrey (E) TCU	1961
Lipscomb, Gene (DT) Miller H.S.	1956-60
Little, Jack (T) Texas A & M	1953-54
Lockett, J.W. (B) Oklahoma Central	1963
Logan, Jerry (DB) West Texas State	1963-72
Looney, Joe Don (RB) Oklahoma	1964
Lorick, Tony (RB) Arizona State	1964-67
Luce, Derrel (LB) Baylor	1975-78
Lyles, Lenny (DB) Louisville	1958, 61-69
Mackey, Dee (E) East Texas State	1961-62
Mackey, John (TE) Syracuse	1963-71
MacLeod, Tom (LB) Minnesota	1974-78

Maitland, Jack (RB) Williams	1970
Maples, Butch (C) Baylor	1963
Marchetti, Gino (DE) USF	1953-64, 66
Marshall, Greg (DT) Oregon State	1978
Martin, Jim (K) Notre Dame	1963
Mason, Lindsey (OT) Kansas	1983
Matte, Tom (RB) Ohio State	1961-72
Matusak, Marv (B) Tulsa	1959-61
Mauck, Carl (LB) So. Illinois	1969
Maxwell, Tom (B) Texas A & M	1969-70
Maxwell, Vernon (LB) Arizona State	1983
May, Ray (LB) USC	1970-72
Mayo, Ron (TE) Morgan State	1974
McCall, Reese (TE) Auburn	1978-82
McCauley, Don (RB) North Carolina	1971-81
McHan, Lamar (QB) Arkansas	1961-63
McMillan, Chuck (B) John Carroll	1954
McMillan, Randy (RB) Pittsburgh	1981-83
McPhail, Buck (RB) Oklahoma	1953
Memmelaar, Dale (G) Wyoming	1966-67
Mendenhall, Ken (C) Oklahoma	1971-80
Michaels, Lou (DE, K) Kentucky	1964-69
Mike-Mayer, Steve (K) Maryland	1979-80
Mildren, Jack (S) Oklahoma	1972-73
Miller, Dan (K) Miami (Fla.)	1982
Miller, Fred (DT) LSU	1963-72
Mills, Jim (T) Hawaii	1983
Mioduszewski, Ed (B) William & Mary	1953
Mitchell, Lydell (RB) Penn State	1972-77
Mitchell, Tom (TE) Bucknell	1968-73
Mooney, Ed (LB) Texas Tech	1972-73
Moore, Alvin (RB) Arizona State	1983
Moore, Henry (B) Arkansas	1957
Moore, Jimmy (G) Ohio State	1981
Moore, Lenny (RB) Penn State	1956-67
Morrall, Earl (QB) Michigan State	1968-71
Morrison, Don (OT) Texas-Arl	1978
Mosier, John (TE) Kansas	1972
Moss, Roland (RB, TE) Toledo	1969
Mumphord, Lloyd (CB) Texas So	1975-78
Munsey, Nelson (CB) Wyoming	1972-77
Murtha, Greg (OT) Minnesota	1982
Mutscheller, Jim (E) Notre Dame	1954-61
Myers, Bob (T) Ohio State	1955
Myhra, Steve (LB, K) North Dakota	1957-61
Neal, Dan (C) Kentucky	1973-74
Nelson, Andy (DB) Memphis State	1957-63
Nelson, Dennis (T) Illinois State	1970-74
Nettles, Doug (CB) Vanderbilt	1974-79
Newsome, Billy (DE) Grambling	1970-72
Nichols, Robbie (LB) Tulsa	1970-71
Nottingham, Don (RB) Kent State	1971-73
Novak, Ken (DT) Purdue	1976-77
Nowatzke, Tom (RB) Indiana	1970-72
Nutter, Buzz (C) VPI	1954-60, 65
Nyers, Dick (B) Indiana Central	1956-57
Oatis, Victor (WR) NW Louisiana	1983
O'Brien, Jim (K, WR) Cincinnati	1970-72
O'Dell, Stu (LB) Indiana	1978
Odom, Cliff (LB) Texas	1982-83
O'Neal, Calvin (LB) Michigan	1978
Oldham, Ray (S) Middle Tennessee State	1973-77
Olds, Bill (RB) Nebraska	1973-75
Orduna, Joe (RB) Nebraska	1974
Orr, Jimmy (E) Georgia	1961-70
Orvis, Herb (DT) Colorado	1979-81
O'Steen, Dwayne (DB) San Jose State	1982
Owens, Luke (T) Kent State	1957
Owens, R.C. (E) College of Idaho	1962
Ozdowski, Mike (DE) Virginia	1978-81
Padjen, Gary (LB) Arizona State	1982-83
Pagel, Mike (QB) Arizona State	1982-83
Parker, Jim (T, G) Ohio State	1957-67
Parker, Steve (DE) E. Illinois	1983
Patera, Jack (LB) Oregon	1955-57
Pear, Dave (DT) Washington	1975
Pearson, Preston (RB) Illinois	1967-68
Pellington, Bill (LB) Rutgers	1953-64
Pepper, Gene (G) Mississippi	1954
Perkins, Ray (WR) Alabama	1967-71
Perry, Joe (RB) Compton	1961-62
Peterson, Gerald (T) Texas	1956
Petties, Neal (E) San Diego State	1964-66
Pinkney, Reggie (DB) East Carolina	1979-81
Pittman, Charlie (RB) Penn State	1971
Plunkett, Sherm (T) Maryland State	1958-60
Poole, Barney (E) Army, Mississippi	1953
Porter, Ricky (RB) Slippery Rock	1983
Porter, Ron (LB) Idaho	1967-69
Porter, Tracy (WR) LSU	1983
Pratt, Robert (G) North Carolina	1974-81
Preas, George (T) VPI	1955-65
Pricer, Billy (RB) Oklahoma	1957-60
Pyle, Palmer (G) Michigan State	1960-63
Raba, Bob (TE) Maryland	1980
Radosevich, George (C) Pitt	1954-56
Raiff, Jim (G) Dayton	1954
Randle, Tate (CB) Texas Tech	1983
Raymond, Gerry (OG) Boston College	1982
Rechichar, Bert (DB, K) Tennessee	1953-59
Reece, Geoff (C) Washington State	1978
Reed, Mark (QB) Morehead State	1983
Reese, Guy (T) SMU	1964-65
Renfro, Dean (B) North Texas State	1955
Ressler, Glenn (G) Penn State	1965-74
Rhodes, Danny (LB) Arkansas	1974
Richardson, Jerry (E) Wofford	1959-60
Richardson, Willie (WR) Jackson State	1963-69, 71
Riley, Butch (LB) Texas A & I	1969
Robinson, Chas. (G) Morgan State	1954
Robinson, Glenn (DE) Oklahoma State	1975
Rowe, David (DT) Penn State	1978
Rudnick, Tim (DB) Notre Dame	1974
Salter, Bryant (DB) Pittsburgh	1976
Sample, John (DB) Maryland State	1958-60
Sandusky, Alex (G) Clarion	1954-66
Sanford, Leo (C) Louisiana Tech	1958
Satterwhite, Howard (WR-KR) Sam Houston State	1977
Saul, Bill (LB) Penn State	1962-63
Schlichter, Art (QB) Ohio State	1982
Schmiesing, Joe (DT-DE) New Mexico State	1973
Scott, Freddie (WR) Amherst	1974-77
Sharkey, Ed (G) Duke, Nevada	1953
Shaw, George (QB) Oregon	1955-58
Sherer, Dave (E) SMU	1959

Sherwin, Tim (TE) Boston College	1981-83
Shields, Burrell (B) John Carroll	1955
Shields, Lebron (G) Tennessee	1960
Shinners, John (G) Xavier	1972
Shinnick, Don (LB) UCLA	1957-68
Shiver, Sanders (LB) Carson-Newman	1976-83
Shlapak, Boris (K) Michigan State	1972
Shula, Don (DB) John Carroll	1953-56
Shula, David (WR) Dartmouth	1981
Siani, Mike (WR) Villanova	1978-80
Simmons, Dave (LB) North Carolina	1982
Simonini, Ed (LB) Texas A & M	1976-81
Simonson, Dave (T) Minnesota	1974
Simpson, Jack (B) Florida	1958-60
Sims, Marvin (RB) Clemson	1980-81
Sinnot, John (OT) Brown	1982
Smith, Billy Ray (T) Arkansas	1961-70
Smith, Bubba (DE) Michigan State	1967-71
Smith, Ed (LB) Vanderbilt	1980-81
Smith, Holden (WR) Cal-Berkeley	1982
Smith, Ollie (WR) Tennessee State	1973-74
Smith, Phil (WR) San Diego State	1983
Smith, Zeke (LB) Auburn	1960
Smolinski, Mark (B) Wyoming	1961-62
Sommer, Mike (RB) George Washington	1959-61
Speyrer, Cotton (WR) Texas	1972-74
Spinney, Art (G) Boston College	1953-60
Stanback, Harry (DE) North Carolina	1982
Stark, Rohn (P) Florida State	1982-83
Stevens, Howard (RB) Louisville	1975-77
Stone, Avatus (B) Syracuse	1958
Stonebreaker, Steve (LB) Detroit	1964-66
Strofolino, Mike (LB) Villanova	1965
Stukes, Charles (DB) Maryland State	1967-72
Stynchula, Andy (T) Penn State	1966-67
Sullivan, Dan (G, T) Boston College	1962-72
Szymanski, Dick (C, LB) Notre Dame	1955, 57-68
Tabor, Tom (DT) Baylor	1982
Taliaferro, George (B) Indiana	1953-54
Taseff, Carl (B) John Carroll	1953-61
Taylor, David (T) Catawba	1973-79
Taylor, Hosea (DE) Houston	1981, 83
Taylor, Jim Bob (QB) Georgia Tech	1983
Thomas, Jesse (B) Michigan State	1955-57
Thomas, Spencer (DB) Washburn	1976
Thompson, Arland (OG) Baylor	1982
Thompson, Aundra (WR) East Texas State	1983
Thompson, Don (DE) Richmond	1962-63
Thompson, Donnell (DE) North Carolina	1981-83
Thompson, Norm (DB) Utah	1977-79
Thompson, Ricky (WR) Baylor	1976-77
Thurston, Fred (G) Valparaiso	1958
Tongue, Marco (CB) Bowie State	1983
Toth, Zollie (RB) LSU	1953-54
Troup, Bill (QB) S. Carolina	1974, 76-78
Turner, Bake (E) Texas Tech	1962
Unitas, John (QB) Louisville	1956-72
Utt, Ben (OG) Georgia Tech	1982-83
Van Divier, Randy (T) Washington	1981
Van Duyne, Bob (G) Idaho	1974-80
Varty, Mike (LB) Northwestern	1975
Venuto, Jay (QB) Wake Forest	1981
Vessels, Billy (RB) Oklahoma	1956
Vogel, Bob (T) Ohio State	1963-72
Volk, Rick (DB) Michigan	1967-75
Waechter, Henry (DE) Nebraska	1983
Wallace, Jackie (S) Arizona	1975-76
Ward, Jim (QB) Gettysburg	1967-69
Washington, Joe (RB) Oklahoma	1978-80
Welch, Jim (B) SMU	1960-67
White, Bob (B) Stanford	1955
White, Stan (LB) Ohio State	1972-79
Wilkerson, Daryl (DE) Houston	1981
Williams, John (G) Minnesota	1969-71
Williams, Kendall (CB) Arizona State	1983
Williams, Kevin (WR) USC	1981
Williams, Newton (RB) Arizona State	1983
Williams, Steve (DT) Western Carolina	1974
Wilson, Butch (E) Alabama	1963-67
Windauer, Bill (DT) Iowa	1973-74
Wingate, Elmer (E) Maryland	1953
Winkler, Jim (T) Texas A & M	1953
Wisniewski, Leo (NT) Penn State	1982-83
Womble, Royce (RB) N. Texas State	1954-57
Wood, Mike (K) S.E. Missouri	1981-82
Woods, Mike (LB) Cincinnati	1979-81
Wright, George (DT) Houston	1970-71
Wright, Johnnie (RB) S.C.—Columbus	1982
Wright, Steve (T) Northern Iowa	1983
Yohn, Dave (C) Gettysburg	1962
Young, Buddy (B) Illinois	1953-55
Young, Dave (TE) Purdue	1983
Young, Dick (B) Chattanooga	1955-56
Zabel, Steve (LB) Oklahoma	1979

The following players and coaches were members of the Baltimore Colts teams that played in the All America Football Conference and then in the NFL during the 1947-1950 seasons.

COACHES

Campofreda, Nick—W. Md	1947
Conkright, Bill—Oklahoma	1949
Crow, Clem—Notre Dame	1950
Defilippo, Lou—Fordham	1948
Driskill, Walter—Colorado	1949
Edmonds, Don—Indiana	1947
Hewlett, Andy—Davidson	1947
Hunt, Joel—Texas A & M	1947
Isbell, Cecil—Purdue	1947-49
Michalske, Mike—Penn State	1949
Milner, Wayne—Notre Dame	1950
O'Rourke, Chas.—Boston College	1949
Pirro, Rocco—Catholic U.	1950
Stidham, Tom—Haskell	1947-48
Taylor, John—Ohio State	1947

PLAYERS

Akins, Frank (B) Washington State	1947
Artoe, Lee (T) Santa Clara	1948
Averno, Sisto (G) Muhlenberg	1950
Barwegan, Dick (G) Purdue	1948-49
Baumgartner, Bill (E) Minnesota	1947
Bechtol, Hub (E) Texas	1947-49
Benson, Warren (C) Minnesota	1949
Berezney, Pete (T) Notre Dame	1948
Black, John (B) Mississipi State	1947
Blanda, George (QB) Kentucky	1950
Blandin, Ernie (T) Tulane	1948-50
Blount, Lamar (E) Mississippi State	1947
Brown, Hardy (LB) Tulsa	1950
Buksar, George (B) Purdue, USF	1950
Burk, Adrian (QB) Baylor	1950
Campbell, Leon (B) Arkansas	1950
Case, Ernie (B) UCLA	1947
Castiglia, Jim (B) Georgetown	1947
Coleman, Herb (C) Notre Dame	1948
Collins, Albin (B) LSU	1950
Colo, Don (T) Brown	1950
Cooper, Ken (C) Vanderbilt	1949-50
Corley, Elbert (C) Mississippi State	1948
Cowan, Bob (C) Indiana	1949
Crisler, Hal (E) San Jose State	1950
Cure, Armand (B) Rhode Island	1947
Davis, Lamar (E) Georgia Tech	1947-49
Dellerba, Spiro (B) Ohio State	1948-49
Donovan, Art (DT) Boston College	1950
Dudish, Andy (B) Georgia	1947
Faunce, Everett (B) Minnesota	1949
Filchock, Frank (B) Indiana	1950
Fletcher, Oliver (E) USC	1950
Fowler, Aubrey (B) Arkansas	1948
French, Barry (G) Purdue	1947-50
Galvin, John (B) Purdue	1947
Gambino, Lucien (B) Maryland	1948-49
Garrett, Bill (G) Mississippi State	1948-49
Getchell, Gorham (E) Temple	1947
Gillory, Byron (B) Texas	1949
Grain, Ed (G) Penn	1947-48
Graves, George (G) Marquette	1948
Grossman, Rex (B-K) Indiana	1948-50
Handley, Dick (C) Fresno State	1947
Jagade, Harry (B) Indiana	1949
Jenkins, Jon (T) Dartmouth	1949-50
Jensen, Bob (E) Iowa State	1950
Jones, Ralph (E) Alabama	1947
Kasap, Mike (T) Illinois & Purdue	1947
Kelley, Bob (B) Notre Dame	1949
King, Ed (G) Boston College	1950
Kingery, Wayne (B) LSU	1949
Kissell, Vito (B) Holy Cross	1950
Klug, Al (T) Marquette	1947-48
Kodba, Joe (C) Purdue	1947
Konetsky, Floyd (E) Florida	1947
Landrigan, Jim (T) Holy Cross, Dartmouth	1947
Leicht, Jake (B) Oregon	1948-49
Leonard, Bill (E) Notre Dame	1949

Lio, Augie (G) Georgetown	1947
Livingstone, Bob (B) Notre Dame	1950
Madar, Elmer (E) Michigan	1947
Maggioli, Chick (B) Notre Dame	1950
Marino, Vic (G) Ohio State	1947
Maves, Earl (B) Wisconsin	1948
Mayne, Lew (B) Texas	1948
Mazzanti, Gino (B) Arkansas	1950
McCormick, Len (C) Baylor	1948
Mellus, John (T) Villanova	1947-49
Mertes, Bus (B) Iowa	1947-48
Meyer, Gil (E) Wake Forest	1947
Mobley, Rudy (B) Hardin-Simmons	1947
Murray, Earl (G) Purdue	1950
Mutryn, Chet (B) Xavier	1950
Nelson, Bob (C) Baylor	1950
Nemeth, Steve (B) Notre Dame	1947
Nolander, Don (C) Minnesota	1947
North, John (E) Vanderbilt	1948-50
Nowaskey, Bob (DE) Geo. Washington	1948-50
Oristaglio, Bob (E) Penn	1950
O'Rourke, Chas. (QB) Boston College	1948-49
Owens, Jim (E) Oklahoma	1950
Page, Paul (B) SMU	1949
Perina, Bob (B) Princeton	1950
Perpich, George (T) Georgetown	1947
Pfohl, Stormy (B) Purdue	1948-49
Phillips, Mike (C) W. Maryland	1947
Poole, Barney (E) Miss., Army	1948
Rich, Herb (B) Vanderbilt	1950
Ruthstrom, Ralph (B) SMU	1949
Salata, Paul (E) USC	1950
Schweder, John (G) Penn	1950
Schwenk, Bud (QB) Wash. U. (St. Louis)	1947
Sidorik, Alex (T) Mississippi State	1948-49
Sigurdson, Sig (E) Lutheran	1947
Simmons, Jack (G) Detroit	1948
Sinkwich, Frank (B) Georgia	1947
Smith, Joe (E) Texas Tech	1948
Spaniel, Frank (B) Notre Dame	1950
Spavital, Jim (B) Oklahoma A & M	1950
Spinney, Art (G) Boston College	1950
Spruill, Jim (T) Rice	1948-49
Stewart, Ralph (C) Missouri, N.D.	1948
Stone, Bill (B) Bradley	1949-50
Sylvester, John (B) Temple	1948
Terrell, Ray (B) Mississippi	1947
Tilman, Alonzo (C) Oklahoma	1949
Tittle, Y.A. (QB) LSU	1948-50
Trebotich, Ivan (B) St. Mary's	1947
Vacanti, Sam (QB) Nebraska	1948-49
Vardian, John (B) Ft. Pierce	1947-48
Wedemeyer, Herman (B) St. Mary's	1949
Williams, Joel (C) Texas	1950
Williams, Windell (E) Rice	1948
Wright, John (B) Maryland	1947
Yokas, Frank (G) Great Lakes NTS	1947
Zalejski, Ernie (B) Notre Dame	1950
Zorich, George (G) Northwestern	1947

Index

Index

Index

Index

Index

Index